this star
won't go out

THE LIFE AND WORDS
OF ESTHER GRACE EARL

esther earl WITH LORI AND WAYNE EARL

INTRODUCTION BY JOHN GREEN

PENGUIN BOOKS

PENGUIN BOOKS

Published by the Penguin Group
Penguin Books Ltd, 80 Strand, London WC2R 0RL, England
Penguin Group (USA) LLC, 375 Hudson Street, New York, New York 10014, USA
Penguin Group (Canada), 90 Eglinton Avenue East, Suite 700, Toronto, Ontario, Canada M4P 2Y3
(a division of Pearson Penguin Canada Inc.)
Penguin Ireland, 25 St Stephen's Green, Dublin 2, Ireland (a division of Penguin Books Ltd)
Penguin Group (Australia), 707 Collins Street, Melbourne, Victoria 3008, Australia
(a division of Pearson Australia Group Pty Ltd)
Penguin Books India Pvt Ltd, 11 Community Centre, Panchsheel Park, New Delhi – 110 017, India
Penguin Group (NZ), 67 Apollo Drive, Rosedale, Auckland 0632, New Zealand
(a division of Pearson New Zealand Ltd)
Penguin Books (South Africa) (Pty) Ltd, Block D, Rosebank Office Park, 181 Jan Smuts Avenue, Parktown North,
Gauteng 2193, South Africa

Penguin Books Ltd, Registered Offices: 80 Strand, London WC2R 0RL, England

penguin.com

First published in the USA by Dutton Books, an imprint of Penguin Group (USA) LLC, 2014
Published simultaneously in Great Britain by Penguin Books 2014
001

Designed by Irene Vandervoort
Edited by Julie Strauss-Gabel

Printed in Italy by Printer Trento

British Library Cataloguing in Publication Data
A CIP catalogue record for this book is available from the British Library

ISBN: 978–0–141–35403–3

www.greenpenguin.co.uk

THIS IS A STORY about a girl that went through a life changing experience known as Thyroid Cancer. It's not one of those dramatic "based on a true story" cancer things, especially since Thyroid Cancer is not as bad as cancer. It's a story about me, Esther Earl, having a sickness that's pretty scary.

MR. CANCEROUS LUMP
Esther Earl,
"Cancerous Lump" journal

To all who long to live fully and love
deeply no matter the obstacle or
length of days

this
star
won't
go out

Abigail and Esther with John Green,
LEAKYCON, 2009

INTRODUCTION
by John Green

bestselling author of THE FAULT IN OUR STARS *and
co-creator of the vlogbrothers channel on YouTube*

My friendship with Esther Earl began, as so many great love stories do, at a Harry Potter convention. My brother, Hank, is a wizard rocker, which means he writes songs about the Harry Potter universe, and so he'd dragged me along to Leaky-Con 2009, a celebration of all things Potter in Boston. The first night of the conference featured a banquet and concert, which of course meant quite a lot of dancing.

The great thing about the Harry Potter fan community is that no one judges you. Being a nerd isn't seen as a character defect. Unironic enthusiasm is celebrated, and never more so than on the dance floor. At a Wizard rock concert, it doesn't matter if you're a great dancer or a terrible dancer so long as you are committed to your dance moves.

Which I am not. I find it impossible to dance as if no one were watching, even when no one is watching. So when everyone rushed to the dance floor, I hung back. My strategy at a dance event is to lean against a column or wall and stare thoughtfully at the musicians and the dancing crowd as if I am thinking Extremely Intelligent Thoughts, so that anyone who happens to glance at me will hopefully feel that I shouldn't be interrupted.

But I was interrupted by a small voice saying, "Are you John Green?" I turned and saw a girl wearing a nasal cannula and a nearly identical girl—her sister, I gathered— holding an oxygen tank. "Yeah," I said. "Hi." What followed was pretty standard: The girl—her name was Esther— liked the videoblog Hank and I make and wanted a picture. Her sister took the picture, and after a quick conversation, I went back to leaning against the wall.

A couple minutes later, a friend grabbed me and tried to pull me onto the dance floor. I spun around in panic and saw Esther and her sister Abby sitting at a table behind the dance floor and said, "I, uh, need to go. I need to go talk to those girls."

This was the first, but not the last, time that Esther Earl saved me from catastrophe. I sat down next to them and began chatting. It turned out that Esther wasn't just a viewer of our videos—she was a hardcore nerdfighter. (Nerdfighters are people who fight for nerds and celebrate intellectualism; the community grew out of the videos my brother and I started making in 2007.) Esther had been watching us for years. She would later help to maintain the biggest nerdfighter fan site, effyeahnerdfighters, with a small group of friends who called themselves Catitude. Catitude also helps run an annual nerdfighter charity project called the Project for Awesome. Hank and I have frequently turned to Catitude for advice and assistance. So it turned out that Esther and I already sort of knew each other.

We talked that evening in Boston for quite a while, boring the hell out of Abby I'm sure, about nerdfighter injokes and Hank's music and our favorite Wizard rock bands.

I kept tabs on Esther after meeting her. We'd sometimes have brief Skype conversations, and I'd jump into the Catitude chat every now and again to discuss the fan site they ran, or their moderation of the forum, or just to hang out. It's impossible to describe the speed at which people typed in those Skype chats: Ten or twelve people could produce thousands of words a minute, and Esther, although she was one of the youngest members of Catitude, kept right up.

I knew Esther had cancer, but I also knew that most young people with cancer get better, and I never wanted to pry too much, not the least because I had been working for years on a book about kids with cancer and I didn't want my friendship with Esther to become a research project. For a long time, there was an element of denial in our relationship. I didn't want to imagine that this hilarious, devoted fan might die, and Esther wanted friendships that weren't defined and circumscribed by illness. Her physical disabilities made that difficult in real life, but on the Internet, she wasn't Esther Earl Who Has Cancer and an Oxygen Tank. She was Esther Crazycrayon the Funny Girl in Catitude.

And then one day Esther and I were typing back and forth when she revealed that she was writing to me from a hospital bed, and—when I pried a bit—that she was actually in the ICU with tubes coming out of her chest to drain fluid that had accumulated in her lungs. Even then, she made it all seem very standard and casual, as if all fourteen-year-olds just occasionally need chest tubes, but I was concerned enough to reach out to her friends, who put me in touch with Esther's parents, Lori and Wayne. Soon after, all of her Internet friends began to realize that Esther was terminally ill.

I realize now that I'm doing that thing where you create distance between yourself and your pain by using cold, technical phrases like "terminally ill" and by describing events rather than feelings, so: I was so angry—with myself for all the times I cut our conversations short so I could go back to work, and with the Earth for being the sort of reprehensible place where children who've done nothing wrong must live in fear and pain for years and then die.

I dislike the phrase "Internet friends," because it

implies that people you know online aren't really your friends, that somehow the friendship is less real or meaningful to you because it happens through Skype or text messages. The measure of a friendship is not its physicality but its significance. Good friendships, online or off, urge us toward empathy; they give us comfort and also pull us out of the prisons of our selves. I imagine that part of Esther was sad to give up the illusion that she was going to be okay with her Internet friends, but what followed was a revelation for all of us. Our Internet friendships were real and they were powerful, and they became more real and powerful when Esther and her friends were finally able to acknowledge and openly discuss the truth about her illness.

A few months before Esther died, those Internet friendships became IRL for a while when several members of Catitude spent a few days with Esther in Boston. I was there for one day. I wish I could tell you how cool and strong I was, but in fact I cried for most of the day and could hardly get out a sentence at times. I wish I'd been more of a grown-up with Esther and her friends, that, like her parents, I could have been a comforting and calming and loving presence instead of a blubbery and scared one. But so it goes.

Still, it was a great day. We talked about our hopes and fears for the future, about the last Harry Potter movie (which sadly Esther never got to see), and about our happiest memories. Esther told me that her happiest memory had occurred a year back, when she was hospitalized with pneumonia and thought to be dying. She spoke about having her whole family around her, holding hands with them, feeling connected to these people who loved her infinitely. She used that word at some point referring to her family's love, infinite, and I thought about how infinity is not a large number. It is something else entirely. It is boundlessness. We live in a world defined by its boundaries: You cannot travel faster than the speed of light. You must and will die. You cannot escape these boundaries. But the miracle and hope of human consciousness is that we can still conceive of boundlessness.

We watched a movie Wayne and Lori had made of Esther's life. We ate Chinese food. We cried a lot together. Esther took breaks—for naps, to throw up, to have medicine injected into the port in her stomach—but she was fully with us, as alive as any of us, as capable of love and joy and anger and grief. And as much as I didn't want our friendship to be about my writing, I couldn't help but be affected by her as a writer and a person. She was so funny, sharp-edged, and self-aware. She had such an improbable capacity for empathy. And most of all, she was a person, complete and complex. We have a habit of imagining the dying as fundamentally other from the well. We hold them up as heroes and imagine they have reserves of strength forbidden to the rest of us. We tell ourselves that we will be inspired through the stories of their suffering—we will learn to be grateful for every day, or learn to be more empathetic, or whatever. These responses, while certainly well intentioned, ultimately dehumanize the dying: Esther was uncommon not because she was sick but because she was Esther, and she did not exist so that the rest of us could learn Important Lessons about Life. The meaning of her life—like the meaning of any life—is a maddeningly ambiguous question shrouded in uncertainty.

Later that night, Esther, her friends, and I went for a walk (taking turns pushing Esther's wheelchair) out into Boston to get coffee and gelato. I will never succeed in explaining to you how fun this was, how much it felt like a grand adventure along the lines of scaling Mount Everest as we wound around the centuries-old streets in search of dessert.

I made a video about Esther a couple weeks later, and she soon became something of a celebrity in the nerdfighter community. For the last months of her life, she handled this newfound attention with grace (which was, after all, her middle name). She even started making her own vlogs, and even though she was very sick and within weeks of death, they were funny and charming and found a broad audience. We stayed in touch, and she kept visiting with her friends in the Catitude chat, even when the conversation at times moved too quickly for her as her condition worsened.

The last thing she ever filmed was part of a Catitude collaboration video for my thirty-third birthday, which was on August 24, 2010. By the time the video went live, Esther was back in the ICU. She died in the early hours of August 25th.

When we think of death, we often imagine it as happening in degrees: We think of a sick person becoming less and less alive until finally they are gone. But even in her final days, Esther was wholly alive, as alive as anyone else, and so even though everyone who loved her understood she was dying, her death was still a terrible shock to me. She did not leave slowly, but all at once, because even when she could not get out of bed, she found ways to be fully alive: to play with her friends, to crack jokes, to love and to be loved. And then she was gone, all at once.

I've said many times that *The Fault in Our Stars*, while it is dedicated to Esther, is not about her. When the book was published, lots of reporters wanted me to talk about Esther; they wanted to know if my book was "based on a true story." I never really knew how to deal with these questions, and I still don't, because the truth (as always) is complicated. Esther inspired the story in the sense that my anger after her death pushed me to write constantly. She helped me to imagine teenagers as more empathetic than I'd given them credit for, and her charm and snark inspired the novel, too, but the character of Hazel is very different from Esther, and Hazel's story is not Esther's. Esther's story belonged to her, and fortunately for us she was an extraordinary writer, who in these pages tells that story beautifully. I find comfort in that, but make no mistake: I am still pissed off that she died. I still miss her. I still find her loss an intolerable injustice. And I wish she'd read *The Fault in Our Stars*. I am astonished that the book has found such a broad audience, but the person I most want to read it never will.

I mentioned earlier that when Esther kept me off the dance floor that night in 2009, it wasn't the last time she saved me from catastrophe. In fact, she is still saving me, all the time. In these pages, and in my memories, she reminds me that a short life can also be a good and rich life, that it is possible to live with depression without being consumed by it, and that meaning in life is found together, in family and friendship that transcends and survives all manner of suffering. As the poet wrote in the Bible's Song of Solomon, "Love is strong as death." Or perhaps even stronger.

Star Pillow,
SAUDI ARABIA, **2000**

Esther at work,
MASSACHUSETTS, **2003**

ESTHER GRACE *an introduction*
by Esther's parents, *Lori and Wayne Earl*

From the time she was little, Esther was certain she was going to be a writer. And we believed her. She loved words, felt their power, and believed in the magic of story. Later, she would keep a running list of ideas and characters she hoped to develop. We encouraged her to write and promised enthusiastically to help her find an audience for her work.

From about age eight, she began keeping a diary and increased the pace of her entries as she grew older. Of course, she didn't keep a diary with the idea that what she wrote down would one day be published. She wrote because she had to. She was passionate about the process and found it essential for her mental and emotional health to be able to get her thoughts out of her head and onto the page. Like many people her age, keeping a journal helped her navigate the passage from childhood to young adulthood; writing became increasingly critical after her diagnosis.

Her writings now belong to you, the reader. We feel certain she would not have objected. She often spoke of her desire to encourage and inspire others and would have done that whether or not anyone noticed, perhaps especially if no one noticed. She was a champion of the lonely, a welcomer of strangers, an inviter.

Esther usually wrote in her journal as the final act of her day, in her bed, and only after first reading something delicious. It's clear that she related to her diary as a person and often reread her entries as she sought to improve her strengths and address what she thought to be her flaws and failings. As the years moved forward, her style and content began to reflect a life of purpose through the perspective of an empathetic and joyful young girl forced to navigate the monstrous reality of a cancer death sentence, while at the same time entering the beguiling world of early twenty-first-century adolescence.

In the face of such an unwelcome intrusion, we often found ourselves feeling helpless as we struggled to stay positive. For us, Esther's omnipresent breathing machine was an incessant reminder that the day was coming when its comforting whirring would be silenced. But Esther chose to see things differently. Throughout her treatment, she felt that, overall, life had been good to her. She had the love of family, friends, and she was daily renewed in her focus on a mission to comfort and care for others. No matter how heavy the assault, until her work was done, she had no plans to abandon her

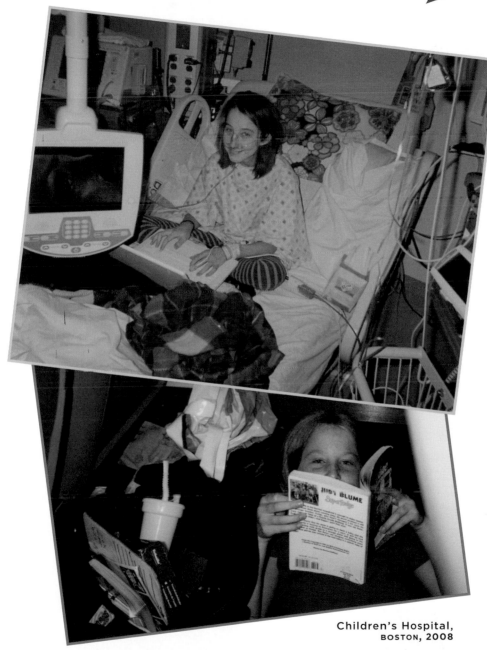

Children's Hospital,
BOSTON, 2008

Flying home from Europe,
2004

15

hopeful post. Two weeks after her sixteenth birthday, she tweeted to friends:

> *Like if I can ask for three talents they'd be: able to reach into bodies (without hurting them) and remove all cancer, able to dance & WORDS*

Creating words that could heal and energetically sharing and celebrating life in the here and now: that's her legacy. We are convinced that this, along with a deep love for others, is how she would want to be remembered.

Her life was her book. She didn't get to choose the ending, but the way she filled the pages makes her story irresistible. Sharing our Star—*our amazing burst of sunshine*—is a way of spreading light. We are so grateful that she graced our lives, if only for a short time. Through reading the words of this young author, we hope that others will be inspired and changed for the good, as we have been.

Untitled artwork,
DECEMBER 6, 2008

AUGUST 3, 1994

Born in Beverly, Massachusetts, to a minister
father and educator mother, ESTHER GRACE
EARL was well loved long before the world met
her. Esther—which means "star"—was named
for the courageous Jewish queen who had once-
upon-a-time risked her life to save her people.

Esther at seven months,
HAVERHILL, MASSACHUSETTS, 1995

HAIR

Our Star was born with wonderful, flyaway hair
that matched her energetic approach to life—
it would not be tamed, so we didn't even try!
Occasionally we'd hear the comment about our
toddler: "Bad hair day, huh?" Our indignant
response was always in the form of a rebuking,
"We love her hair!"

The Toddler,
WARD HILL, MASSACHUSETTS, 1997

CREATIVITY

Just two years old, Esther drew a picture of a
boot with shoestrings and a smiling face. Her
dad wrote about it in his journal:

"Esther, did you see that drawing
somewhere?"

"Nope."

"You just thought it up in your head?"

"Yep, I saws the boot, Daddy, and made a
face fer it! You like it?"

"Yes, Esther, yes. I like it very much."

Daddy's boot,
1996

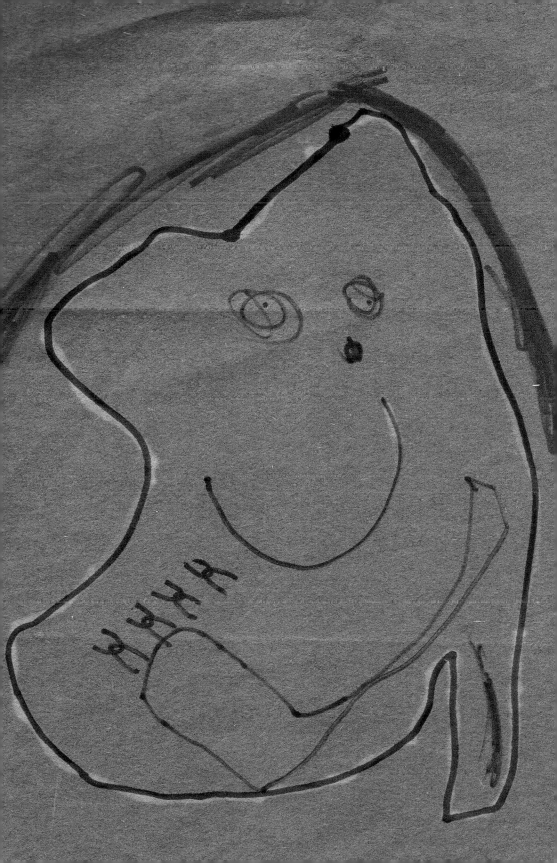

EMPATHETIC

When Esther was four we took a teaching contract in Saudi Arabia. Esther's world revolved around family, including big sisters, Abby and Evangeline, and little brother, Graham.

Esther's empathy, already clearly apparent, was demonstrated the day she generously applied sunscreen to Graham's face. When he began crying because she got some in his eyes, Esther quickly intervened. "No, Graham, see, it doesn't hurt!" and she put some lotion in her own eyes to show him. They both ended up screaming in pain as they ran off to find help!

Esther and Graham,
GERMANY, 2000

25

READING AND WRITING

In 2001 our family returned to Massachusetts,
where Esther's dad took a position with a church.
By now an avid reader, she also found many
opportunities to write stories and other things,
including e-mails to friends and family such as
this one to her dad from October of that year.

> Dear Dad,
> I hope you're doing ok. I made two more
> stories, "Scary Cat Ruins Vegetable City"
> and "The Easter Duck" and I'm doing well in
> school. I'm just kind of sad 'cause you're gone.
> I love you and pray for you. And I thought
> about what I want from where you are and I
> want a stuffed animal or a Kinder Egg, I don't
> care it's just you can't get me a beanie baby
> because you don't know which ones I have so
> that's why you can't get me one.
>
> Love and kisses from Esther
> XOXOXOXOXO

Esther Grace,
BAHRAIN, 2001

Third Grade,
KINGSTON, MASSACHUSETTS, 2003

ALL ABOUT ME

Esther was one of only two students in the entire second grade to clamber up the rope ladder at her elementary school gymnasium and reach the top, proudly winning the honor of writing her name on the ceiling!

"All About Me" Poster

FIVE WORDS TO DESCRIBE ME ARE: nice, smart, fun, funny, sweet

ONE THING THAT MAKES ME SPECIAL: My middle name is Grace

MY FAVORITE BOOK IS: *Harry Potter*

MY FAVORITE FOOD IS: pizza

MY FAVORITE SPORT IS: soccer

MY FAVORITE ANIMAL IS: a cat

WHEN I HAVE TIME TO MYSELF: I like to read and write

WHEN I GROW UP: I want to be an author

NINE YEARS OLD

Baby brother Abraham joined the family the year Esther turned nine. She was present for his birth, and cut his umbilical cord. Her aside to everyone in the delivery room was clear and adamant: "I'm adopting!"

Esther loved the ocean. Even her face seemed made for the sand and sea, breaking out in splashes of freckles at summer's first light! Her joy is reflected in the following poem she wrote while sitting at the beach.

Apple Picking,
NORTHBORO, MASSACHUSETTS, 2003

<u>The sea is very dear to me</u>
Every time I look at it,
It looks back at me
I love the sea, its waters are blue
And the sky is too
And the sea is very dear to me
If when I grow up and the sea is still there
Then I'll open my eyes and smell the fresh air
Because the sea is very dear to me
The sea is very calm and that's why I like it there
The sand is brand new and the wind blows in my
        hair
And the sea is very dear to me.

FIFTH GRADE

From a wall poster labeled, "Interview with the Class," here are a few of the questions Esther answered about her life as a fifth grader.

> Q. What do you like best about yourself?
> A. My hair and my freckles, babay!

> Q. What would you do if you saw someone being made fun of for stuttering?
> A. Ask if they want to sit with me at lunch; play computer games at my house.

> Q. Fears?
> A. Crashing in a plane, car, boat, or getting hurt while alone at home.

> Q. Nicknames?
> A. Estee, Star.

> Q. Heaven?
> A. I think it will be perfect and everything will be cooler than cool!

Allée Centrale,
PARIS, FRANCE, 2004

FRANCE

We moved to France in December 2005 to work with a nonprofit, fulfilling a lifelong dream. The kids dropped into immersion programs in the French public schools, and Esther especially seemed to adjust to all the change with ease. She must have fit right in as one day she came home from gym class—where they'd been skiing in the Alps!—to tell us an amusing story of being pointed out as a "pretty little French girl" by a British family.

Esther and Abe,
ALBERTVILLE, FRANCE, 2006

ESTHER GRACE

After nearly a year, the kids were adapting well to our new life in Europe. But in the midst of the fairy tale came the cancer. Our slim, muscular, energetic, never-tired twelve-year-old found she was fatigued walking even a short distance. She needed to rest, and she began coughing. Fears of pneumonia or TB led to hospital visits, and then the worst news: thyroid cancer.

Sixth Grade, Collège Mignet,
AIX-EN-PROVENCE, FRANCE, 2006

DIAGNOSIS & TREATMENT
by Dr. Jessica Smith

Boston Children's Hospital, Attending Physician, Endocrinology

In 2006, when she was twelve years old and living in France with her family, Esther started to find herself unable to keep up with her well-traveled family of seven. In retrospect, Esther had noted several weeks of chest pain, cough, and difficulty breathing, particularly upon physical activity. She went to the Hôpital de la Timone in Marseille, France, where she was originally thought to have pneumonia. Then, surprisingly her chest X-ray showed fluid and nodules in both lungs.

Esther was immediately admitted to the hospital and after extensive procedures she was diagnosed with metastatic papillary thyroid cancer, the most common type of thyroid cancer in children. That November Esther underwent surgery to remove the thyroid gland and numerous lymph nodes in her neck. After her surgery, she struggled with serious complications which required her to permanently take thyroid hormone, calcium, and vitamin D supplementation. As part of her cancer therapy, Esther received also two doses of radiation therapy.

* * * * *

I first met Esther and her family in August 2007 at Boston Children's Hospital as they hoped to find assistance in finding a remission and cure. In general, the long-term prognosis of pediatric thyroid cancer is quite good with up to a 90 percent survival rate at twenty years. But Esther's case was different; she presented with more extensive disease. Her cancer had spread throughout her body and had resided in the lymph nodes in her neck and lungs. A team was assembled, including a thyroidologist, (doctor who specializes in thyroid cancer), pulmonologist (doctor who specializes in lungs), endocrine nurse (nurse who assists in hormonal disorders), and social worker (specialist who helps with financial and emotional hardships and adjustments), to assess Esther's medical status.

Typically, patients with thyroid cancer require visits to the hospital every six to twelve months, but Esther needed to be seen much more regularly. Our first approach was to administer high doses of radioactive iodine (radiation) to target the disease in her lymph nodes and lungs. Not only did this require an extremely restrictive diet, but it also necessitated further isolation from friends and family. Although Esther began to respond to therapy, both she and her family began to experience many additional challenges associated with her treatment. Esther was no longer able to attend school regularly due to the number of doctors' appointments. The amount of medications she was required to take on a daily basis grew dramatically, and the stress on her body resulted in daily headaches, nausea, and further weight loss.

I was cautiously optimistic about Esther's response to therapy until June of 2008 when she began to take a turn for the worse. She was no longer able to breathe on her own without the assistance of oxygen, and her weight loss was quite striking. Esther very much resisted the idea of having a tube placed in her stomach to help with nutrition and medication delivery, but after an extensive discussion about fashion forward ways to hide the G-tube, we finally agreed to have it surgically placed. Then, in October 2008, Esther arrived in the ICU with a major setback after experiencing two episodes of bleeding from her lungs. Esther did not tolerate the sedation, and moving forward, she was quite adamant about mind-altering medications.

After her admission to the ICU, I had an extensive discussion with Esther and her family in regards to the next steps of her care. We decided to consult with the Dana Farber Cancer Institute and pursue a new, experimental therapy. Although it would not be curative, it could potentially provide more quality time for Esther.

The risks and benefits were reviewed with both Esther and her family, and although the decision was difficult (further bleeding into her lungs was a potential outcome), Esther was willing to trial this new therapy. During this transition, she required additional nursing support at home and was no longer able to sleep in her own room. The family transitioned their dining room into Esther's room as she could no longer walk up and down the stairs.

Over the following eighteen months, Esther fought valiantly and was transitioned between two different experimental therapies. During this time, her oldest sister became an outstanding caregiver and spent a lot of time transporting her to and from the hospital. Esther developed many side effects, including hair loss, fluid overload, rashes, nausea, and headaches, but despite these, she was always positive. Over the summer of 2010, Esther developed kidney failure. Throughout all of her medical experiences, Esther was greatly involved in her medical decision making.

I felt blessed to be present on a warm summer night in August of 2010 when Esther peacefully passed away in the presence of her family due to complications related to her thyroid cancer.

I was asked to contribute a small portion of this text to the dedication of Esther Earl. The medical piece, although a painful reminder of a beautiful life lost, is a part of my livelihood as a physician. I had the great fortune of meeting and caring for Esther and her family. I also faced the difficult task and associated challenges of explaining her long-term prognosis, which was accompanied by great anxiety, shock, and unexpected disappointment.

But the life lessons that Esther taught me and the ability to have been present for this life-changing experience with Esther and her family are truly a gift. To summarize my thoughts and feelings for Esther in just a few words is nearly impossible. Upon meeting Esther, I knew instantaneously that she was a star. She lit up the room with her smile, and she had an ever-present aura that immediately warmed the room. Her sense of humor was dry but endearing, and her laughter illuminated the darkest of days.

Early in our relationship, Esther stood out as a quirky and highly intelligent caffeine-drinking teenager who was wise beyond her years. She always listened quietly but attentively to our discussions, and her questions were not only smart but also medically astute. Even when she was thirteen, Esther was able to respectfully challenge medical decision making and provide thought-provoking inquiries. As our relationship grew and she began to trust me, we developed a bond that was simultaneously jovial and deep with honesty and integrity. Esther was never willing to accept failure, yet she accepted her destiny and was able to express herself clearly and emote with such wisdom and confidence. As her disease progressed, she fought with such poise and dignity.

Esther allowed each and every person to feel unique and special through her blogs and formed lifelong relationships among strangers that would grow over time. Her love of literature, friendship, art, and the overall creative process allowed for her circle of friends to grow stronger, and it continues today. Esther developed her own support structure, one that allowed her family and friends to garner strength in the setting of her own illness.

One has to be incredibly resilient in order to achieve such a success in a disease process that afflicts so few. There is not a day that goes by in life that I do not think of her. Her contribution to my work has allowed me to strengthen my own dedication to my career and personal development. There is not a talk or lecture that I will ever give in which she will fail to be mentioned. Despite her short time with us, her longevity and legacy will forever be present in many different media. For me, I will always know where to find her—in my heart.

One of Esther's favorite pastimes was to create a work of art and then give it away. These treasures might include something handmade, or hand picked, such as a bouquet of daises, or sewn, or painted, or collected, like a cup full of seashells. Her offerings were always accompanied with a note or longer letter: the true intention of her giving, her real gift. Though the flowers may have withered and though the artwork has begun to yellow, her cherished letters of love endure. —ESTHER'S PARENTS

Untitled,
2009

Wayne & Lori Earl...

It's your anniversary! Do you guys know
what that means?!? you've been together/marr
23 (or was it 24?) years! Cool.

Well, I'm sorry that we cant do anything more
special or romantic for your birthday! seriously...
who wants to have a lame anniversary? Well, it
shouldnt matter if you love each other :

*Parents, I love you two. So much. I am so
lucky to have such amazing people raising me.
Because... really, I wouldnt be who I am today
if not for the love and care of you two. Please
realize that you are amazing. I thank God that
He blessed us with such loving people.

Cancer is hard. I wouldnt have made it this
far if it werent for my family. Thankyou, very
much for being here for me. It makes it seem less ha

I know I sound pretty sappy, but I cant write
~~~~~~~~~~~~~~ in pen how much you
two are to me. Just know that I love you.
and I wouldnt trade our poor, houseless family
full of love for the world.

Please, guys, have a fun day! despite
the fact that nothing cool is planned. We love
you and wish you the best anniversary ever.

Love you lots,
Your Estee

Letter, June 2, 2007

Wayne & Lori Earl . . .

It's your anniversary! Do you guys know what that means?!? You've been together/<u>married</u> <u>23</u> (or was it <u>24</u>?) years! Cool.

Well, I'm sorry that we can't do anything more special or romantic for your birthday. Seriously . . . who wants to have a lame anniversary? Well, it shouldn't matter if you love each other :)

Parents, I love you two. So much. I am so lucky to have such amazing people raising me. Because . . . really, I wouldn't be who I am today if not for the love and care of you two. Please realize that you are amazing. I thank God that He blessed us with such loving people.

Cancer is <u>hard</u>. I wouldn't have made it this far if it weren't for my family. Thank you, very much for being here for me. It makes it seem less hard.

I know I sound pretty sappy, but I can't write in pen how much you two are to me. Just know that I love you, and I wouldn't trade our poor, houseless family full of love for the world.

Please, guys, have a fun day, despite the fact that
nothing cool is planned. We love you and wish you the
best anniversary ever.

> Love you lots,
> Your Estee

LETTER, June 3, 2007

Dahling, it may be French Mom's Day,
But WE'RE CELEBRATIN' IT!

Mommy,

I love you. There's no other way to put it. You are an
amazing woman, did you know that, Mom? I find that
us kids are the most lucky kids: we have "no" money—
to replace it we have love from two wonderful parents,
we don't have a house—but with you, I think we're
always at home . . . with you, the guardian angel God
sent to love us (:D), I think we don't have to worry.

Mom, I know that I'm just a child, but can I just
say that going through cancer has helped me grow.
Sometimes, when I ponder just why it had to be me,
I get some "answers"? Like, before La Timone, I was
not really close to God. I didn't wanna deal with Him.
I liked enjoying the material things that don't matter
. . . But one day I realized, without God, <u>nothing</u>
matters. So, I asked Him into my heart. Look, I don't
understand anything, basically, about God except
He loves me, He made me, without Him I'm lost. I
wouldn't have realized any of this without you, Dad

Dahling, it may be French Mom's Day,
But WE'RE CELEBRATIN' IT!

Mommy,

I love you, ~~there's~~ no other way to put it.
You are an amazing woman, did you know
that, mom? I find that us kids are the most
lucky kids: we have "no" money, ~~we have~~ to
replace it we have love from two wonderful
parents, we don't have a house - but with you,
I think we're always at home,...with you, the
guardian angel God sent to love us (:), I
think we don't have to worry.

Mom, I know that I'm just a child, but can
I just say that going through cancer has
helped me grow. Sometimes, when I ponder
just why it had to be me, I get some "answers"
like, before La Timone, I was not really close
to God. I didn't wanna deal with Him. I liked
enjoying the material things that don't matter.....
But one day I realized, without God, nothing
matters. So, I asked Him into my heart. Look, I
don't understand anything, basically, about
God except He loves me, He made me, without Him
I'm lost. I wouldn't have realized any of this
without you, dad & Abby telling me to read
the bible and reading it into me, too. Thank you.

Another thing el realized is that your friendship is so very important to me, and I wouldn't
have such a close one with you had it not been
for all this. And if I had the choice of going
back in time, somehow, and preventing the
cancer, I wouldn't, since it would change so
many ~~of these things since~~ things.

I just wanted ▬▬▬ you to know that maybe
I don't really care that I have cancer. It's a part
of me at the moment, and I find I'm quite
fortunate. What I mean is that thyroid cancer
is treatable with radiation, and I'm barely affected
by that! I feel differently about chemotherapy.
I mean... that's tons of poison, killing good stuff too.
I hope they find a good cure for cancer soon. cause
well, if I hadn't gotten sick, I wouldn't have thought
twice about all the patients that suffer from it....

and Abby telling me to read the bible and reading it to me, too. Thank you.

Another thing I realize is that your friendship is <u>so</u> very important to me, and I wouldn't have such a close one with you had it not been for all this. And if I had the choice of going back in time, somehow, and preventing the cancer, I wouldn't, since it would change so many things.

I just wanted you to know that maybe I don't really care that I have cancer. It's a part of me at the moment, and I find I'm quite fortunate. What I mean is that thyroid cancer is treatable with radiation, and I'm barely affected by that! I feel differently about chemotherapy. I mean . . . that's tons of poison, killing good stuff too. I hope they find a good cure for cancer soon, cause well, if I hadn't gotten sick, I wouldn't have thought twice about all the patients that suffer from it . . . I would have "ohh . . . too bad" sympathy, instead of <u>earnest</u> sympathy. Sometimes I just feel the urge to scream and have a fit because doctors can't find a cure for this disease . . . oh, it's painful.

(Wow! I just realized it seems a bit like I'm talking to my diary, not to you. Oh well!!!)

I just thought you should know that I accept the fact that I had thyroid cancer. It's fine and I'm <u>NOT</u> in denial or anything, I just know everything's okay with God and a protecting, loving, caring family helping me through it.

Okay, so, sorry to change the mood but it's your . . . what is it? . . . 18th <u>Mother's Day Day!!</u>

P.S. I'm better at writing on paper than talking. Seriously. Even to Angie. Oh, that reminds me . . . you know that even though I can't open up to [you] as <u>much</u> as I can with her, you do <u>realize</u> that I appreciate your friendship more than <u>a lot</u> of things? Cause I do. And Mom? Babe, I love you, and there's no other way to put it.

PS. tell Dad I say thanks . . . without him I wouldn't be here . . . <u>literally</u>!

Happy Mommy's Day!

I love you.

Ich liebe dich.

Je t'aime.

+ and some hundred or 10 other languages

Your's Forever,

And ever,

And ever,

And ever,

And Infinity,

<3 Estee <3

Mother and daughter,
PLYMOUTH, MASSACHUSETTS, **2003**

Beach Boardwalk,
SANTA CRUZ, CALIFORNIA, 2004

June 5, 2007

Life is going ok right now.
Really, it is.

Mom & Dad had their anniversary on June 2—but they
had their anniversary dinner in town on the first. I
wrote them a card and left it by their door during the
night. They said they "loved" it.

Then at about 11 PM—June 2—, me and Angie decided
to do something for Mother's Day—June 3. (the rents
were in bed—asleep) We used white paper & cut out
"HAPPY MOTHER'S DAY!!!"—2 letters per each page.
We set them on the dining room table, with a card I
wrote Mom (long one!) & a little note Ang wrote. We
decided it looked too plain, so we went out the gate and
got lots of flowers (some from peoples' yards . . . :D). It
was soo fun cause it was about 12:30! And we were ditzy
& blonde. Funerooo.

June 20, 2007   3:00 PM

You know, I have a really great attitude about all this
cancer thing. I smile, laugh and joke about it. I only have
meltdowns like, <u>once</u> every month. And . . . I normally only
have them in my room—away from people. Angie's never
even see me cry about it but it really is hard. It's not like
anyone's here to comfort me now. We're stressed. We're
going to another country tomorrow . . . continent, actually.

What am I supposed to say when people say like,
"Toughen up, you've only been through surgery," just
as Angie just did. It's just . . . surgery doesn't seem the
problem. It was like, 6 months ago. Surgery is gone and
done. But I still have cancer in my body. I'M the one that
God didn't heal. I'm not mad at him, though. He has
reasons for everything. But . . . I just want someone to
ask how I <u>really</u> feel. I still hurt inside, no matter how
happy I am on the outside.

Sorry that I seem so depressed when I talk to you. It's just
. . . you're the only 'person' besides God that I can talk to.
I'm so glad God loves and cares for me. It makes me feel
really safe . . . REALLY. Sigh. I've gotta go clean now.

<3 Later xoxo

Evangeline, Abraham, and Esther,
La Grand-Place,
BRUSSELS, BELGIUM, 2007

It's now June 22 and we're in the states!
Lots to tell . . .

So, I woke up Thursday (21) at 6:40ish, though I wasn't
that tired since I'd fallen asleep before 11. Anyway, we
went on the 8 o'clock bus to Aix, got on the navette to
Marseille airport, and were there soon enough. Then
we got ready to go to the first plane to Munich. So I
was pulling two little suitcase carry-ons, carrying a
little duffel bag, and my mickey. So I was getting really
tired from all that pulling, and everything was getting
heavier, and heavier, so I stopped and said, "Mom,
I can't carry all these bags!" of course whining a bit
(emotions, sleep deprivation). So Mom says "Daddy, can
you pull one of these?" and he comes over and goes,
"Oh ESTHER! Don't do this stupid whining thing!" and
it hurt. I got this stomach-clenching thing I've been
getting lately—when mad, or jealous. And I got sad
and angry, and Dad came to get the bag, all angry and
flustered. As he grabbed the bag, I pulled away with my
now "only" 3 bags, and said "Stop it, Dad!"—my voice
cracking.

I went to the check in/waiting/BK room, and then
walked to the bathroom (without the bags, duh). I went

pee, and cried for . . . 2 (?) minutes, then sprayed water on my face and as soon as I had gained my composure enough, Angie came in.

"Are you ok?"

I walked past her, going out the door. Taking my anger out on her, I guess. "I'm fine."

I walked about 2 feet and then went back in the bathroom, trying not to cry. I burst out in tears, and Angie hugged me, for a long time.

It was really comforting. Really. I'm so glad I walked back in there. I said a bit of what had been on my mind lately. Such as the fact that I feel so alone. And this whole thing is so hard. Cause, it really is. I can't . . . well. She is an amazing friend and sister.

Exact date unknown

Love, intensity, value, passion, rejection, hope, care,
failure, joy. What life throws at us never makes sense.
Thinks we're at life's dispense. How long we wait for
life to change us. How long we should try to change
ourselves. The weight of death, the weight of fear.
The burden of stress, the pain is here. Never to know,
never to guess, never to know, how much mess. Do not
show care, do not have love, do not feel joy, or you may
change.

To feel

The weight of death, the weight of fear,
the burden of stress, pain is here.
Never to know, never to guess.
Never to know, how much mess
Do not show care,
do not feel joy,
do not have love,
life's not a toy
and yet we feel,
we have,
we show,
who knows . . .
I do not know.
I do not know.

(2007) September 9

Wayne, Papa, padre, papi, daddy...
Daddy...

Happy 40th!!!...

you're almost **50**, almost an old guy, wrong choice
of words, i mean a M<u>ATU</u>RE guy. ☺ Duh.
   I just wanted to let you know, dad, how dear you
are to me. you've watched over me and loved me
through everything that has happened. like while
i was in the hospital bed - my hair, a wild mane,
my face, white as the sheet covering me, tubes in
my nose, arms, sides ooo neck at one point! not
to mention my legs were as hairy as yours!-
but throughout this whole episode, you held
my hand and prayed and cared for me. and
loved me. and this is all i need to know you
are the most amazing dad. who knows, maybe
someday this picture of me, sick, tube filled
and peeing in a bed pan, will come back
one day. but if it does, i know you'll

9/16/07

Wayne, Papa, padre, papi, daddy . . .
Daddy . . .

Happy 48th!

You're almost <u>50</u>, almost an old guy! Wrong choice of words, I mean a <u>MATURE</u> guy. :) Duh.

I just wanted to let you know, Dad, how dear you are to me. You've watched over me and loved me through everything that has happened. Like while I was in the hospital bed— my hair, a wild mane, my face, white as the sheeting covering me, tubes in my nose, arms, sides . . . <u>neck</u> at one point! Not to mention my legs were as hairy as yours! : / But throughout this whole episode, you held my hand and prayed and cared for me. And loved me. And this is all I need to know you are the most amazing dad. Who knows, maybe someday this picture of me, sick, tube filled and peeing in a bed pan, will come back one day. But if it does, I know you'll be there, helping me understand it's all worked out in God's eyes; helping me know God loves me even more than you and Mom and everyone put together, times infinity. And Dad? A couple more things . . . without you, I would be a poor, sick, hopeless, girl, but instead I'm just a sick girl. But I'm only sick in my body for the time God wants me on earth, once I get to heaven I'll understand my time on earth was a piece of my time—not even. And that the second God's ready for me to party with him, all the sickness goes away. So that's what gives me hope. Daddy . . . I want to say that I know how much going to work in Switzerland meant to you, how much you were ready and excited and willing to go, and I'm quite sorry that I messed up your plans—but thank you for giving it up for me and everything I need here, in Boston showing me you wouldn't give a second thought about going after the doctors told you what I'd need means so much to me. Just . . . thank you, Daddy, thank you. So much. For everything.

On that note, I'll switch to a different subject.

Happy Birthday!

I hope you have a fantastic birthday, Daddy. I love you too much to express.

> xxoxoxoxoxoxoxoxoxoxoxoo
> Your daughter,
> Esther Earl

Father and daughter,
BOSTON, 2009

September 17, 2007 (Monday at 12:11PM)

You know, I think for a while there my entries were happy ones, the ones where I was like, "yes, life isn't so bad, ladida." And the times when I thought that after all I'd gone through, life was A-okay. Well, life is, I guess, not that bad, but I feel worse than ever. I feel tired, lazy, helpless . . . I don't know. Today I'm feeling sick— my head hurts, my tummy aches, I feel flushed, but I took my temperature and it's a normal 98.0. So yeah yesterday was Daddy's birthday and it was good. On Friday I had started making a cross-stitch of a duck, and (in church!) on Sunday I finished. It had a yellow duck with a blue ribbon on his neck and it sayyyed [sic] . . . "I'm ducky for you, DAD!" or so. I had sorta followed a little duck pattern, so mmhmm. Dad kinda liked it. We also gave him a napkin holder (*snicker*) and a back scratcher (*choke*) and I gave him a letter that I cried while writing (*aww* ;))

Ahh yes, here comes mister serious for a visit—and look he brought Mr. Sober and Mrs. Pleasefeelsorryforme! Wow, what a party. :'\

A while ago, I think on Wednesday the 12th . . . Mom and Dad went to the doctors. They came home with some news! Yeah. —The "!" just exaggerates how upset I am. >: (Quoth Mom (as I can remember) who quoth the doctor. Quoth, "We found more cancer than we suspected in your lungs. Our plan is to do a large dose of radiotherapy in January, to give Esther's lungs time to re-fix themselves." Unquoth. Of course that was a ginormously brief summary, it was way more hesitant, emotional, longer, more detailed, but yeah. I didn't cry until the 'rents left the room after telling me. Me and Angie (I told her it all) hugged and cried. :\ Anyway, what it means is the cancer is more advanced than they thought—more spread. Oh yes, I also have a teensy kidney stone. ☹ Doctor Jessica Smith said it will most likely dissolve and I'll "urinate it out, without noticing . . . may experience little or no discomfort . . ." but I'm really worried for it.

All yesterday I read some of Exodus . . . it was interesting. I read of Moses and God seems so stern. I didn't know he was so strict! Like with the pharaoh why did he cause him so much pain?? Couldn't He (God) have used Moses to open pharaoh's heart?

September 17, 2007

Hey . . . tru? I don't want to grow up. It's so hard. Abe's so oblivious to the pain we experience once we understand more . . . He's so lucky! Do you know that—I've been noticing this for a bit, but—people/adults talk, and I now find their discussions interesting. But they talk like . . . well, here's an example . . . "So I talked to Bob today, and he said Aunt Ronda has cancer now. Yes, terrible." "Joy said <u>Opa's</u> cancer has spread!" "Esther, did you know Keri's mom's dad has cancer now, too?" and cancer pops up in so many conversations and the 'rents talk so openly about "he died of this cancer, and her of that . . . " that I feel so sad, like I'm gonna die! Oh, didn't I tell you? Before, when I had NORMAL THYROID CANCER, I fell into the 99.6% <— (around there) of kids who cure fine. And OK I fall into the 0.4% of kids who cure, and then it comes back again sometimes and they die, or they die right away, or they are as Mom put it, "you fall into the 'unsure category.'" Fun, eh? So I could die. Scary . . . But I feel so peaceful. I truthfully think a lot of the time it's worse for the friend or family member who doesn't have cancer, and isn't used to having a different person with sickness and weakness, or when they die . . . But oh it's just difficult being so different. I

don't mind as much as I used to, but if it hadn't spread, I might've been cured now . . . so it's getting to me a bit again. Other than that were all fine! : D tired—g'night.

xoxo <3 Esther Earl

Bubble Girl,
MEDWAY, MASSACHUSETTS, **2009**

Thursday, September 20, 2007

Hi :) sorry about being such an emo-sounding person,
it's just I'm always quite depressed at night, and also
you're the only person . . . thing? . . . I can release my
sadness to.

Doctor Smith e-mailed Mum and Dad today, telling us
she's scheduling an MRI, a date with her, I THINK with
the physical therapist and also someone else. I looked
up MRIs on Google Images and it looks like the picture
as I can draw it on the next page. I'm nervous for it not
only because I have to go through some claustrophobic
thing, but because there's a chance it could have spread.
And it's already so, so hard. Today I said to Mom, "What
would happen if I have cancer in my spine?" And as she
talked about how serious that would be, and how if it
spread *pause* it would first go to leukemia . . . it hit me
that I have cancer.

CANCER! The kind of sickness that people die of —often!
It's not like I dwell on it that much—but I sure don't like
the fact that I do have cancer. And I might die. It's more
serious of an illness I never thought I could have—not
even during surgery. I mean right before surgery funny
enough I didn't feel too sad. I was just thinking of when

I went into surgery—to switch subjects. And right before I did, Opa prayed and prayed, and Mom and Dad did too, but I remember feeling so full of peace. I remember that I talked/prayed to God while I lay on my surgery bed thing, unable to move because the shunt in my side hurt. And I remember telling God that whatever happens, happens. I remember telling myself "He's in control." I remember that I didn't even feel nervous going in—just a little sad about maybe (if things went wrong) never seeing my family again. Ha, I just had a sobbing attack. I was just thinking how I don't know if I'll live. I'm so scared. God means so much to me, but I wish He could heal me. Is that vain? selfish? stupid? That I want to be better is, I think, any sick child's wish. You know how God especially loves children? I'm a child —right? Well, I just want him to lift me up and hug me, like in all those pictures of Jesus and the children . . . Is that too much to ask for? Maybe so, I don't know. I'm off reading Esther in the Bible—there's one verse that I'm especially looking for.

GOODNIGHT! <3 Esther

Esther 8:3 *"If I have found favor with you, O king, and if it pleases your majesty—grant me my life—this is my petition."*

things i'm thankful for:

- my cats!
- my family:
- oxygen machines
- air conditioner
- weight
- God
- our house

things I'm thankful for:

- my cats!

- my family!

- oxygen machines

- air conditioner

- weight

- God

- our house

CARINGBRIDGE
ESTHER EARL / JOURNAL
Esther Grace Earl's Journal

The CaringBridge site for Esther began after she had come precariously close to leaving us during an extended stay at the hospital in October 2008. As she lay unconscious over several days, many people became aware of the seriousness of her illness for the first time. Since her diagnosis, we had communicated updates with family and friends through e-mail and phone calls, but suddenly there were far too many new sympathizers! Lori looked around and decided that CaringBridge would be the perfect vehicle for getting the news out about her condition more efficiently. On November 1, 2008, Esther's father wrote the first Guestbook entry:

Dearest Estee Star,

I love you loads and loads and you are on my mind even for those moments when I'm not by your side!

Always and Forever,

Daddy

Esther's CaringBridge continues to remain active and people are still writing encouraging notes to her and to our family. As of November 1, 2013—five years since opening the site—there have been over 84,000 visits.

At Children's Hospital,
BOSTON, MASSACHUSETTS, **2009**

75

Saturday, November 1, 2008 12:30 PM, EDT

The last week has seen some good improvement in
Esther's energy level and appetite. She ate servings
of Mom's stuffed grape leaves, and last night enjoyed
African curry! Talk has been of sending her home next
week to spend some time at home, once the logistics of
getting her back and forth for hospital visits at her high
oxygen settings is worked out. We'd love to have her
home, and she is so anxious to see her kitties, Pancake
and Blueberry.

Monday, November 3, 2008 11:28 PM, CST

Okay, so this is the journal on this site! Apparently it's where we'll be updating the main things that go on with me (Esther). Most of the time mom (also known as Lori) will be updating it, but I want to say hi sometimes too. :) Even if I don't always respond or write stuff, I'd just like to say that I love all the messages and cards and thoughts and prayers and all the people that think about me, and us. I'm so thankful for everything. Thank you all so much. :) So just to say really quickly that I feel good, and going home tomorrow is being talked seriously about! Yes:D

-Esther

Me and Blueberry,
FALL, **2008**

Tuesday, November 4, 2008 10:18 PM, CST

On this election day, as you await the results with either joy or fortitude, here's something to REALLY celebrate!!! Esther Earl is home tonight from the hospital! In sharing with a fellow teacher today, I stopped in mid-telling to exclaim—"This is what happiness feels like!"

While Esther's diagnosis is unchanged, and her oxygen settings are very high (5 liters), the doctors felt she was stable enough to come home as long as she is able. We are thrilled, and she savored the freedom of leaving Children's Hospital after 32 days of incarceration! Her kitties, brothers and sisters welcomed her home, and we plan to enjoy each moment God may give us with Esther, whether that is a few months or years. Rejoice with us!

Thursday, November 6, 2008 5:40 AM, EST

Early Thursday morning, and Esther has been holding her own here at home! A few panic moments here and there, like the fuse blowing 4 times in a row in her room due to all the machines going at once—some adjusting of what's plugged where, and so far so good! (We're also getting the landlord over to see if he can update the electricity upstairs in this old house!) Then, Esther woke me at 4:30 this morning because her oxygen count was really low—we checked it out, and her biPAP was going, but the oxygen wasn't connected. Oops!

Esther's visiting nurse yesterday said her numbers look good. We got to practice French with her, since she is from Haiti. Thanks to all of you for your encouragement: spiritual, emotional, and financial. Happy Thursday!

Saturday, November 8, 2008 3:51 PM, EST

Saturday—We're getting used to our "new" routine, making sure Esther has her medications at the right time, making sure everything is hooked in and turned on! She had a LONG hot shower yesterday, and feels like a new woman. Amazing how we can appreciate small things as luxuries, when we've gone without them . . .

Some have asked what Esther enjoys. She likes reading Archie and Garfield comics, and teen & fashion magazines. She plays computer games on her Mac, and has a few favorite TV shows like "What Not to Wear," "Jon & Kate + 8," and "Grey's Anatomy." She loves painting her nails (latest models were white, sporting dots like dice!). We never know what new activity will catch her fancy—in the hospital she did 8–10 huge puzzles. We're just so happy to see her enjoying life!

Sunday, November 9, 2008 1:29 PM, EST

Thought you'd enjoy Esther's thoughts on what makes a good nurse:

- They can get blood out of your veins on the first try.
- They don't wake you up in the morning.
- They know how to put on and take off duoderm without taking off your skin too.
- They don't talk to me as if I'm a baby.
- They don't wake me up when I'm sleeping.
- They're patient even when I'm grumpy.
- They listen to my requests with respect.
- They don't wake me up!

Most of the staff at Children's Hospital were wonderful, and we appreciate all they've done for us. The few who were challenging gave us opportunity to grow! So thanks to them, too!

Tuesday, November 11, 2008 11:25 AM, CST

MAKE A WISH

Esther had a great day Monday! It started off with our first appointment at The Jimmy Fund cancer clinic in Boston which was a positive experience as our primary caretakers there are a joyful duo, perfectly suited for Esther. All told, she was off the Bi-pap machine for 16 hours, drew some cool pictures for friends, ate some Chinese food, texted big sister Abby and visited long and well with the dog, sundry cats, mom, dad, Abe and Angie.

Last week the Make a Wish people stopped by but couldn't get any ideas from our Star. She simply does not wish for anything—except to be well of course. Recently she dreamt that she was in France walking briskly along with her sister when suddenly she noticed she didn't have her oxygen tank! She began to panic when she happily realized that she no longer needed one! That's the stuff of wishes . . .

What do you wish for when you already have all you want and need? She said she'd like another cat but we told her she'd have to trade one in first! (Had we the room, she'd have many and varied members of the animal kingdom.) She mentioned she'd like to visit India because she loves the color and cuisine there, but she can't travel. She'd like to swim again . . . There isn't anyone she'd like to meet, nothing she longs to have. Her ideas are always about what she'd like to give and not get. Any ideas for such a hard case?

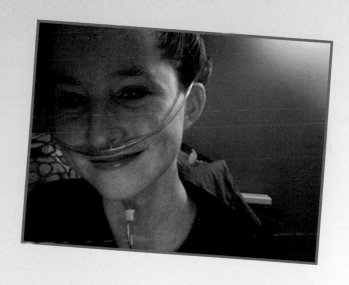

Esther's room,
QUINCY, MASSACHUSETTS, **2009**

Wednesday, November 12, 2008 7:26 PM, CST

Hi there. :) Quick update to let you know I'm doing good! I had a hospital appointment in Children's on Monday, and that went really well, even waking up at 8am was . . . okay. Hahaha. And Tuesday some friends came and visited for a while, which was wicked fun. We took a lot of pictures and played Scene-It, and hung out. :) Then Wednesday and today I've just spent time with the family, watched tv, played games and stuff. So yeah, things are going good, I've been feeling alright. I love reading all the messages and cards people send! Also wanted to post a link to a site (it's called Flickr) with many more pictures of me and the family. Go <u>here</u> to see them!

Love Esther

Friday, November 21, 2008 6:07 PM, EST

Esther had her second visit to the Jimmy Fund Clinic
yesterday. It was a four hour, big excursion for her,
since she doesn't leave the house except for those
visits. Getting down the stairs, out to the van, into
the hospital, blood work, check up, and back home,
all in about 30 degree weather . . . whew! She does
have constant throat discomfort and they said her
recent, and intense stomach pains are probably due
to the acidity of the chemo drug she's been taking.
Unfortunately, for the first time her red blood cell
count is now down—undoubtedly why she's been
more fatigued than usual. So next Wednesday morning
we'll be going in at 8 am for her first 2-3 hour blood
transfusion. Some have wondered whether Estee is in
remission; no, that would mean that she was cancer
free. She is unlikely to ever experience a remission and
it is hoped that the present chemotherapy will stop
further tumor growth and possibly even destroy cancer
cells. But that's a best case scenario and her medical
team(s) really doesn't know if she'll live sixty days or
sixty years. They have been clear that it will take a
miracle for her to see adulthood. We've talked about it,
about dying, her odds and she's aware of what we are
writing here. Dad reminded her about 2am yesterday

that to be absent from the body is to be present with the Lord. For a young woman who wants nothing more than to be present with her Lord, that's not a bad deal. Of course, she, and we, prefer she stick around to bless her great-grandchildren! Our family is really looking forward to Thanksgiving. We've decided to fix just a tiny turkey breast so that we can focus on the fixin's that we really love! Roasted veggies, lots of mashed potatoes (this is the one thing Esther's craving!), olives and other condiments, and pumpkin muffins and pumpkin pie. We hope all of you consider God's blessings along with us this holiday season.

Thursday, November 27, 2008 12:11 AM, CST

Dear Friends,

It is now Thanksgiving, a day to gather with friends and family and together express gratefulness and appreciation for our many blessings. Today also marks exactly two years since we first heard the words, "Esther has cancer." We've been thankful for each day we've had and especially encouraged by Esther's recent blood transfusion which pushed her numbers from 23 to 38! Also, after two full days of antibiotics, she has begun healing from an infection and is now feeling much better. You can see Esther sharing various thoughts in her own quirky way by clicking the link to youtube here on this site.

We also answered the door today to learn that a friend had submitted our names to a local radio station and we'd been chosen to receive a full Thanksgiving meal! So, we will be cooking an entire turkey after all!

Monday, December 1, 2008 6:30 PM, EST

I'm glad so many are interested in our Esther. The many
notes and expressions of caring encourage us all. Wayne
and I think of each of you, even if we don't respond with
individual emails back!

Thanksgiving was emotional for me. It was supreme
happiness to be together as a family, and to share lists
around the laden table of what we're thankful for. But
I'm often overwhelmed by grief that Esther is so much
worse than a year ago, even. Last year we went to the
Quincy Christmas parade and to a Christmas farm to
cut a tree for the season. This year Esther's only outings
are likely to be doctor visits, although we're hoping to
get her to Angie's Holiday Concert at North Quincy High
School. We should be able to take her in a wheel chair,
with oxygen in tow . . .

The reports from her blood work today are good, with
red blood cell counts staying up this time. She has a
continued infection near her g-tube site, and hasn't
been able to eat much because the rash on her face is
now internal as well, and it causes too much discomfort
to swallow more than necessary. We may have to take
her in to the Clinic tomorrow to check things out and

see what medication they can prescribe for these side effects. Lately she's been enjoying her new journal, and we've caught glimpses of drawings of her cats in her sketch book.

We are consciously thankful each day.

Selfie,
BOSTON, 2008

Accio Pooh!
QUINCY, MASSACHUSETTS, **2008**

JOURNAL, December 2, 2008

This is my <u>new</u> journal.

Right now I'm sitting here watching *Jon & Kate Plus 8*, which, by the way, is my favorite show. At the moment the Gosselin's and all their 8 kids are going on the Oprah show to talk about all their problems.

I read their book, *Multiple Blessings*, about a week ago. It's mainly by Kate and her good friend Beth Carson, and it's about being pregnant with sextuplets, and going through all the financial and emotional and physical difficulties. The book is full of stories of their faith, and many times when they basically gave up, but God came through! Those stories inspire me and made me remember it's God who's getting me through all MY difficulties.

What are <u>my</u> difficulties? Hmm. First of all, and definitely most difficult, I have cancer, and I'm sick. Second, our money and income stuff is slightly in shambles; though it may not be, I never really hear about our money stuff. Third, I guess there's not that much of a third, just that I'm getting older, I guess. So, let's talk about that wonderful cancer topic again . . .

Ah, I'm not sure exactly where to start. I'll start with the whole friggen story! Yeah, that's a <u>great</u> place to begin.

Let's see, when I was twelve, actually no I was eleven, we were living in Plymouth, MA, duh. So then Mom & Dad decided it'd be just grand to move to France. We moved sometime toward winter, was it November?, to a town called Albertville in the Alps of France. That was an . . . experience. Maybe you'll hear about o'l [sic] Albertville another time. After—wait, no. While living in Albertville my all-French 5th grade class went to a pool for Gym and we had to swim—I remember feeling so out of breath while having to swim four laps without stopping. Also, we had to run laps around our school yard, and I thought it was weird that I had cramps on my rib cage, but I thought I was just out of shape.

Also in Albertville me and Angie began walking on walks around town, basically at least every other day. We continued doing that all the way until we moved to a new town in France called Aix-en-Provence.

One time, somewhere between the summer and fall, we went on a long walk to a park site sort of nearby. We brought the keys from our apartment and were just getting ready to go inside our apartment again when we couldn't find the keys. Suddenly I remembered leaving them on the grass and Angie and I walked part way back. Angie told me to go the rest of the way by myself. I got the keys and went back home.

My side hurt and I was extremely out of breath. I caught my breath in an half hour or so.

That whole losing-my-breath, coughing, pain-in-my-side thing started maybe in September or October. I thought the pain was regular old exercise pain or period pain. I also thought I was out of breath because I exercised too much.

While we lived in France, Abby was going to boarding school in Germany that was English speaking. Me, Mom and Angie went to visit her for two or so days.

When we got back, Dad figured any cold or trick-to-get-out-of-school that was causing my cough would be gone. When it wasn't, Dad said, "Let's get an X-ray." So we did just that, and the X-ray showed loads of fluid in my lungs. The doctor said to go to the hospital. >:,S

We went to the hospital, and I think it was the next morning, they sent me into surgery for a tube in my side that would drain out the liquid.

Going in was definitely scary. I just laid on the bed and prayed so hard, asking God to just take care of me. A

very nice surgeon lady held my hand while they shot sleeping medicine in.

After surgery, I slept for the next day or two, in and out of consciousness. The tube itself was like a quarter of an inch, and was in my left rib, going through to the lining of my lung (not my actual lung, ha!). It drained a load of liquid.

A few days later, in the hospital still, they had tested and poked me, trying to figure out why I had liquid. They thought it was TB or pneumonia, or something

Kandern, Germany,
JUNE, 2007

like that. However, on Thanksgiving, the doctors came in and said I had cancer. **crap**

I'm not sure when it was, but a little bit later I had a lump in my neck removed, along with my thyroid and one (or two, or three?) para-thyroid.

A few days later, I was moved to La Timone, Marseille's Children's Hospital. They were more experienced with cancer in children, however thyroid cancer in children is especially rare, so they weren't that experienced.

I had a dose of radio-iodine treatment, which was a pill that didn't have many side effects. About a month or so later (maybe 2 months?) I had another dose, and a while later another.

They planned to do another dose when we got back from America, where we were going for two months? But it turned out we ended up staying in America for forever.

So coming to Children's Hospital was a lot different than La Timone because they seemed to know what they were doing more. I had a dose of radio-iodine therapy, much larger, and worked on feeling good.

Then, 2 months ago, just a week or so away from another radio-iodine dose, I felt a large rumbling in my lower left/ middle lung, and figured it was another wheeze. I was on the toilet peeing, so I breathed in and out and it rumbled a lot. I coughed, expecting mucus, and instead saw blood.

You don't know what it felt like to look in my tissue and see blood. My heart thudded so fast, my stomach sunk and I got light-headed. I yelled for Mom, but I was so worried my voice cracked. She heard and Mom and Dad came running up. After coughing some more into a bowl, Dad took me to emergency. By then I was feeling fine, still unnerved, but fine. My oxygen was cranked up from 2 to 4, but I was fine, fine. I was checked in and they said I bled mainly because being off my thyroxin (in preparation for radio-iodine) my lung tumors had become über active.

A few days later I had my radio-iodine dose. I was fine for the first day. Second day I was headachey. Third day I was on a new air machine, "BiPAP," and on morphine. I only remember sleeping, Mom came in and woke me and said Abby and Angie were there, so I drowsily hung out for a few minutes with them. Mom and Dad stayed in my room, sometimes switching and going out for a while because of my high radiation levels.

Apparently everyone highly, highly thought I was going to die. That's why, despite such high levels of radiation, Mom and Dad spent so much time in my room, and Abby and Angie came to see me. But I didn't know I was close to dying, I just figured because this dose of radiation was so much higher I was feeling quite sick.

Fortunately, praise God, I made it through! It wasn't until like a week later, in the ICU where I was staying, that Mom told me about the dying thing. Hearing that made me think more about dying, death, heaven, hell. I'd always thought I knew how scary death was.

I thought you died, and then went to where you were supposed to go, but I didn't think too hard about it. <u>Now</u>, being at a point in my life where doctors say I'll live 6 days, or 6 months, or 6 years, or <u>60</u> years, they don't know, I've had more time to say, if I died tomorrow, what would happen?

Even having all this time to think, I don't think my views of death have changed too much. I guess now I figure you die, and then you have a sense of looking at your body from above, as Dad has said when we've talked about it. And then maybe you meet someone who takes you to where you go. Or maybe you're already there, I don't know. I wonder if anyone on earth's idea of death is spot-on.

December 3, 2008

Since I'm sick, obviously, and in a way that really keeps me room bound most of the time, I don't see many people. Part of that is that I don't <u>want</u> to, so we ask people not to visit. I mean, who wants people they barely know to come into their house and be like, "How are you?"? That's just weird stuff that has happened to me before. Haha :\

But I also feel like I'm cut off the world. One day a week ago or so, my best friend Alexa and my good friend Melissa who I met through North Carolina, came to visit for 3 hours. It was pretty awkward at first, but after a while it was so fun!

So I would like to have some form of human contact in my life, but the want for social stuff comes and goes spontaneously (if that's how you spell it . . .). Maybe one day we'll figure this out.

. . .

Okay, so this is slightly embarrassing, but when I'm bored, (aka every second of every friggen hour) sometimes I film myself doing something on the computer and post it to . . . <u>YOUTUBE!!</u> How lame am

I? Oh man, so lame. But so far I have an intro video, titled, what else?, "Intro to YouTube," a "favorites" video where I show my favorite things, and now "That's so Funny" where I talk about those annoying people who say "that's so funny" all the time. Even when it's not.

When Mom and Dad bought this journal for me (which I titled Daisy, though that may change), they also bought a sketch book where I've been drawing some stuff. Recently I drew an eye, eyebrow, nose and lips on a page. It's supposed to look like half of her face, not many detailing on the nose and rest of face. I must say I'm really proud of the eye. I was thinking when I can't think of what to write and the mood strikes, I'll try to redraw it here.

ooh dude that looks FREAKY. but dont you love the gorgeou

iris? ☺

December 5, 2008

Ugh. Ugh, ugh, ugh.

Do you know what happened the day before yesterday?
I had a migraine. Then yesterday I went to the hospital,
where, by the way, Annette my nurse said, "Whose
blood was drawn here? Your numbers look amazing!" :)
After getting home I was so completely exhausted. Then
later a migraine popped up. I took a 4 hour nap and
then was up for a while when, another migraine popped
up. Joy. I don't know what's causing them . . . tiredness?
Chemo? Stress? Tumors? Ahrgh.

So, I'm embarrassed to say this mainly because I know
one day Dad and Mom will be reading it, but too bad.
You know how my life is full of problems teens shouldn't
have to deal with? AKA cancer? Well, when I get to do
"normal" things, like watch a movie with my sisters, get
out of the house, or just get downstairs, I tend to feel
better. Tired, but good.

And lately, I've been thinking about boys, uh-oh. It was
weird, cause I had this dream where I kissed a boy (I
don't know who), and then kissed him again, and that's
why I have been thinking about boys. So yeah, lately

I've really, really thought that if and when I die, I'd like to have one more normal teen thing, which is kissing a boy. =) And I feel stupid thinking that because in the midst of wanting to spend more time with my family and becoming closer to God, there's this huge want for a first kiss. So hit your knee and call me Sally I friggen want a kiss. It's something normal I may never have, <u>another</u> thing I'll miss out on. Sigh.

I can't think of what else to write. I'm afraid to write random thoughts cause this book is gorgeous and I don't want to ruin it..! :D

Oh! CHRISTMAS! <u>SO</u> EXCITED FOR IT! I've kind of thought of what I'd like. S'quite a bit of stuff, shall I include it? Yeah? Okay. ;)

<u>List:</u> 1. <u>Matt and Kim</u> CD (self titled)

~~Phantom Planet CD~~ 2. Makeup 3. SOCKS!

4. Matt and Kim <u>Grand</u> CD (not out til January . . .)

5. gift cards/money =)

6. Regina Spektor CD

Sunday, December 7, 2008 8:07 AM, EST - Lori

It's early Sunday morning, and a light snow is falling! Our first this season. The boys couldn't sleep in, of course, and are already out playing in the backyard, with my frequent "Shhh!" so they won't wake up the neighborhood! I'm on Craigslist trying to find a futon since Abby will be with us over the Christmas vacation.

Esther had a good visit at the Jimmy Fund Clinic Thursday. Her nurse practitioner came back in with an excited, "Whose blood is this? It's perfect!" We're so glad her body is showing good signs of underlying strength. She came home with two new antibiotics for blood in her urine, and a lymphnode in her neck that seems infected—better than it being another tumor, though! Also she has a medication to take every eight hours that will coat her esophagus. Last night she was already able to eat more than she has in a week or two, since the pain had gone down a lot. Last night Wayne was plotting out all of her meds on an hourly chart—complicated, since some require an empty stomach, some you can't eat after for 2 hours, others must be taken alone . . . it requires a degree to figure it out!

Later today Wayne is going to pick up a cut tree—no tree farm this year. Then we'll bring Esther downstairs to decorate tonight. A fire in our beautiful old brick fireplace, and some freshly-baked pumpkin muffins with cider are on the agenda!

Daily Booth photo,
QUINCY, MASSACHUSETTS, **2008**

December 8, 2008

You know what's kind of weird?

Every night, almost, while I'm going to bed, I talk kind of to myself and kind of to God (my form of prayer, I suppose). And while I'm talking to God, it's no doubt I talk of my pains and also of cancer. That is not the weird part. The odd part is that I usually end up having tears roll down my cheeks, but I'm not sure why since daily I'm not (<u>too</u>) sad about cancer. Maybe it lets off some of my emotions that normal* people direct in everyday social situations . . . I have no idea.

So to change the subject, lately I've been thinking about my identity. Why, you ask? (Maybe you're not asking, but you're my journal, so you're gonna ask!) Well I drew this very not-so-good self-portrait of myself the other day, and Abe saw it. He was like, "You drew that? Without any picture?" and was slightly in awe, which was cool that at least Abe was . . . in awe. And then he said, "but where's your nose thing?" pointing to my nasal cannula. To me it seemed more insightful than something that bothered me. However Mom heard, and Dad too, and later Dad said Mom cried.

It is kind of sad I guess, to see my energetically, enthusiastic 5-year-old brother not remember the days when he was 2/3, and I would take him to play on the bars in Albertville, or he would watch me do flips all around the bar. But I kind of think of Abe as not remembering, but everyone else as. But now I'm realizing that it has been over <u>2</u> years, and memories began to fade, and are replaced with making a "HUGE" trip out to dinner, or something. I hope not all the memories are bad. :\

Another thing Abraham said which was funny and not sad (woo!), and also quite original, was, while we were decorating the tree, Abe said, "Oh! Just <u>one</u> more!" as he tried to pick up Mom. It was funny funny.

Oh yeah! We decorated our Christmas tree last night! Dad and the boys went to Home Depot and picked a pre-cut one that they brought home and set in the corner of the living room. We then ate dinner, which was stew, and, yes!, I did go downstairs to eat with everyone! Minus Abby though. :P After dinner Angie went to bed and we all decorated the tree. Abe loved the ornaments of him*, and Graham seemed to like hanging the ornaments, "down low so they would fall on the tree skirt not break" he said.

So that was <u>loads</u> of fun! I wish Angie had stayed upstairs long enough. However she has a "life." Two nights ago she "slept" over (aka stayed awake over) her friend Michelle's house. Apparently she was tired last night, go figure.

I think that because I have cancer, I spend a lot of time with the 'rents. And because of that I think I get along best out of us sisters, because of it, with the parents. Abby does, I guess get along with them but doesn't <u>always</u> respect them. I think Angie respects them even less, just by the way she treats them, but maybe not. I've never asked her . . . But anyway, the way she treats them gets on my nerves lately, and because of it sometimes I don't say that much to her, and then my head says, "don't do that Esther." So I'm nice to her again. But by that time she's gone back under "her life" rock, which she would do anyway if I were nice or mean. I'm <u>usually</u> always nice though. I think I just completely contradicted myself there, hah.

*Normal?! What the heck is normal? Healthy is, I guess, my definition of it. Apparently.

*ego maniac! Nahhh :D

December 11 / December 12, 2008

It's 2 in the morn'!

Wow, today was one of the most eventful days in a while, for me. It started at 9:30 am, I woke up feeling nauseous, so I called Dad and he came up to my room and gave me my nausea helping pill. Then I got myself all pretty, got ready, and me and Dad left for Jimmy Fund at 10:30am-ish. We got there at around . . . 11:30. I got my blood drawn, got new high scores on the Webkinz games site (GEEK!) and peed in a cup. When they drew my blood they missed friggen vein and had to do the other freaking arm.

(You know, at one point I would have screamed and cried if they tried to take my blood; a bit later than that I would tear up and have to take large breaths; little bit later if you tried I would get watery eyed when it went in; and now when they do it, I take a long breath in, I don't know why, and they do it. It really just pinches.)

What <u>did</u> annoy me about this time—other than missing the "freaking arm"—was that one of the nurses was like "does that hurt?" as she's moving the needle around in my vein. I did my best duh/confused face and she kept asking. I know it's her job, but of course it hurt! Afterward, with my Band-Aids all on and blood drawn, she's like, "does it hurt" pointing to the Band-Aids. I said no.

It's insane how little things that are meant by no means to be personal, or even close to what I'm currently worrying about can make me angry, or sad, or lonely, or happy. Like, well, I can't think of any examples right now. Oh well, if I do I'll include it in here.

Oh yeah, I was talking about my day. So after I did all that I weighed (<u>88.2 POUNDS</u>!!) and got my temperature and blood pressure. And whenever they do blood pressure, they wrap the wrap part around your upper arm and you (me . . .) straighten my arm and it tightens so hard—so hard, in fact, that I get cuts from it. Not bleeding ones, just under my skin. Then the blood pressure is unwrapped, and mine's been good. Which is good, cause for this new experimental drug, high bp is common, so they're watching mine.

After vitals, Annette came in and we went over my pains from toe to head. Lower body's fine, arms are okay, my g-tube is still acting odd, it's slightly infected. My throat/neck still has that weird lump thing going on. I'm not sure what it is, neither are they. My head has a new pain,

I don't know how to describe it well . . . Hm, the back left, near my ear, and down toward my neck, too, I get this come-and-go pulsing kind of pain. It comes when I change positions, and it's like, "no pain, RUSH OF PAIN, no pain." It's rather odd and it was yesterday and day before, more annoying than painful, however now it's been hurting more. Yeah.

So after we went over that we chatted a little, I saw Dr. G! He's funny. He definitely is a cheery person that makes you feel better just by seeing him. Plus he treats kids and adults the same—same tone. No talking to me like I'm 5 years old, which is quite enjoyable. After that, we, would you believe it, got in our car! Then me and Dad decided to go to OLIVE GARDEN! So I ***walked*** from the car, into the restaurant, down past many seats, to our seat. That is a load of walking my friend! Like no joke. We ate their delicious chocolate cake and their wicked good salad! And we just talked about whatever, nothing deep! It was nice hanging out with Dad. He's a pretty cool guy—for a dad. ;D

Then we walked to the car—in the rain!—and got home, and then I walked up the stairs to my bed and sat down. And now, after hours, here I sit.

So, I was thinking, if I were to describe my family now,

as they are now, what would I say? And what would I do to draw them? In a silly way, I thought I'd give it a shot.

Nevermind. That was an awful idea. But I <u>do</u> have a good one! Ready?!

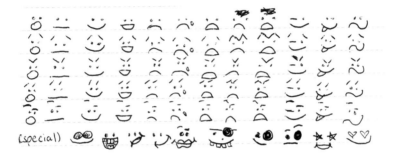

Those are (only some of) my fantastic, fabulous assortments of goodies! Smiley goodies, that is. Doncha love 'em? My fave is <;) which looks different than the last every time I do it! Although I can't remember ever actually doing that smiley . . . heh. Smilies are fun.

December 12, 2008

Noticed my "Holiday page decor"?

Abby and Elise came home today, and they'll be here till Sunday, which is 2 days away (it's Friday). Tomorrow we're going out to a restaurant called Tia's, and we're gonna have LOBSTER! I don't even like, know if I like lobster, but I'm hoping I do. We were going to go to No Name but Tia's is better because it's more fancy schmancy.

Oh, so you know how I was talking about how little things sometimes set off some of my emotions? Yeah, I was talking about that yesterday. Anyway, today Dad was frustrated about something and he snapped at me last night and a few times today. And I realize he's not "being personal" but I just felt like crying. I don't ever cry during the day. If I have to I hold it in and plan to cry that night. Sometimes I do or sometimes I don't. If I don't, the repressed emotion is added to my emotion pot, and if the emotion pot fills, I break down.

So when Dad was snapping I felt like it's my fault he's stressed. And lately I've been like, well DUH, it's my fault my parents are stressed. If it weren't for me they'd be in

France still, or where they want to be. Obviously they don't say that, but it's true. When any type of sickness is in your house, there's of course gonna be added stress and frustration . . . thus it's my fault.

Another thing that I've sensed, but have over-thought, is that Mom and Dad think I'm lazy. They do, but wouldn't say so because they wouldn't want to hurt my feelings. I think I'm lethargic and I could do more, but I AM like, limited. I get disoriented if I walk somewhere, and out of breath.

But I could do more and I would do more, but finding the motivation for doing stuff comes in really small amounts. Like really small. :\ If I felt more motivated, I'd probably do more, but I feel like doing stuff is pointless. AGagh.

Well, I'm off to put on my BiPAP and think of life. Joy to the world . . . <:D

Oh, also, what do I draw? My sketch book has been ignored for days! I can't think of anything. D:> I don't like "still life," I think I like more imaginary or fantasy things. Meh.

December 15 (the 14ᵗʰ at 12am . . .), 2008
Dish on Lobster dish.

Last night, Abby and Elise and Mom and Angie, and I,
went out for dinner! We stuffed 2 big oxygen tanks in,
and 3 little ones, for a just-in-case pleasant evening. So
we drove in the car to the restaurant! We were going to
go to Anthony Piers 4 in the most original plan, but that
was loads of moolah so we decided on Tia's. Mom called
them and found out they were closed for winter! Ick. So
Mom picked the not-too-fancy, not-too-casual Barking
Crab. We got there and got our table by the fire*.
*But not too close . . . no one wants an oxygen tank
explosion. <:]

Unfortunately, we were also by the door, and every
time it opened we'd feel a rush of cold air. Brr! D: Other
than that it was comfy. Apparently the bathroom was
outside, but only Elise and Angie had to pee, so, haha!

We got a bucket of crab legs for appetizer, onion rings
too. The crab legs looked so odd. And we had no idea how
to get the meat out of the shell, so we asked, and the lady
waitress brought us a huge rock to smash it with!

So you stick the crab leg in the middle of your paper
plate and fold over half of it. Then you take your rock

and hit the folded over plate, on top of the crab, until you hear a crack. Then you open the plate, take the leg and peel off shell until you see the meat. Then you take your fork/fingers and slide the meat off and eat it! I wasn't a huge fan of it, but it was okay.

Then I got lobster. A WHOLE lobster. With antennae and legs and everything. They pre-cut it where it needs to be cut, and "all I had to do" was 1. Twist the claws off, there were two! 2. Pull the body backwards so the tail comes off. 3. Stare/laugh/gag at the poop stuff that falls off after unhinging the tail. 4. Peel away the tail shell. 5. Pull the meat off the bone stuff. 6. Dip the <u>meat</u> in butter and <u>eat</u>.

At the Barking Crab,
BOSTON, MASSACHUSETTS, **2008**

Not too hard. Sadly I kind of liked the taste, just not the texture or the I-don't-know thing about it. Ickay. :/ I ate a little, Abby ate the rest, and I ate loooads of onion rings. They were so good.

Hey, I was thinking, you know how people have things on a list of stuff they'd do before they died if given the chance? I want to do something like that. I don't know yet. There are some things I'd do if I had no breathing problems:

1) Make a stand in a downtown area with the sign "free hugs" and give a hug to anyone who wanted.

2) Somehow do something for sick children.

3) Taste lots of different foods.

4) Go to India

5) Witness something truly amazing

6) Do more.

But I don't know. I'd like to do stuff and, just LIVE, because if I do die soon, sitting in my room with the occasional movement will not work. It's just hard moving around. You know wha'm <u>sayin'</u>? G'nizzle. (night . . .)

Monday, December 15, 2008 5:54 PM, EST

Esther is doing pretty well these days, which makes for a happily anticipated Christmas season! This weekend Abby was home from Gordon College, and a close friend of hers from Black Forest Academy days was visiting from college in Missouri. I took all the girls out to a little seafood place a few miles from us, on the wharf in Boston, since Esther felt up to an outing and said, "I've never tasted lobster!" A couple of us had fish, Angie had asparagus, and Esther tried lobster. She didn't like it ... but she filled up on onion rings and we had a great evening. She did super with her oxygen tank (I think we took 4 tanks with us, just in case ... !).

Our Christmas Tree looks wonderful, even though it's from Lowes and not handpicked by us from the farm. This little house has a brick fireplace, so we've been enjoying some warm evenings near the tree. Wishing you all a great week as you wind down (or rev up!) for the holidays!

Monday, December 15, 2008

I had that huge adventure (because apparently I'm an adventurist . . .) on, um, Saturday, the one with the lobster, and it was fun. It was also extremely exhausting, and that night I slept pretty much without waking. The next day, (yesterday) I woke up at like 5 pm, even though all my lights plus my TV had been going since 2 when Dad started to "wake me up." BAHA! So yes, I was quite a bit tired. Yesterday was slow and lethargic— Although I DID make a new YouTube video? Excitement

THIS morning I woke up around 6am and felt soo nauseous. That's happened a few mornings since starting chemo, especially if I forget my nausea pill the night before. Which I did last night.

So yeah . . . wake up at 6 and called Mom's cell, because I figured she was at home (disorientation . . .) but of course she was at school, so I called home, feeling so sick. Dad came up and stuck a bowl in front of me as I threw up. That was good timing, since otherwise it'd be up-chuck-bedding.

Can I just say, my esophagus has that "mucicidos" thing

going on, which is like a rash inside my esophagus. So I'm taking medicine for it, and thank goodness the pain I had been experiencing in my middle chest area went away. But if I eat meat, or eat something irregular to my diet, I get really bad acid reflux, which burns.

That's what my throw up was like: it burned my throat and esophagus area, and just flat out <u>hurt</u>. It didn't stop hurting for like 2ish hours. It really, really was not cool.

After the throw up episode, I couldn't fall back asleep so I got up. I filmed myself and was gonna post it as a YouTube video but it was lame. I spent an hour or so praying and just plain hanging out with my brother Abe. We drew some pictures together, and I got <u>out</u> of bed (!) to see his new room arrangements (his bed was moved around by Dad). And it was fun spending time with Abe.

Later, at like 9pm, I started getting tired, and then later I couldn't keep my eyes open. But by the time I was tucked in bed (11? 12?) I got my second wind. So here I am! :D and . . . I think I'm getting tired again.

I'll write more tomorrow—I'm trying to think of a cool cartoon character that I can make cute cartoons with— just a random person/creature that I like. We'll see. If I can think of anything, I'll draw it here. Duh. BYE!

Tuesday, December 16, 2008 11:31 AM, EST

Esther is slowly moving toward a "normal" schedule.
She typically sleeps 12 hours a day, from 2am–2pm. We
are trying to arrange a more balanced 12am–12pm time
table which ain't easy. Problem is she insists that we
be around to tuck her in (which we're glad to do). We
sometimes retire to bed and have her call (by phone)
when she's ready to sleep. There are night time meds
and a feeding tube to prepare and lotions to apply
and blankets to settle and re-settle. Sometimes a long
talk and/or general silliness. I occasionally bark at her
though she's never been unreasonable or demanding.
In the daytime, there are still more medications and
weekly hospital visits and just hanging out time.
Yesterday she was up at 7:30am and had a great day
drawing pictures, writing in her journal, watching
anything on the HGTV station and perusing old sitcoms
(she especially likes Cosby, and a few other shows that
I think peculiar . . .). Today, though, she'll pay for that
good day and struggle to join the daylight. She writes
well and with depth (not that I would know . . .) and
draws amazing pictures of cats, people, and sundry
other things such as landscape scenes. She recently
drew a fabulous cartoon of Graham and Abe diving

into a pool (they are taking swimming lessons at the Y).
We retrieve any art or prose she tosses out which she
discourages and finds bizarre but mom and I are trying
to save so many snowflakes . . .

Be sure to check out her mostly unique and often
hilarious youtube postings which you can find on the
Links section of this site. All our love to you dear reader!

Snowflakes,
MARSEILLE, FRANCE, **2006**

December 18, 2008

Wow, okay so today was the second eventful day in one week! :) It's crazy!

I woke up at 10:30 am today, and decided to just stay up from then on. But then Dad reminded me that Angie's Christmas choir concert was later, so I took a nap from around 3 pm–5 pm, when I woke myself up. So, since I fell asleep at around 3:30 am last night, I got a total of around 8–9 hours. Not that great, but alright.

Anyhoo, I got up at 5 and got all dressed and ready (and stressed . . . I get stressed easily . . .) and by like, 7, we left. I <u>walked</u> into the concert hall/stage and me, Mom, and Abby sat in the front row.

At first I felt like everyone was looking at me, which I'm sure a lot of people were, because let's be real and completely honest here, a girl with a tube coming out her nose attached to a huge tank attracts some lookers. But only for a few seconds was I self conscious, after that I was like, whatevs. I mainly focused on the singers and tried to forget people may be able to see me. Besides, I can't stop what people think. They think what they think. :\

(merry christmas!)...

I wish I was better at describing my feelings, **dear, PARENTS...** because there are so many things I would like to say. First of all, sorry if my writing is hard to read: I try, and, like, epic fail, but I think it's translate-able ☺ Secondly, it feels ~~great~~ to be here, 2 years (plus) since being diagnosed, and many insane thinggs later. I mean, not all of them were insanely bad, some were good ☺

Like, remember wheeling me in the wheel chair down Cors mirabeau road in the Christmas time? There were all those Christmas kiosks, and stands and all those rides. I remember riding that ride that you sit in and watch a movie of, like star Wars, and the ride jerks around like your falling and stuff. Me and Graham went on once, and the second time Abe came, and he was so scared I had to **hold him** and use my feet to hold myself. hah, we decided it was a wee bit too scary for him ☺

oh! And do you remember, I won that Winnie the Pooh stuffed animal from that claw/crane/grab machine? I still have it! it's so cute.

Another memory I have is going to the Wringley Brothers carnival thing! The **elephants** and **clowns** were so cool! Well, the ELEPHANTS were cool, anyway.. ☺

Christmas 2008

dear, Parents . . .

(Merry Christmas!) . . .

I wish I was better at describing my feelings, because there are so many things I would like to say. First of all, sorry if my writing is hard to read: I try, and, like, epic fail, but I think it's translate-able. :) Secondly, it feels great to be here, 2 years (plus) since being diagnosed, and many insane thingys later. I mean, not all of them were insanely bad, some were good. ;)

Like, remember wheeling me in the wheelchair down Cours Mirabeau road in the Christmas time? There were all those Christmas kiosks, and stands, and all those rides. I remember riding that ride that you sit in and watch a movie of, like *Star Wars*, and the ride jerks you around like your falling and stuff. Me and Graham went on once, and the second time Abe came, and he was so scared I had to hold him and use my feet to hold myself. Hah, we decided it was a wee bit too scary for him. : D Oh! And do you remember, I won that Winnie the Pooh stuffed animal from that claw/crane/grab machine? I still have it! It's so cute.

Another memory I have is going to the Wringley [sic]

Brothers carnival thing! The elephants and clowns were so cool! Well, the ELEPHANTS were cool, anyway . . . : (

Were there trapeze people too? I feel like there were. The stuff that I can <u>remember</u> was fun! haha . . . oooh! One of my *favorite* memories is my 13th birthday! We (including Keri, duh) went out to a Chinese restaurant and I opened all my presents, except one. So I opened the last one and it was a <u>BAG</u> <u>OF</u> <u>CAT</u> <u>FOOD</u>! (with other cat stuff.) I remember freaking out! Whew, I was so excited. Of course, what followed the news that [I] was getting a cat was the news of "not yet," which, let me tell you, then followed with the longest week ever. But then I got not one but TWO cats, which was amazing. The night we brought them home, Pancake and Blueberry slept in between me and Angie. AWW.

I love the memory of last Christmas, too! Going Christmas tree hunting, "letting" Graham pick out the tree, Dad "trying" to cut it down. bahaha : D We walked all over looking for the right one! Then we went to that cabin-place with the fire and that, err . . . santa. Oh, and there was cider. OH MY GOSH! Getting my nano last year was real exciting! I watched the video of my reaction today—so funny! I was not expecting it :)

So, I totally know I'm missing out on writing so many more good memories, but oh well. I look forward to getting old and wrinkly and talking about that crazy "Esther–year" . . . Get it? Like "yester-year" but it's "Esther" instead of "yester"! HAH!

We'll make more memories, for sure. Some <u>may</u> even pass up the great ones I mentioned! : D <u>Maybe</u> . . .

SCREEEECH!! . . . sorry, but now I have to change my song and dance from the hip, hop, happenin' tunes to the slow, blue-y, melodramatic. Not because I'm trying to be mean and make you cry but because I'd like to be slightly sentimental. :)

And I'd also like to share some of my feelings, since I'm not always a talker. If you don't want to know some of my feelings, um, I don't know. I'd find that somewhat odd . . . : (heh, heh . . .

Well, you of all people know more than anyone (except myself) what it feels like to hear I may only live a short time. It sucks, man. But I mean, it's the truth, and the truth is icky. I guess until I had that bleeding, I figured I was getting healthier. I wasn't feeling any different, but I thought I was. And then the bleeding knocked the sense out of me and I had no idea where I thought my . . . "health scale" was at A-one, I guess. So then I talked a bit to you guys about dying (a <u>bit</u>) and thought I'd be fine. Another bleed . . . Well, who knows. Radiation was taken, and I almost died. Now I'm getting healthy again and the only bad thing left (I'm exaggerating) is death. You know? Maybe I should not have shared that with you. Uhh. Scratch that? Nah, now you know what I was thinking? Yeah. Wow, I'm babbling! Yikes! : O

But rereading what I just wrote, it's not really <u>all</u> what I think. I mean, I'm confused as to whether or not God's plans include me dying soon or living till I'm 104. But I do know God has a plan. It's not like He's sitting up in Heaven and . . . NOT having a plan! He is in control, but I'm still worried. I take each day, say thank you for it, and then worry,worry,worry. So at one point in time I tried to fix,fix,fix, but then that didn't work, So now I . . . worry,pray,worry,pray,worry,sleep. Hahaha : P

I do think about dying a lot, but I don't know. I feel like I've finally like, grasped that I'd no longer live on Earth. But I'm working on the actual progress of death and the people missing me part, you know?

Maybe, (or maybe not) you're interested in hearing "my" heaven? My heaven would be this all green hill-side with a really blue sky, and lots of pink and colorful flowers, that's completely calm and serene, that I could run and run and run through—without oxygen. It'd just be really nice.

Maybe, (or maybe not) you're interested in hearing "my" heaven? My heaven would be this all green hill-side with a really blue sky, and lots of pink and colorful flowers. that's completely calm, and serene, that I could run and run and run through ~ without oxyegen. It'd just be really nice.

Maybe one day I'll get to do that ☺

Maybe one day I'll get to do that :) I don't even remember what I thought about anything even a year ago. Maybe you don't either. Maybe brains just forget what they thought earlier or something.

I do hope that when the day comes, whether in 1, 10, or 100 years, I don't want you to think of me and feel sad. Even now, while I'm alive, don't think of me and say, "Poor girl. It's sad she's sick." Not that you do that. Think of me and think of the sunshine, and how I looove animals, and drawing something nice. Like this smiley -> :) <- AW! I'm such a good smiley artist :) Speaking of that . . .

: O madamoiselle esther made a faux pas! : (

That's not what I was speaking of. I <u>was</u> speaking of how good of a smiley artist I was, and I <u>WAS</u> going to go on to say I have great facial expressions, but now I don't think I will. : (

Now I'd like to say thanks. <u>Seriously.</u> Serious thanks. <u>Thank</u> you, Mom, for being my mom. When you're with me, I feel peaceful, and when you take charge I know my needs are met. You put up with more than any woman should—ever. You are my friend, my mom, my inspiration, when I'm sad, your hug reminds me I'm not alone. You make me feel better. When we chill (and also known as hang out), and laugh at that, "I love you more. No I love you more, because I gave you medicine!" commercial or watch HGTV I feel happy! <3 Thank you for watching out for me and telling doctors and pulmonologists to go away! You are so kind, and your genuity (is that a word?) is inspirational. If one day I grow up, I hope to be like you. I <u>completely</u> love you! Thank you, for everything. Dad, thank you for <u>being</u> my dad. You are my favorite person to talk to about odd studies or when I have questions about big stuff. Your laugh is contagious and your jokes <u>sometimes</u> make me laugh along. :) If I feel restless or slightly confused, your presence gives me back my senses. You are such a good listener and a great friend. I love you for all that you do, thank you.

You two are raising me, (and have so far raised me) very well, and with this whole cancer thing you've been amazing. I know without you both I would not feel as good as I can. And even through my struggles you stick with me through everything. I just want you to know you're not only my "parents" but my rocks. God is the reason I'm surviving, but he's sure used you in my life wonderfully. I love you. I wish there was a less sappy way to say it, but I do. I just love you. Thank you.

You two are amazing.

What is this, she's not <u>done</u>?!?! AHHHHHHH!

Oh no, you have created a daughter with an extremely strong hand that can write useless information for PAGES!! AND PAGES!! Nah, this page and maybe more (I don't know how much I'm going to write yet, you see.) are just random thoughts I have during the day I'll jot down. Maybe doodles. Who knows? . . . I can be deep, or not so deep. You'll see. (just for the record, the following words are <u>MAINLY</u> pointless . . .)

It's CHRISTMAS! Happy Christmas! Can you believe 3 years ago we had Christmas in . . . where was it? Let's see, last Christmas was Quincy, before that was France, before that was Germany, before that Plymouth, and on, and on . . . Hey look at the spiffy thing below that "S"!

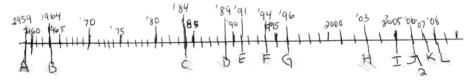

A= 1959. Wayne Eugene Earl II is born.

B= 1963. Lori Lanei Krake is born.

C= 1984. Wayne and Lori get married.

D= 1989. Abigail Cherisse Earl is born.

E= 1991. Evangeline Danei Earl is born.

F= 1994. Esther Grace Earl is born. <- me!

G= 1996. Graham Kenneth Earl is born.

H= 2003. Abraham Judson Earl is born.

I= 2005. Earls move to Albertville.

J= 2006. move to Aix/Marseille.

J^2= 2006. Esther's diagnosed <- : O

K= 2007. Move to U.S.A.!

L= 2008. LOTS OF STUFF <- zzzz.

If you don't mind, I think I'll say something "deep," also know as "serious." haha. :)

In Jon and Kate's book <u>Multiple Blessings</u>, they talk about the hard stuff they've gone and still go through, and how they were hopeless many times, and helpless. I think we of all people know what helpless feels like, (think Fuveau, when we had that week of eating only beans?) and I don't know about you but I've lost hope quite a few times. When I lose hope, and feel like there's nothing I can do, I basically just bawl!

Yep, I bawl. <u>And</u> sob. <u>And</u> talk to God. And while I'm talking to Him I usually stop feeling that way. But sometimes, like today for instance, I felt like I was on the verge of tears and I felt like everything negative was directed toward me. Which it wasn't, but that's how I feel when I'm in those "zones." But I was saying, today I was in those "zones" and I was sad and slightly angry, and finally after praying and taking a breather, I'm feeling better. So it's good. :)

As I was saying (before the previous page ripped and had to be trimmed), <u>Multiple Blessings</u> talks of the Gosselins' hardships and ALSO their . . . easyships . . . haha, what I mean is [it] also talks of all that God provides and their faith in Him. The stories of their faith really inspire me, and the last chapter really made me thank God more, and feel less helpless. That last chapter includes 6 things to remember when feeling slightly . . . agitated.

(1.) God is in control. (2.) God is gracious and strong. (3.) God can be trusted. (4.) God is love (5.) God will provide. (6.) Give <u>God</u> the glory and praise!

I think we can understand why these are important. It's easy, to me at least, to forget it's God who is controlling it all. I sometimes feel like <u>I</u> want to control, but I know it's always God. I most <u>definitely</u> know God is strong. If he were weak he would not have been able to hold me when I'm tired, and he does. His graciousness is wonderful, when we get annoyed at him he says "I Forgive You" always. God can always be trusted, and we, or at least I, have found that not trusting God to keep me safe through all this cancer stuff would drive me crazy. He always is trusting. God is love. Just like you say to me "I love you more," God loves us even more. That's a lot of love. God will provide, of course we know this is true. Even during the times when we had no money in our account, and not much money coming our way, we've had a roof over our head—enough food to keep us from starving, and each other. Even though it's not everything we ever wanted. He never keeps us from having too little. The last to remember on this list is to give God the glory and the praise. When you found the teaching job at Hanover, Mom, we say thank God. And God is the reason I'm still here. I mean he gives people talents, like Doctors, and they use them. Like Dr. Smith who's helped me, and stuff. But God should get the glory. You know? Yeah.

Anyway, those are not the only things to remember, but I do agree with Kate And Jon :) Gosselin that those are very important.

Wow, so this "letter" went from a note, to a letter, and now it's like my journal! Yikes. I do think I'm done now. :) For now. No more. I swear. Maybe a word. I'm done. I'm DONE . . .

Merry Christmas!

favorite . . . verse

Isaiah 40:31

"Those who hope in the LORD will renew their

*strength. They will <u>soar</u> on wings like eagles; they
will <u>RUN</u> and not grow weary, they will <u>walk</u> and not
grow faint."*

I love you two :)

Love, Esther

Sun, December 27, 2008

It's been Christmas eve, it's been Christmas, it's been <u>many</u> things since I last updated this journal (which at one point I wanted to name Delilah? It now has no name). I actually wish I was writing in this a lot more than I am, but oh well. I suppose I'll try.

So I don't really remember what I've been doing lately, but I can go back to Monday, December 22. Me and dad went to the Jimmy Fund, and it was just a regular visit. We got this teddy bear from there, which we saved for Abe, for Christmas. That was an alright day.

December 23 was GOING to be the day that Alexa and Melissa came up, but I was wicked tired and didn't want them to come then. So we re-scheduled and that day (it was Tuesday) was just a sleepy day. Oh and we watched Elf. :D

December 24, Wednesday, was a day we all know . . . CHRISTMAS EVE! Holy crap that was a fun day. I made a new YouTube video while I was wrapping presents, and then I went downstairs (at like 11pm) to chillax with the fam. (Oh, earlier we had watched "Can't Buy Me Love," just me and Angie and Abby, which was fun.)

Graham's presents "were not there" so Graham opened
Dad's two presents. Then Abe wanted to open two,
then we figured we all would . . . of course, afterwards
Graham just happened to spot his presents under the
tree. Anyway, I got Wall-e, the DVD, and a pillow. I forgot
to mention we always open one present each year, it's
like tradition. =)

After we opened presents, I went upstairs and fell
asleep. Yo dawg I was tiyed. I'm like tawking all coo. ;)

Thursday, December <u>25</u> was . . . C-H-R-I-S-T-M-A-S!

Christmas was great! I woke up at, what? Ten, eleven,
<u>AM.</u> And I went downstairs and Abe was itching to
open his presents, and Graham's presents "oddly" had
a rip in them . . . pahaha! So yeah, Dad read the story
of Jesus being born, and the Angels were frightening
the Shepherds, and the men were wise, and 3. Yeah.
It's really, not sarcastically, a nice, calm story. I'd like to
read it again. After reading that story Abe opened the
first prez . . . which was his skate shoes! He loved them!
Graham got some too, but was not as excited as Abe.
Let's see if I can remember who got what . . .

<u>Abby:</u> Grey's Anatomy s.1, a drawing of a daisy and a
note from me, an anatomy book, other stuff?

Angie: yoga matt, shampoo, others . . . ?

Abe: lots of clothes, skate shoes, toys

Graham: same as Abe

Me: Sexy metallic leopard leggings! And a bag full of makeup, another bag with nail polish, drawing stuff, other things?

I'm not the best at remembering things. But me and Abby (with Angie, kind of) painted pictures of me, Abby and Angie. And stuck them all in this frame. I think there were a total of 15 photos? Yeah, well it looked sweet and we gave it to Dad, and sort of Mom, for Christmas. (t)he(y) loved it!

Overall, Christmas was a good day.

Tuesday, December 30, 2008 12:37 PM, EST

Christmas memories made together . . . That's what will
hang with us as we recollect these past weeks in future
years. Nothing dramatic, no bells and whistles—just
living life. We enjoyed a "quiet" Christmas with our five
children. Can you believe that Abe and Graham opened
their stockings when they got up at 7:15, then waited
until 10 to open gifts, the earliest Esther was willing to
agree to?! (So what if a few of the gifts labeled "Graham"
had slightly loosened wrappings from hard-to-contain
peeking!) And did you know, as Abe informed us
during the reading of the Christmas story, that the
angels surrounding the shepherds in the fields sang
"Jingle Bells!"? Perhaps they did . . . Later, we enjoyed a
relatively calm meal of baked ham, mashed potatoes,
stuffing, green bean casserole, and Dream Pie for
dessert. The next day Uncle Jerry and cousin Michaela
arrived from California, which demanded a visit to the
Aquarium, a trip (including Esther) to see the Christmas
lights at LaSalatte shrine, and a night out at the movies!

A HUGE thank you to the many who blessed us and
Esther this Christmas with cards, prayers, and gifts.
While you are not named here, you have warmed

our hearts and helped to lighten our load. May God abundantly meet your needs as well!

Esther had a long day yesterday at Children's Hospital and the Jimmy Fund, with full PET and CT scans and blood work. We left home at 7:15 a.m. and returned at 6:00 p.m! On Wednesday Wayne and I go in for a full team conference to hear her status, with any improvements or concerns, especially regarding any changes since she began taking the experimental chemotherapy drug. We are nervous . . . Keep us in prayer, and watch for an update.

Thursday, January 1, 2009 7:17 PM, EST

Wayne and I braved the snow storm yesterday to attend the meeting with Esther's primary doctor at the Jimmy Fund Clinic at Children's Hospital yesterday. The short of it is that after reviewing her PET and CT scans from Monday, scans reveal that in the two months since starting the experimental chemo the tumors in Esther's lungs have reduced slightly. At the least they were hoping to see NO growth—shrinking is even better news (the only thing better, said her doctor, would be a miracle!). So she will continue to take the chemo for now, working to keep side effects contained with various medications as we are doing currently.

They were clear with us that studies have found this chemo to work for an average of 8 months before ceasing to continue helping. When the effectiveness wears off, then they would expect the growth of the tumors to begin again. We compare it to a war in which we're outnumbered, yet we are gaining in the battle for the moment. We will take the weeks and months reprieve with thankfulness . . . !

Happy New Year, everyone!

CRAZYCRAYON BLOG

Friday, January 2, 2009
Emphasis on one

If one person sits down at their computer one day and types one word, does that affect the future? If that one person didn't type that one word, would the future's history be changed? Does their one word even mean anything? Does my one (times a lot) word mean anything? Does that one person's one word even get read—once? If I wasn't sitting here writing my words, would my future be different?

No doubt it would. I'm sure I'd get much more accomplished in life if I weren't so caught up in thinking about these things and then writing them down . . .

I think in total I've had somewhere between 10–15 blogs. Maybe that's not a lot? I don't know what the number of blogs a person has usually is. I feel like 10–15 blogs is kind of a lot. I mean come on, why would I write so much down and then decide I don't like my blog, just to start a new one, after deleting the other blog, some months later? Really.

Do my words make sense? Whenever I write
something and then reread it, it makes little sense.
Maybe I'm just too smart for my own brain. (;

"Too smart for my own brain."
QUINCY, MASSACHUSETTS, **2009**

CRAZYCRAYON BLOG

Sunday, January 4, 2009

some content deleted

Oh, my, gosh. Can I tell you about the worst day ever? It's pretty bad. Here goes: 2am: I go to sleep.

7am: "Esther wake up I overslept we have to leave now!" "SHUSH!" "Come on!"

7:20am: We leave. (Me and Mom)

7:50am?: We get to Children's, and I go with Mom to the room where I'm supposed to have my 1-2 hour lay-flat-on-your-back scan. They ask if I haven't eaten for 4 hours. We tell them I stopped feeds at 7. "Uh-oh," they say, and poke my finger for blood to test my gluclose (?). Turns out it was alright, so I go lay down for 1.30 hours of a scan.

Next me and Mom go eat food and I get an IV put in. OOPS, they missed. Then they do it again. They made it, and I lay down for 10 minutes of a CT scan. After that we go to the Jimmy Fund where they need blood. I had already taken out my IV because it hurt, so they poked me. Later Annette comes in and says they need more blood. Shut up. They poke me again and get blood, and my spot where the IV was starts bleeding. It finally stops and Annette talks to us about stuff. We go home, by which time it is now exactly 5pm. BAH.

I forget what day that was but it sure sucked. :\ The next few days my lungs felt bruised from lying flat for so long. Ay yi yi. Now I must part for sleep, because it beckons me.

Farewell.

Sunday, January 4, 2009

I've gotten more into YouTube these past few days/past week. Not like I've posted more videos but I've found a few people who are nice, funny, and have not too many subscribers . . . I don't like when there are over a certain amount of subscribers on someone's channel because then all of your posts are replaced by others in the next five minutes—not so fun.

Also, I started a blog, yes, blog, where I've posted 2 entries thus far. I have one "follower" and 3 people I "follow." To me I feel as though a blog is like a public diary: you write your thoughts but edit to sound more impressive. Mine are FAR from impressive, but, yeah. I forget what I was saying. Oh well.

CRAZYCRAYON BLOG

Sunday, January 4, 2009

. . . let me count the ways.

I like a lot of things. I like books, ones with a
meaningful message but with humor, or a comic book.
I like movies, mostly classical romances and comedies,
but I like those odd artsy ones too. I like music, indie
stuff, but I don't like liking music that other people
like. I like food, really only Olive Garden and my mom's
cooking. I like the Internet, and going to my favorite
websites twenty times a day. I like coloring books,
especially when I use those metallic, shiny crayons.
I like animals, I communicate better with them than
that "human species." I like snow, when it's untouched
and all white and I'm inside. I like leaves, the crunchy
kind that you can step on and crush into smithereens.
I like when the sun is shining on your arm, and you
feel it and it's all warm. I like stuffed animals, smallish
ones that fit on my bed but end up under my mattress.
I like quiet, where I can sit, and just sit, and do
nothing else. I like vases filled with flowers that look
effortlessly placed, all spread apart equally. I like a lot
of things.

I also love many things. But what I really love, what I really, really, really truly love is definitely easy to say . . .

I love Neverball.

"Jughead, my one true love."
QUINCY, MASSACHUSETTS, 2009

Game Boy time,
ALBERTVILLE, FRANCE, **2006**

Lady of the Beach,
QUINCY, MASSACHUSETTS, **2009**

CRAZYCRAYON BLOG

Tuesday, January 6, 2009

I don't know a lot of stuff

I wish I was a better person. I try to do good things, but really? I think I do but I don't. I don't know. I think I'm one of those people that think about their own problems, even though I wish I could do something resourceful. Now I'm one of those people that think about their own problems and then blog about how they wish they could do something to make a difference. Perfect.

I also wish I were a bit more creative. I always want to blog, but I can never think of anything interesting to say. I could fill you in on my life story, but I'm sick of it. Maybe one day I'll be bored enough to type it all out. All out? Ha, I think I think I'm older than I am. Seriously, fourteen years is like nothing, and maybe you're like, "snap girl, you know nothing about life!" (because don't we all talk this way?) and maybe I don't. I don't really know.

I'm listening to Regina Spektor. I don't usually like women's voices, but she has such beautiful songs . . . they're making me cry. I don't even know why. I'm not even sad. Maybe I am. I honestly can never decipher my emotions.

Labels: I don't know, regina spektor, thoughts, tired

Posted by Esther at 8:48 PM 0 comments

The Earl children,
BRAINTREE, MASSACHUSETTS, 2010

CRAZYCRAYON BLOG

January 16, 2009

I have been in such a bad mood lately. I hate it. I'm mad at my brain for being mad. And I'm mad at my body for being tired. I hate being mad. I hate hating being mad. AGHHHHHHHHHHHHHHHHHHHH.

I'm getting a haircut tomorrow. It's going to be short and angleafied. Because that's a word. And after cutting it I'm dyeing it orange with purple streaks. That's right.

Sunday, January 25, 2009 11:28 AM, EST

We are now well into 2009 and are grateful for every
moment with our Star (Dad's nickname for Esther).
Sadly, because of the chemo, she's been slowly losing
her recently brightly colored, pumpkin-orange hair.
Her eyelashes, eyebrows and skin have been affected,
too. She's brave and shrugs it off but we know it can't be
easy to go through this. On a very positive note, Esther
did pass 90 pounds this week!! She was 20 pounds less
not too long ago so this is fantastic news. In fact, 100
pounds for her size and body type is the ceiling for
her. This weight gain is a strategic part of her battle
and we're glad to report she's winning there. Also, her
numbers (I am lumping in a bunch of info here) have
been quite good and we were told this week that there
is a chance that she may respond to additional, related
medical therapies once the present plan runs its course.
Good news, indeed!

Her weekly routine includes visits to the cancer
clinic in Boston (though we were there twice for her
this past week and nearby for a third appointment
for Graham). If we let her she would easily sleep 16
hours a day but we try and keep it to 12. We are still

struggling to contort her sleep/wake patterns into our daily schedule. She's never happy being awakened for medicine or whatever. She sleeps with a mask on as her small Bi-pap machine forces air and oxygen into her lungs which works to ease her part in breathing with less discomfort. During the day she breathes via a nasal tube attached to either a portable canister (for going downstairs or out of the house) or to the oxygen machine itself, a permanent fixture in her bedroom.

She loves to eat a spicy Chinese vegetable food dish from a nearby restaurant and asks for it at least twice a week. She likes the chocolate cake from Olive Garden, too, which we sometimes pick up after a trip to the hospital. She enjoys painting her nails strange colors and her little brother Abe likes to have her paint his nails regularly as well (he also demands that she routinely paint his face as some superhero, though not with nail polish! Her artwork on skin or canvas, is always amazing). She adores her cats and would like to have a third or fourth cat running around (ain't gonna happen: Dad). Her cats sleep on her bed, taking turns sleeping on her tummy! She said she'd love to live somewhere where she could have animals of all types running around to enjoy (for now, she prefers that idea over hanging around people). She is reading bits and pieces in several subject areas, but mostly lives on her computer, writes, paints or watches TV leaving her room every day or two to play board games and visit with us downstairs. She is still the positive, cheerful girl we have always delighted in! In spite of this awful cancer and its cruel side effects, at 14 1/2, and a few months away from beginning high school, there is no stopping Esther from turning into the young, beautiful woman we always dreamed she would become.

Saturday, February 7, 2009 6:51 AM, EST

This week has been a bit tough, with a new type of headache that has kept Esther from sleeping and kept her in quite a bit of pain. The result now is that her schedule is completely upside down—awake through the night, and finally able to sleep through part of the day.

Her doctors are working on medications, and have taken her off her chemo for a few days to see if it is because of the larger dose she's been taking for the past week or two. So right now we're living on pain meds . . . trying to keep them in her system constantly so she gets some relief.

Other than that, her numbers are still good. Hopefully just a small thing to get through.

Grandma sent her some toys for her kitties—we've laughed and laughed at the "feathers on a fishing pole." When they manage to catch the pile of feathers, they try to sneak off with their "bird" but of course get pulled up hard when they get to the end of the string we're holding! Hilarious, as they will do it over and over. Esther also got a package this week with a colorful lap quilt from some friends. She and I have been enjoying the antics on American Idol; Esther has been painting, reading (when her headache is down), and of course "computering"!

Tuesday, February 10, 2009 5:38 PM, CST

The good: Thankfully, we just found out that Esther's CT and MRI scans from yesterday are normal! Everyone was worried about about the cancer having spread to the brain, etc which would have caused these recent symptoms.

The bad: Though her parents and medical team are overjoyed, she still has the intense headaches. We hope to get a different pain medicine approved and that should help (though so far the insurance co has denied it). She's miserable and just wants to sleep. Waking up over the last several days hasn't been any fun as it involves vomiting, nausea and migraines.

Keep praying and hoping!

5am February 1 / 2, 2009

I feel so useless. And I know it's late and I'm tired and I'm upset and I should be sleeping but I feel the need to write. This will probably be short. I feel so useless because I don't know. It would make no difference if I died. What I mean is not that I'm suicidal, I just have not done anything other than get on the computer for the past year. Yeah, I can't do much else but seriously?! I want to make a difference, to help someone. And I don't know how. Helping someone would make me feel good, like I did something productive for a change, thus helping myself, too. Maybe one day.

Saturday, February 21, 2009 11:54 PM, EST

Dear Estee's Friends, Esther is doing pretty well
these days! Between working with her medications
and wrestling with God in prayer, there has been
improvement! Thank you for your part in this. Though
her headaches are not all gone, they are manageable for
the time being. Also, her sleep patterns are improving
and her last few weekly visits to the cancer clinic have
revealed excellent progress overall! These things are
enough in themselves to be ecstatic about but since
we last wrote she's also been busy with a few other
happenings: had a couple days surprise visit from a
lifetime friend (yeah, cool Andrew from NY!), went to
the mall one afternoon for three yummy, warm pretzels
with dad (though she felt kind of conspicuous with non-
stop stares in the direction of her ever present oxygen
tank), painted Abe's face twice (both times as a super
scary super something), played piano downstairs a
few times (we love that), watched American Idol with
mom (they love that- go Danny!), entertained big sis
Abby once (hard to get Abby away from her beloved
chemistry books more than that!), ate a few delicious
(ahem) home cooked meals at the table like a regular
kid and made a general blessing of herself on a regular

basis. Hope that encourages you. From where we sit today, we're especially grateful for these and many other daily gifts!

Wayne

Sunday, March 15, 2009 10:39 AM, EDT

Dear Friends,

Haven't been keeping up too well on updates, which is after all, a good thing! No news usually means no new bad news! We find that one of the most difficult things about Esther's cancer is finding the right balance in approaching life. We often feel like we're waiting, but we want to feel like we're LIVING. Finding the way to live life with the right perspective is a big part of what living a Christ-following life is all about, isn't it?

So, the nitty gritty for those of you interested! Esther's weekly visits to the Jimmy Fund Clinic (the outpatient branch for pediatric cancer at Dana-Farber/Children's Hospital Boston) have been positive, with slight improvement in her various blood counts, oxygen functions, and overall health. We're constantly adjusting medications, as new health concerns come and go. This week it's an oral medication to get rid of the thrush which started after the steroid treatment to break her week-long migraine a few weeks back. She has also contracted Clostridium difficile (or C-dif), so yesterday we started a new antibiotic for that. Her calcium levels had dropped, so we're back to taking a calcium supplement. There's some concern about slight blood count in her urine—waiting to hear how much of a problem that is. As you can see, status quo isn't really status quo—it's just calm concern, versus overwhelming.

On the social front, our Esther has been a butterfly! Went to see a movie with Abby and Angie last week, since Abby was home from Gordon College for the week. Also went this past Thursday evening as a whole family to hear Angie's (wonderful) voice recital at North Quincy High School. And Esther is spending most evenings competing on Game Cube with her brothers—there is nothing Graham and Abe love more than finding out if she's awake when they get home from school, and ready to play! Someday we'll update to Wii, but they still love their antique system, and at least used games are cheap so we can keep adding new ones!

Graham turned 13 ten days ago, and I wish you could all have heard his prayer as we gathered around the table for his birthday dinner. We had been watching old family videos, and his heartfelt prayer was for Esther to walk and run like she used to . . . we were all pretty teary eyed!

Thank you for praying—we'll keep you posted!

Monday, March 30, 2009 10:42 AM, EDT

Keep Scootin', Esther!

Esther was 'out and about' on Saturday; first as a face painter at a special education conference that mom helped to organize and then to high-coffee with mom and sister, Angie. After that, the girls went grocery shopping which was a *big* deal because, as best we could figure, Esther had not been full blown food shopping for nearly a year! While the others walked, she scooted around driving one of those engine driven carts for a while without incident until she rounded a tight corner and bumped up against a stack of something-or-others. Other than that, not too shabby for someone who has never been to driving school!

Beginning this week, along with her regular visits to check up on her general status, Esther starts twice weekly visits to a physical therapist. She now has at least three separate appointments a week in Boston (two trips total though, thankfully). Also, within the next week or two, her growing medical team (oncology, endocrinology, etc) will meet to confer about the next step. There are some differences of opinion on how to go forward in her treatment so they, and we, need wisdom. The great news is that they have instructed us to think in terms of a "*long term*" care plan! What this means we are not quite sure, but it sounds pretty good! We'll take this news as they intended it: great news, *indeed*.

4pm-ish Tuesday, March 31, 2009

I had this weird dream last night. It was spectacular. You know how I've complained about wanting to kiss a boy? Sounds dumb but I want to like someone and someone to like me. Eesh I sound like a 2nd grader. Whatever.

In my dream we were watching tv or something, and this boy I was with kissed my cheek and I got all tingly and it felt amazing. (haha not like I was getting turned on, oh geeze this sounds wrong.) Then he traced my neck and kissed the back of it. Oh my goodness it felt nice. But there were like people watching us, or something, so we went into another room. We played GameCube and watched tv, and I put my lips like near his face or something?? But nothing happened.

Then I woke up and felt sad cause it wasn't real. But then I was thinking and I was like, who was the guy? hahaha.

I also had this dream about the B-s boys. They came and I hugged Bruce and he lifted me up really high or something? Then I went to hug JT but he just waved his hand. Then I went and waved at Ryan. They were all scowling.

Later I asked them why they seemed so upset, and they said cause it was Graham who was sick. But he wasn't . . . so odd.

So yeah I thought the kid in the kissing dream might be Ryan? But then I remembered I had a dream about Jake S (cohenism) and he's awesome so it might be him?

Or just some guy as made up as those kisses.

Oh and I don't know if I've said this before, but I can't even kiss a boy now because my chemo from my spit could harm him. Kinda makes you sad when something you want can't even happen.

Hmm. Speaking of wants, the LeakyCon 2009 is happening from May 21-24. IN BOSTON.

Wtheck is this you ask? It happens like once every two years. Harry Potter fans from around the world meet up to hang out and listen to Wrock—hP music—and HANK AND JOHN GREEN ARE GOING TO BE THERE. IN BOSTON. IN BOSTON AT THE LEAKYCON!!!

I want to go awfully bad. SO bad. But tickets cost 195$ a piece, plus 30$ to hang out with the Greens. Plus I don't know anyone going. But like Mom or Abby and Angie could [go] with me! Sadly we really don't have money. I could do this for Make-A-Wish . . .

could harm him. Kinda makes you
sad when something you want can't even
happen.

Hmm. Speaking of wants, the Leakycon 2009 is happening from May 21-
24. IN BOSTON.
Wtheck is this you ask? It happens
like once every two years. Harry Potter
fans from around the world meet to
hang out and listen to Wrock -hP music.
and HANK AND JOHN GREEN ARE
GOING TO BE THERE. IN BOSTON.
IN BOSTON AT THE LEAKY
CON!!!
I want to go awfully bad. So bad.
But tickets cost 195$ a piece, plus
30$ to hang out with the Greens Plus
I don't know anyone going. But like
mom or Abby and Angie could with me!
Sadly we really don't have money.
I could do this for Make a wish....

WHAT TO DO..

Eek anyway I wish I could go and I wish I could kiss someone and I kinda wish I could make friends with someone going to the magical LC09. Sigh.

Anyway this was an incredibly immature and frivolous entry. Thinking of this more than health.

Oh, on a good note, I made a "pal" on OMGPOP.com/#/ balloono (haha), and we make designs out of balloons and kill ourselves with it. Like stop signs, triangles . . . it's cool and it makes me happy. :)

Okay bye.

Untitled,
APRIL 10, 2010

Wednesday, April 15, 2009 12:55 PM, EDT

Esther's team of doctors at Children's, Dana-Farber and
Mass General Hospital are very happy with her progress
so far! After much discussion and review of her case,
their recommendation at this time is to continue with
her Sorafenib (a "smart" drug) chemo treatment which
she takes twice daily at home, and NOT to treat her
at this time with I-131 Radiation. Fortunately her side
effects to the chemo have been minimal compared to
what some suffer (she has some rash, hair thinning,
stomach discomfort). I have to admit I'm happy to hold
off on the radiation, since last October is when she had
her last treatment and got so sick we were afraid we'd
lose her. The doctors are also waiting to see the result
of her CT scans/PET scan next week on the 23rd. If they
see either continued shrinkage of the tumors in her
lungs, or no change for the worse, then we'll continue
with her current treatment schedule.

On another note, this week Esther got a Wii video
system! Since she just started physical therapy when
we go in on Thursdays to the Jimmy Fund, it's perfect
timing! She will be able to do therapy while playing
bowling, tennis, golfing, and of course all their old

GameCube games which also work on Wii. This purchase was thanks to two very generous people. Thank you, Lee and Freeda! Esther (and the boys, of course!) are very excited!

We also had a big day on Good Friday, when Esther had her g-tube of one year replaced with a PEG (or Mickey) tube. I tell her it looks like a beach ball fastener. Due to Esther's compromised lungs they did the procedure without any medications—I think with all the chemo and radiation her tube had been through a lot, and it was much stiffer and tougher to pull out than they'd expected. But they managed, although Abby said she'd had no idea Esther had the strength to squeeze her hand so hard!

Easter Sunday we all visited our "old" church together here in Quincy. It was wonderful to have Esther with us for the morning and the church family was happy to see her. Then a vegetarian Mexican Easter dinner with two of Abby's college friends—it was a day of contentment. Just like Abe loves finding hidden colored eggs and counting them, we celebrate hidden blessings and treasure each one . . .
(written by Lori)

"Dreams are Weird" April 21, 2009

I always have very, very odd dreams. Like, really, they're usually quite strange indeed. Last night I had a dream where I was chasing this car, it was a red car, and it stopped at a stop sign, so I ran up to it and knocked on the window. It rolled down and this person with big, anime-like eyes stared at me, and then his eyes filled up the whole screen, like a movie sort of, and I was standing in a pool of water. Out of the water these dolphin-like creatures came out and started singing about aliens. Then one of the dolphins walked (??) toward me, and smiled, and then kissed my cheek.

Then I woke up, and my cat, Pancake, was licking my face. That was one of the weirdest dreams I've had yet, and I sort of blame it on Doctor Who. That's all I've been watching lately, seriously. I'm on vacation this week, so I have nothing to do. I wake up around 3 in the afternoon, eat some breakfast, talk to people on Skype, and then watch Doctor Who. I'm on the last episode in season 1, finally :O

This afternoon I went to the mall and purchased season 2 and season 3! Stupid series 3 cover gave away something that happened to someone, but I don't know if I should say, since I hate giving away secrets. But yeah, the series 3 cover made me angry T__T. I also got some pretzels from this store in the mall called Auntie Anne's, and ZOMG the pretzels are fantastic! They're kind of sweet, but not in a cinnamonny way, and they have salt, but not in a gross, I-don't-want-to-ever-eat-sodium-again way, and they're super soft. Oh man, I want some more now . . .

Anyway. My brain is tired. I did too much homework today. Now I must sleep! Oh, and I posted my video for my failboat channel! You should watch it. :D

Blueberry,
DECEMBER 5, 2008

Monday, May 4, 2009 6:29 AM, EDT

Well, if you only like reading bad news, then quick, close the page! Because we only have good news to share about our Esther today. The PET scans came back saying "little change." But the CT scans can show smaller differences, and they register continued shrinkage of up to 15% in the size of some of Esther's multiple lung tumors. Her doctor said that of the possible scenarios, this was the best they were hoping for. Current studies show this new chemo benefitting for up to 24 months, before the cancer outsmarts the smart drug. So we feel a bit like Christian on Pilgrim's Progress, seeing ahead a distance of smooth, straight road—we'll take it!

So we are on to the task of LIVING. Esther has started on her Algebra program, and we are working with her school to get an official pass from 8th grade. High School next year has to be figured out—probably online, but maybe a combination. We'll have to see how the summer goes.

We'll keep posting here from time to time, as the journey isn't over, of course. Esther continues to use oxygen 24/7, but her doctors are encouraging her that she might be able to get off of it for periods of time. We have our share of side effects from the many drugs she takes, but they've been very manageable so far. We keep working on Esther's sleep schedule, as she has a hard time falling asleep, then sleeps too late in the day (or is that because she's a teenager?!). Thank you for praying, caring, and celebrating with us!

Lori (for the gang of us!)

Saturday, May 23, 2009 8:30 AM, CDT

Hello All,

Esther is having a great time this weekend as she continues to attend the LeakyCon conference here in Boston. It began Thursday and continues through Sunday. She has absolutely loved going and meeting in person many of her online friends and heroes such as writer John Green. Big sister Abby has trailed along and has fit right in but only after Estee's extensive coaching. "It's Griffendorf, not Huff in Puff." **(no dad, no. It's Hufflepuff, not Huffinpuff, and it's Gryffindor, not Griffendorf. bahaha)** Say, "Oh, Ministry of Magic is my favorite." Abby is probably a closeted nerdfighter anyway if the fun she's been having is any proof. Angie will help lug the oxygen around today and she'll fit right in as she at least knows what language to use. Mom and Dad are not *quite* sure what the appeal is, but Estee is in heaven and that's alright with us. Check out the www. leakycon.com web site for a better sense of things. Also, Esther's Facebook has current photos.

In other really good news, after nearly a year of going in to the clinic in Boston once a week, Esther was recently upgraded to bi-weekly visits! Kind of like moving from coach to first class with more leg room and free peanuts.

All for now,

Wayne

At Leaky with Alex Day!
BOSTON, MASSACHUSETTS, **2009**

Friday, July 3, 2009 11:11 PM, CDT

Hellooo everyone. This is Esther, and I figured I'd update, and stuff, because it's been quite a while since that last happened.

Nothing very significant happened in June, which I suppose is both good and boring news. I started a better schedule of home physical therapy (every Monday), and I'm still going to Jimmy Fund every other Thursday. Medicine is the same and the next scans are this Monday, July 6, so we'll tell you how that goes.

A week or two ago I went to a concert nearby with my sister, Angie, and that was awesome. We danced and I was exhausted the next day, but dude, it was so worth it. I have these two "liquid" oxygen tanks, and they last about 4 hours each, so I take those with me whenever I go out. If we ever go somewhere and I need more than 8 hours of oxygen, there's also a few big tanks that hold 3 hours worth.

Oh, this past week my mom and dad (or you could say Wayne and Lori) went to an island for a belated anniversary trip. Abby and Angie were in charge of my medicine/keeping Abe and Graham occupied, and I must say they did a brilliant job. We didn't really do anything major, but we made coffee cake, and stuff. :)

Haha and yesterday, Abe, Graham and I squirted out the contents of an entire shaving cream can and played with it. It may sound boring but it was awesome. Seriously, squeezing a handful of shaving cream is AMAZING.

Hummm I can't think of anything else to say. OH. This year for school, I'll be going to freshmen year at Angie's high school, where she's a senior. I think I'm doing three days a week, two or three or four classes on the days I go? Yeah, we haven't figured it out perfectly, but the main idea is that. I'm going to take a photography class, and Angie will actually be in the class with me, so that's sweet.

Tomorrow being July 4, I'm not sure what we're doing O_o Probably go see fireworks nearby, or something. haha

I have this huge bag of cards I've received, and yesterday while cleaning I read them all, and it was so cool. Thank you guys for all the well wishes, gifts, prayers, thoughts,

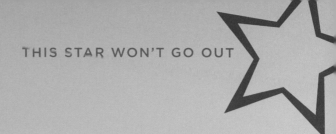

e-mails, everything you've given us the past three years. Although we tend to forget about replying to most of them (hi, we're the Earls), they DO mean a lot, and I'm really thankful to have so many people supporting me, and us. Hope you all have a lovely July 4th.

-Esther

With Paul DeGeorge of Harry and the Potters,
BOSTON, MASSACHUSETTS, **2009**

Saturday January 31, 2009

Obviously I'm a rather . . . "unique" person. I mean I dislike being with other people besides my family, and even then I only like short visits. It's not that I don't LIKE people, or LOVE my family, I just get annoyed with them.

I also do not like sports, thus cutting me out of the "sporty" type of people; I'm not very artsy, I'm not very nerdy, I'm not very cool, I'm not very funny/class-clowny. I'm not very rebellious. I don't fit in with any group.

Although, lately I've been watching a lot of YouTubers, and my favorites are these channels:

fiveawesomegirls—five girls who take turns posting videos on weekdays, their main "topics" are Harry Potter, Wrock (bands based upon Harry Potter), theater and nerdfighteria (more on that below/—>)

hayleyghoover—one of the 5AG, she's the funniest and makes me laugh :)

italktosnakes—another 5AG, her name's Kristina and I just like her personality :)

turns posting videos on weekdays, their main "topics" are Harry Potter, Wrock (bands based upon Harry Potter), theater and Nerd-fighteria (more on that below/→)

hayleyghoover - one of the 5AG, she's the funniest and makes me laugh :)

italktosnakes - another 5AG, her name's Kristina and I just like her personality ;o

rhymingwithoranges - Jazza - he's cool, funny, he sings :)

vlogbrothers - two brothers started vlogging and stopped textually communicating for one year, so awesome!!

Okay, so the "vlogbrothers", John and Hank Green, started calling their viewers Nerdfighters, which are basically nerds made of awesome. As I said before I'm not totally nerdy, but I like to think of myself as a nerdfighter because of the nerdy things I love: youtube, iiwy.com, Harry Potter, Wrock, and... um... I guess that's it.

But yeah, to become an official nerdfighter
I have to come up with a verse to a song
about the nerdy things I like. :) Better go
crackin.

dont forget to be awesome

5:am   February 1/2, 2009
   I feel so useless. And I know its late and
I'm tired and I'm upset and I should be
sleeping but I feel the need to write. This
will probably be short. I feel so useless
because I dont know. It would make
no difference if I died. what I mean is
not that I'm suicidal, I just have
not done anything other than get on the
computer for the past year. Yeah, I
cant do much else but seriously ?! I want
to make a difference, to help someone.

rhymingwithoranges—Jazza—he's cool, funny, he sings
:)

vlogbrothers—two brothers started vlogging and
stopped textually communicating for one year. So
awesome!!

Okay, so the "vlogbrothers," John and Hank Green,
started calling their viewers nerdfighters, which are
basically nerds made of awesome. As I said before
I'm not totally nerdy, but I like to think of myself as a
nerdfighter because of the nerdy things I love: YouTube,
iilwy.com, Harry Potter, Wrock, and . . . um . . . I guess
that's it.

But yeah, to become an official nerdfighter, I have to
come up with a verse to a song about the nerdy things I
like. :) Better get crackin.

DFTBA don't forget to be awesome :) 8) :D 8D

1am Thurs, February 12, 2009

50 pages. I haven't re-read them lately, but fifty—50—
pages of me writing about pointless stuff is surprisingly
not as much as I thought I would have written. 2
months after getting Mr. Diary, I honestly thought I
would have it full—all 234ish pages. That be a lot of
writing but I thought I'd have done it. Ah well, I'm not
complaining, just wish I'd write more. :|

Well, I'll fill you in on the deets and then—if my hand
doesn't hurt ☌ I'll get more "personal" . . .

I'd say about February 1 or so I got one of my migraines
during the day and had to rest until it left. Just to be
clear, my migraines start with bright lights sticking in
my vision. It looks like a camera flashed and the flash
just won't go out of my eyes. After about 10–20 minutes
of the lights—or "aura"—I get a headache. Usually an
hour, about, later the aura's gone and I'm just left with a
headache for the remainder of the day.

So yeah—Sunday :) , Feb Uno (I think) I got a migraine,
and it went away later. Then the next day I got a
migraine, took a nap, it went away and then I got
a-NOTHer migraine later that day! The following day I

had two separate migraines <u>again</u>.

The day after that, Wednesday, I got another migraine but that one had more pain than I'm used to. I think I slept quite a bit, trying to sleep off the migraine. The day after <u>Wednesday</u> was, *gasp* <u>Thursday</u>, which is my weekly doctor visit.

We went in at like 11? or something? And Dad had to go with Graham and Abe over to Children's while I stayed with Annette. So I told her about the headaches and whatever, and then an "activity lady" came in. We did like collaging (me and her, not Annette LoL) and I started to get a faint headache.

By the time Dad came back, along with the psychiatrist (:D) my head was really hurting pretty bad. So even though Dad wanted to leave, I waited for Annette to give me pain medicine, just oxicodone and tylenol.

That helped, I think. And we left for home. And I slept at home but got another awful headache . . . and slept on and off taking lots of pain medicine. The next day, also known as Friday in some places, was pretty much just as bad, if not worse. I think I slept all day, my head pounding, my neck sore, anything I did made me feel nauseous or worse. I was taking pain medication <u>every</u> 4 hours, a mix of oxicodone and tylenol. The next day was just as bad; I wasn't eating anything, threw up a little at least 2ce in the morning, and literally anything, except lying completely still, amplified the pain.

I think on Sunday the pharmacy gave me a medicine I had used in the hospital for painful headaches—but only 2 pills—one to take and the other to take 2/3 hours later. Just because they're so expensive . . . But that medicine made me feel better. I was awake for once and my head <u>almost</u> stopped hurting. I was able to get on the computer a bit, I think.

Monday they told us to come in for scans to make sure nothing serious was causing the pain. So I went in, every sound and movement sending a soft thump of pain to my head. The funny thing was I felt much better that day than I did all week. Still a lot of pain but they made sure I stayed pain-medicine-d up. Which helped.

First I had them stick an IV in me and—oh!—miss! >:[They did it again and wiggled it around until it made it into my vein. Whew. Then I went and had an MRI, which makes so much noise and [I] was slightly panicking. But I did good. First 45 minutes were almost relaxing, the machine made a lot of vibrations and lots of rumbling, second 30 minutes were too long but it wasn't too bad. I was just happy my headache was almost completely gone. Then I had a 10 minute CT which was fine. Then we went back to Jimmy Fund Clinic . . . and waited.

They came back and said everything looked good, which is great 'cause they were worried about tumors, or bleeding. So thank God! ':D ← (sweating person nervous thing) They said the headaches are a mixture, most <u>likely</u>, of sleep deprivation and dehydration so I'm supposed to be going to bed at the same time-ish, every night.

My headaches have definitely been less severe since Tuesday, although they're in no way gone. I'm stuck literally not moving and when my head feels better my neck starts to hurt. They have me on a steroid for yesterday, today, and two other days, :D, which is funny, but it does seem to be helping.

I'm going in again tomorrow at 12:30, appointment's at 1.30, and I think I'm meeting to talk with a neurologist and sleep specialists to see if they have any brilliant ideas . . . I'll fill you in later (with the emotions). I'm too tired for that.

But I am extremely thankful to the doctors and Mom and Dad for their constant help, they've been unbelievably patient with me. Also thanks to God, for never making the pain last too long. The pain sucks so bad, but it always goes away.

ex, oh, ex, oh :)

"You Are the Moon,"
QUINCY, MASSACHUSETTS, **2009**

CATITUDE:
Finding friendship and community online and IRL

by Lindsay Ballantyne

When people ask for a History of Catitude, it's hard to pinpoint what's important to share, and even more difficult to figure out the time line of events. Our paths crossed in a lot of different ways before we all came together. Many met in the chat rooms that accompanied live shows run by the Vlogbrothers or the Harry Potter Alliance on a site called BlogTV. The Vlogbrothers BlogTV chat was also used in its off hours as a meeting place for enthusiasts of This is Not Tom, a series of online puzzles interwoven with a mysterious story written by John Green.

In April of 2009, a few of us took part in an event spearheaded by author Maureen Johnson called Blog Every Day in April (BEDA) and were matched up by Maureen as "BEDA buddies," giving us a support system to get through the month. Other to-be Cats watched the Scripps National Spelling Bee together in May, and the enthusiasm from that event has carried on in annual viewing parties. We were all pretty prolific on Twitter and would have pages of conversation in messages of 140 characters or less.

BEDA is where it all started for me. We had created a Skype chat that was meant for brainstorming blog ideas but it ended up as a shared stream of consciousness. When BEDA ended and our chatting slowed down a bit, Arka mentioned he'd been talking with another girl he thought we'd like—Esther. A new chat was formed so that we could talk with Esther, and we never looked back.

When I first met Esther she was so well spoken, thoughtful, and kind. I thought she was too wise to be my age, so imagine my surprise when I discovered that at fourteen ("almost fifteen!") she was five years my junior. When I met the rest of Catitude it was the same story. I quickly learned that my age gauge would never be accurate when it came to this extraordinary group of people. Not long into our collective friendship, Esther said, "I feel as though we're all the same age. I don't know what age that is, but yeah." It was true. We could go from debating which would be better to eat, chocolate-flavored poop or poop-flavored chocolate, if you *had* to choose one (a dispute that has lasted years and proved to be our most controversial discussion), to sharing our deepest thoughts and desires without missing a step.

Very early on we discovered that Valerie was a Harry Potter virgin. Because many of us had first met through our involvement in the Harry Potter fan community, we felt it was our civic duty to correct this. It was the first time many of us had spoken, and so as virtual strangers we organized "Operation HP Valerie." Our mission: get Valerie to read Harry Potter by annotating the books and mailing them around the country. Two or three people were assigned to each book and we kept track of it all in a very complicated spreadsheet (a time-honored Catitude tradition).

There were countless chats in early- to mid-2009 that frequently evolved to suit the current need, but it's generally agreed upon that Catitude as we now know it shares its birthday with Esther. The day she turned fifteen coincided with her return from a weeklong vacation without Internet, so we gathered as many friends as we could, including anyone who may have known Esther even tangentially, into a massive celebratory Skype chat.

from **JULIAN GOMEZ**

"Esther, I remember I met you on the day of your birthday, which was basically the inception of what Cat-i-tude is now. We had a party for you on Skype and the first impression I had of you is 'I really want to be her friend.' I'm so happy we became good friends."

Excerpt from "Birthday Chat"
8/4/09

[11:12:20 PM] JULIAN GOMEZ: Why did no one tell me about this collab thing?

[11:12:27 PM] ARIELLE LINDSEY ROBERTS: *finally playing truth of fail*

[11:12:28 PM] LINDSAY: teryn organized it

[11:12:30 PM] ARIELLE LINDSEY ROBERTS: Teryn organized it

[11:12:36 PM] ESTHER: TWINS

[11:12:37 PM] KATIE TWYMAN: TERYN FAIL. D:<

[11:12:38 PM] LINDSAY: she said she DMed everyone in the chat

[11:12:39 PM] BLAZE MITTEFF: #blameteryn

[11:12:44 PM] JULIAN GOMEZ: Oh, Teryn hates me apparantly

[11:12:44 PM] ESTHER: hahahha

[11:13:00 PM] LINDSAY: D:

[11:13:05 PM] [MORBLES.]: I feel like I've been ignoring you guys >.<

[11:13:08 PM] JULIAN GOMEZ: Last DM I have is from ncacensorship

[11:13:10 PM] ARIELLE LINDSEY ROBERTS: Julian did you see my tweet to searchlight?

[11:13:15 PM] JULIAN GOMEZ: YES

[11:13:21 PM] ARIELLE LINDSEY ROBERTS: how awesome would that be?

[11:13:35 PM] JULIAN GOMEZ: Very haha

[11:13:37 PM] ARKA: holy crap how many people are in this chat?

[11:13:45 PM] VALERIE: 21!?

[11:13:46 PM] JULIAN GOMEZ: We tweeted at the same time

[11:13:49 PM] ESTHER: MANY AWESOME PEOPLE

[11:13:54 PM] [MORBLES.]: 21?!?!

[11:13:54 PM] BLAZE MITTEFF: over 9000

[11:13:59 PM] JULIAN GOMEZ: 1337

[11:14:00 PM] [MORBLES.]: I feel special

[11:14:03 PM] ARIELLE LINDSEY ROBERTS: no one comes to florida =(

[11:14:04 PM] [MORBLES.]: but lame at the same time <3

[11:14:09 PM] ESTHER: LAME?

[11:14:12 PM] BLAZE MITTEFF: I came to florida >:(

[11:14:16 PM] JULIAN GOMEZ: Sounds like a personal problem, Morgan

[11:14:19 PM] [MORBLES.]: hahahaha

[11:14:22 PM] [MORBLES.]: thanks Julian
[11:14:24 PM] ROY DUKE: I just got searchlights CD, it's AWESOME
[11:14:28 PM] KATIE TWYMAN: LEAKYCON. FLORIDA. WINNN.
[11:14:28 PM] JULIAN GOMEZ: np <∞
[11:14:30 PM] ARIELLE LINDSEY ROBERTS: sorry correction no bands
    come to florida

"The Four Corners of My Life,"
QUINCY, MASSACHUSETTS, **2009**

As happens with any large group, people drifted away from our carved-out corner of the Internet. The twenty-five or so who remained would come to be known as *Catitude*. Skype chat rooms can be given a name by anyone in the chat, and this feature was often abused by us for comedic value. It was very late at night (when we're at our silliest) that the title was changed to "Cat-I-Tude" and the few of us online couldn't stop laughing about it. Whenever someone would change the chat name we would change it back to Catitude. Ultimately, once John Green and Andrew Slack began referring to us collectively as Catitude, it just stuck.

You could sign onto Skype at almost any hour and someone would be there to greet you. Many of us had trouble sleeping, so we kept each other company in group calls or video conferences, playing multiplayer games online until the sun came up.

Katy said, "We were united by some common factors: a slight addiction to the Internet, a love for John and Hank Green and nerdfighteria, and we all knew Esther. She really was the lighthouse of Catitude. She created the open environment; she had this wonderful way of drawing you in, of making you feel like you were the only person who mattered."

We talked easily and endlessly about our common obsessions, making stupid jokes that only we would find hilarious, taking quotes out of context and posting them on Twitter. Everyone was acutely aware of how Internet friendships are generally perceived and we mocked the connotation constantly. We would call each other "stalkers," some even going so far as to write details about the group in their own "stalker notebook," and routinely joked that one of us was actually a forty-seven-year-old man.

We watched *A Very Potter Musical* together, counting down in an attempt to hit play at the same moment, then cast each other in the roles of the musical. Esther and I ended up as Voldemort and Quirrell, respectively, mainly because the characters share a robe back-to-back the majority of the play and we thought our height difference would increase the hilarity. Soon after, she sent me this letter and illustrated poem:

For several months none of us knew Esther was sick. We had seen a few pictures with oxygen tubes, but whenever someone got up the courage to ask her about it she would just say she had "breathing issues." During one of our late-night video calls I remember thinking, "How does Esther's hair always look perfect, even at three a.m.?" It was, of course, a wig.

The Internet was one of the only places Esther could go and not be treated as Cancer Girl. Looking back, I am extremely grateful I had that time to get to know Esther, the real Esther, free from the constraints that are inevitably put on a relationship when something like cancer is thrown in the mix.

Then one night we decided we didn't know enough personal details about each other, so we took turns posing and answering questions. This excerpt begins with Esther's answer to the question, "What do you want to do with your life?"

9/12/2009

[10:01:19 PM] ESTHER: I've always been really interested in the medical field. I have a lot of health issues that have resulted in me spending a lot of time around hospitals, and curing people is such a great thing. I just don't know if I'd be able to deal with the other side of the medicine industry, like the death and stuff. I know there are jobs that have you not have to deal with that side constantly, but yeah. not sure what I'm doing with my more obvious future.

[10:01:45 PM] KATY: what health problems have you had, Esther?:/

[10:01:54 PM] KATY: slash do you have

[10:02:02 PM] TERYN: :/

[10:02:02 PM] TERYN: I've been wondering myself a bit, too.

[10:02:08 PM] ESTHER: aha. long story time? I'll probably [be] writing for a while yeah

[10:02:13 PM] TERYN: yeah, what Katy said.

[10:02:15 PM] KATY: we're here for you lady

[10:02:25 PM] TERYN: okay well, take your time.

[10:02:26 PM] LINDSAY: yeah, i know a bit but not a lot

[10:02:27 PM] TERYN: we're here <3

[10:05:49 PM] ESTHER: I've never really talked about it with internet people, so telling people things in text is kind of awkward. um, in november 2006 I was diagnosed with thyroid cancer, which is not seen like, ever, in kids. it had spread to my lungs, which was not that great. so they removed the tumor, but there was still a load of crap in my lungs, where like you can't remove things from. so they did some treatments a few times, and it worked a bit. I was in France at that time, then in 2008 we moved back to the US, and they started me on other treatments that worked better. last christmas I had a really serious time where I was pretty seriously sick, but I've been improving loads. so um, my diagnosis is thyroid cancer, and it just brought on a load of other problems, which bring other problems. erm. don't know what else to say about it but I probably didn't give you like any information on it wohkay.

[10:05:54 PM] VALERIE: ho man

[10:05:57 PM] VALERIE: i love you guys

[10:05:58 PM] ESTHER: aha that was a lot.

[10:06:01 PM] TERYN: *reads*

[10:06:26 PM] KATY: oh Esther <3333333

[10:06:28 PM] LINDSAY: *reads esthers*
[10:07:04 PM] DESTINY: Esther <333333333
[10:07:09 PM] VALERIE: freaking heck i don't want to go to bed now, i wanna talk with you guys
[10:07:13 PM] VALERIE: and esther <3
[10:07:18 PM] TERYN: oh Esther <33333333333333 *loves*

[10:07:20 PM] ARIELLE: esther <3
[10:07:25 PM] DESTINY: as soon as I typed in Esther, I want candy by Aaron Carter came on
[10:07:31 PM] LINDSAY: esther <33
[10:07:34 PM] ARIELLE: haha destiny
[10:07:34 PM] ESTHER: *is candy*
[10:07:41 PM] LINDSAY: oh baby
[10:08:01 PM] ESTHER: I'm totally fine talking about everything, I just don't know how to bring it up or what to say about it.
[10:08:03 PM] KATY: I love you gusy!
[10:08:11 PM] DESTINY: same, Esther
[10:08:14 PM] TERYN: Got it, Esther.
[10:08:15 PM] LINDSAY: so are you in remission or what exactly?
[10:08:17 PM] KATY: are you gonna be ok, though, Esther?
[10:08:19 PM] LINDSAY: I LOVE YOU GUYS TOO
[10:08:21 PM] LINDSAY: SO MUCH
[10:08:23 PM] LINDSAY: gusy
[10:08:24 PM] VALERIE: gah i really really have to go now I love you all A LOT and i hope we will have more talks like this
[10:08:32 PM] KATY: WE WILL <3

[10:08:32 PM] DESTINY: aw bye Valerie!

[10:08:36 PM] VALERIE: <333333

[10:09:08 PM] ESTHER: goodnight valerie <3

[10:09:11 PM] ESTHER: I love you lots <3

[10:09:35 PM] ESTHER: oh and no, I still have cancer and probably won't be officially cured of it. but it's looking good, I guess. still have a lot of other things with it. don't really know what the future is going to bring, so I tend not to really live ahead :\

[10:09:46 PM] KATY: aww Esther </3

[10:10:03 PM] TERYN: aww Esther

[10:10:06 PM] LINDSAY: esther <333

[10:10:06 PM] TERYN: *loves*

[10:10:11 PM] ESTHER: *loves back*

[10:10:11 PM] TERYN: <3

[10:10:21 PM] LINDSAY: i don't know if i should say this but i'm totally crying right now

[10:10:22 PM] LINDSAY: </3

[10:10:23 PM] TERYN: esther you are amazing

[10:10:32 PM] ESTHER: I love you all so much.

[10:10:33 PM] LINDSAY: YOU ARE SO AMAZING

[10:10:35 PM] LINDSAY: I LOVE YOU

[10:10:35 PM] ARIELLE: yes esther you are totally amazing!

[10:10:36 PM] KATY: Lindsay, I'm close

[10:10:37 PM] KATY: </3

[10:10:44 PM] ESTHER: I'm pretty freaking close to crying

[10:10:45 PM] TERYN: I'm tearing up

[10:10:52 PM] KATY: #girly

[10:10:52 PM] ARIELLE: me too

[10:10:52 PM] ESTHER: I'm kinda shaky

[10:12:23 PM] TERYN: God Esther, I like . . . you're awesome. That you keep going. I know that may seem sort of strange, because you didn't really have a choice, but seriously. It makes you epic. And keep going. And I love you.

[10:12:39 PM] ESTHER: <33

[10:12:40 PM] LINDSAY: yeah

[10:12:42 PM] TERYN: <3

[10:12:55 PM] LINDSAY: esther has always been epic

[10:12:58 PM] LINDSAY: this just adds on

[10:13:04 PM] ESTHER: hahaha <3

[10:09:27 PM] ARIELLE: okay so here's a question: Other than nerdfighting and harry potter what is something you are really passionate about?

[10:30:18 PM] ESTHER: I haven't found my one thing to be passionate about, but childhood cancer sucks. and I know that there are so many amazing causes that help, but going through it kind of changes the way I view things and it's just, I don't know. not really finding a cure, cause I don't have the resources for that. but helping people who have to go through that feel better.

[11:00:45 PM] ARIELLE: i love you people

[11:00:50 PM] KATIE: God, seriously.

[11:00:56 PM] ESTHER: yeah, I'm so glad ALL OF YOU are here, right now, talking to me. I've never talked about anything with anyone from the internet that was serious, but I'm so happy for your guys <3

[11:00:58 PM] LINDSAY: i can't stress enough how much i'm here for you guys

[11:01:08 PM] LINDSAY: like, really

[11:01:10 PM] ARKA: guys talk about something dumb for 5 minutes I have to get on the laptop

We grew closer that night. People shared their insecurities, struggles with anxiety and depression, and many of the biggest trials life had thrown their way. Our little Skype chat became more than just a place to have fun; it was a place full of unconditional love and support.

Learning of Esther's cancer didn't affect the group

dynamic as much as one would expect. There was always that worry at the back of our minds, but Esther was really good at downplaying the situation, and we knew her well enough to think of her outside of her disease. Catitude proceeded apace, becoming even more active in our community by starting a tumblog together dedicated to showcasing the creativity and awesomeness of nerdfighteria.

S ometimes I just sit and watch the chat and everyone is so funny and intelligent and caring for one another. It's like this truest, purest, most wonderful form of love and friendship. I don't know. It's just the best. And Esther was part of that. She was that. The best." —ALYSIA KOZBIAL

I think there were a number of reasons we all immediately fell in love with this little chat we had. Obviously, a lot of the appeal was that we were all interested in similar things: we all met through various online communities like nerdfighteria, the Harry Potter Alliance, and fan forums for bands like The Mountain Goats and They Might Be Giants. The mutual interests made the initial get-to-know-you's simple and comfortable. Still, in only a few months, we became inseparable from each other, and I think that was because of much more than common history.

It seems to me that we were each at a bit of a crossroads in our life; we all were questioning things about our lives that we may have taken for granted previously. Many of us were coping with anxiety, depression, and other mental health issues. Even more of us were making plans for college and careers, beginning to explore what adulthood might look like. With growing up comes insecurity and uncertainty. Catitude did something to put all of our minds at ease.

Catitude was important because it was exactly what we needed it to be at any given moment. We spent an inordinate amount of time making complete and utter fools of ourselves. Entire nights were spent in Skype calls, playing multiplayer games online with each other. I remember making jokes about poop, going far out of our way to make each other uncomfortable, and laughing at things like a bunch of over-sugared six-year-olds. And then there were the nights when someone showed up in the chat, obviously hurt or bothered. Everyone would stop what they were doing, and all attention would turn to the person in need. Nothing else would matter until that person was properly cared for. It was impossible—not—to trust everyone in the chat with the most vulnerable parts of yourself. —KATIE TWYMAN

"The Arms of Catitude,"
LEAKYCON, ORLANDO, FLORIDA, **2011**

I have had a lot of online friends over the years, but in general I've found that it's a lot more difficult to have personal, intimate conversations online than in person. Maybe it's the overwhelming availability of entertaining and mindless culture to absorb, or maybe it's just the awkward barriers of clunky keyboards and hundreds of miles. Maybe it's just residual warnings from parents not to talk to strangers in chat rooms. This isn't to say that it's impossible to talk about serious issues, since it's easy to discuss such things abstractly and impersonally, but rather that it's hard to talk seriously, with something at stake, about simple, personal, hidden details. In fact, some of these might be so mundane and obvious that it doesn't occur that they are being withheld.

It was no exception talking to Esther for the first time online. We talked about online games, Harry Potter, and how weird some other online communities were. When I remember the first couple of months of knowing Esther, I mostly remember laughing a lot, and thinking what a fun, witty person she was. It's strange, but after being Esther's friend for not too long, she already felt like a little sister, albeit one who happened to be halfway across the country, and whom I'd only seen in blurry YouTube videos. We would make fun of each other's typos; we would have passionate, late-night discussions about Harry Potter, about the latest film in the series, about how a certain scene was just perfectly rendered; we would have the most inane chats with our other friends, with the unrivaled silliness of teenagers and young adults. Being friends with Esther was just fun, and sometimes it seemed like that was all there was to it.

It wasn't long after we became friends that I realized that there was something else about Esther that made a deep impact on her close friends. It's hard to describe this characteristic, but I think it was ultimately a profound capacity for compassion. She would simply, once in a while, avert our attention from fart and poop jokes, and transform our chat into an intimate space to let other people in to the parts of you that you show hardly anyone. She made it a natural transition, and I think that we were all yearning for moments like this. It's hard enough to let new people in to our unattractive, uncomfortable, shadowy inner selves in real life; online, it's easy to have acquaintances you regularly talk to through multiple platforms, but never really open up to. The Internet doesn't demand the same expectations of social interactions, and most of social media doesn't have the same directness of one-on-one interactions.

As I see it, it takes a lot of bravery to break away from the silly, lighthearted chatter, and actually ask your friends to delve into the deep recesses of their lives. Esther would manage to break through the layers of ironic humor and aloofness, to get us to talk about our families, our pasts, our fears and anxieties, our faults. She made our chats seem inviting and completely non-judgmental. She gave you the impression that she's honestly concerned about you, that she really cares about more than you than just your talent for puns. At least largely thanks to her, our group of friends went from being jokes and random nerd enthusiasm, which bears no fault in itself, to becoming a safe, comforting online space of love and compassion. Before I had met Esther, I didn't think of the Internet as the kind of medium for friends to spill their souls out to one another. I couldn't have imagined I would get to know online friends just as well as friends I see every day. These are the things Esther means to me: being able to care deeply and ostensibly for your friends, and being able to make yourself completely accessible and vulnerable in their presence.

Sometimes, though, I forget an equally important part of Esther. It's incomplete to characterize Esther as having been completely open and vulnerable. I forget, even though I constantly remind myself, the Esther who was a young, scared, sick, lonely, flawed girl. I forget, because it took me several months to find out that she had cancer. I forget, because there were far fewer conversations when she told me how sad and depressed she was when her friend passed away, or how futile waking up seemed when she would only go back to sleep, or how isolated she felt even though with the rapt attention of her loving friends and family. I forget, because even though she was a few years younger than me, sometimes it seemed as if she had the maturity and wisdom of an old sage. I forget, because I don't have to think about death every day except in philosophy classes. I forget, because it's hard to realize that the same person who gives you so much love, and to whom you give so much in return, can go through the kinds of pain and suffering that nothing you do can alleviate.

Maybe this is why it's painful to remember Esther. It could have been easy to just recall her laugh, her idiosyncratic typing, her sense of bouncy fun, even her unbounded love, but it's more true to her own way of loving to remember all the little cracks in her image through which she occasionally permitted us access to her deepest concerns and fears. She would want us to remember her authentic self, including all the imperfect parts. What's the point of opening yourself up to your friends if they don't notice you in your vulnerable state? The point of it all is to love friends completely and utterly, at their best and worst, and to love more than just the good things. It's about showing that you're willing to accept them for whatever they are, that they should not feel insecure or self-conscious in your presence, which can be a hard

task to achieve. Esther really knew how to make you feel
constantly that she cared deeply about you, to show that
she loved you with or without saying so.

—ARKA PAIN

Make-A-Wish!
Esther, Teryn Gray, Lindsay Ballantyne, Katie
Twyman, Madeline Riley, Abby Drumm,
BOSTON, MASSACHUSETTS, 2010

Catitude is a really difficult thing to try to describe—even I have trouble trying to articulate the weird and amazing relationship between all of us. I have other friends who have said they are envious of the total openness and uninhibited love that exists between all of us, Catitude, as friends. I guess that's a pretty great thing to be a part of. There has never been a time where I have felt like I could not share anything and everything with someone in the chat. I'm not sure if that unique aspect comes from forging our friendships online, but I am sure that it has a lot to do with how we came together through Esther.

"Esther shared herself through this chat and through us and so, in turn, we shared right back. It became an open platform for discussion on all of life's problems and curveballs, but also a place where we could race to see who was the fastest at answering Harry Potter trivia (something Esther and I constantly battled for the winning title). We trust and accept each other in a way that we can't always trust and accept ourselves—through the loving of each other's faults, we grow to become okay with our own."

—TERYN GRAY

The *Will Grayson, Will Grayson* event was my first IRL (in real life) meet up. It was Esther's too.

On my end, I was terrified. I had to drive

a few hours to go to it. Everything was planned. That day kind of solidified everything. Friends that had been friends before an actual meet up all seeing each other for the first time. Too nervous to laugh too loud, talk too much, hug too much, say the wrong thing. All I wanted to do was stare at them to make sure they were real and they wouldn't run away from me. That was one of the scariest/most rewarding days of my life.

—SIERRA SLAUGHTER

Will Grayson, Will Grayson release,
CONNECTICUT, **2009**

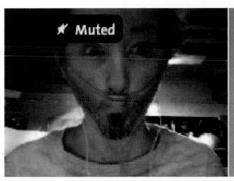

The following excerpts are taken from one of Catitude's earliest abandoned projects. In the course of sending each other snail mail, someone came up with the idea of a shared journal. Esther was the second and last to receive this notebook that we had planned to send through the group multiple times. This is the epitome of us as a group, diving in with gusto and following through on maybe half of what we set out to accomplish. It's a snapshot of Catitude as we were in 2009, including a lot of our running jokes. Esther refers to Valerie as a dog, calls herself "unmanly" when she's tired, and casually slips in quotes from A Very Potter Musical.

—LINDSAY BALLANTYNE

"Manly" Esther with friend,
2009

CATITUDE STALKER NOTEBOOK
September 17, 2009

HI EVERYONE, THIS IS <u>ESTHER</u>, AND I LOVE THIS NOTEBOOK. I'm on an actual IRL phone call with Lindsay Ballantyne, the awesome person. She just set her phone down to put her hair up and I could hear her make noises like "nghngg" eheheh.

I'm trying to do our adorable apostrophe character apostrophe on paper and Lindsay wants me to try to draw a D with eyes but somehow make it look like a pipe. Oh Lindsay here I go . . . 'D' wtf 'D' wtf 'D' Lindsay what the hell am I supposed to draw I do not get you : / (<3)

And now she's telling me about rooming with Geri and her other roommates. They would send videos through Facebook. My pen ink color changed! :O!

Oh man so Lindsay and I are still talking. we've been at it :)for 4+ hours. We called Arka and then we called Abby because she was jealous of our CALLNESS and then we called Teryn to say hello. We called Katie to say hi but she wasn't there so we left her an awesometastic message and didn't know how to hang up so it went on and on (and nerimon) and then we called Valerie for like 5 minutes to say hi. Oh and we talked to Abby for a half hour or so and then she went nappy-nap. Me and Lindsay are in the closet. Separate closets, unfortunately, but later . . . later I'll be in hers. >:)

Lindsay just asked me "when you Google mapped my house was it white or blue?" quite randomly. eheheh I love creepy.

SO IT'S 10:25 PM AND I'M SO FREAKING UNMANLY. School is turning me into this monster. This frilly, flower smelling, bow-sporting monster! I hope tomorrow (tomorrow being Friday) UM, I went to sleep and now it's 11:32 AM, September 18, 2009. I don't know how that sentence was going to end. SUSPENSE.

Today I had French but my French teacher wasn't there so all I did was draw dots on my notebook while the substitute yelled at us for talking even though we weren't. He's a weird teacher . . . right, I drew dots and wrote out VPM quotes. Like:

ooooh it's a FOR REAL new page! eeeeeeeeee! (that was so I want to try "umm" like Abby did. hokay here: a fun to write!ummmmmmmmmmmmmmmmmmmmmmmm mmmmmmmmmmmmmmmmmm

OOOH that was FUN! #coolformsofentertainment

When i rule the world, I'll plant flowers!

When i rule the world, I'll have . . . snakes! >:)

Photo booth with Katie Twyman
and Lindsay Ballantyne,
QUINCY, MASSACHUSETTS, 2010

Sunday 9/20 11:41 AM

hihihihihihihihihihi I haven't forgotten about you, Mr. Notebook, I've actually thought about you many times. I just haven't written in you. IDK WHY. Just haven't.

Last night was pretty freaking great. We tokbox'd and ummm. What else did we do? (besides, you know ;) hmm. It was the #manlies left. (me, lindsay, arka, geri, obviously) I love tokbox'ing/calling/chatting with you guys so much. : D

So I keep going between wanting to use correct grammar, punctuation, capitalizing skills and overall good writing, and not worrying about it. See, that night there was a briiiiiilliant LOL VIDEO! I meant sentence. bah aha oh man. #nerd

mmmmmmmmmmmkay what now. What do I discuss what do I share what do I think of life and all its great mysteries WHO KNOWS not I!! #wtpuff

Damn my phone battery just fell out of my phone onto the ground. I don't want to go get it :/ okay I got it DUDE. DUDE. I'm gonna bring this notebook oh wait oh man I want to oh man I'm not sharing this it'll be a surprise that some of you won't care about HA!!! </spaz>

9/22/ 4:22 PM

I am feeling weird. I had a really really terrible day like, okay, it was actually fine, like nothing terribly bad happened, I just felt meh. Then I got home and felt insanely meh. My house is stuffy but I have nowhere to go. So I slept. then I went to the dentist and lalala had a filling and like anxiety medicine or whatever that lovely crap is called. Also had to have two gum/cheek/oh anesthesia shots on mah cheek/gum/whatever 'cause my teeth are bad. yay! But then my dentist told me his son was a nerdfighter cause we started talking about John Green and he's a sophomore and he goes to my school and my dentist's daughter is a seminerdfighter and she's a junior at my school and just : D I love when nerdfighters live near me. I'm going to see them TOMORROW at SCHOOL.

aaaaaaaaaanway I'll try to think of better things to write in here and I'm sending it soon I SWEAR. K going to sleep or I don't know something BYE.

Sunday 9/?lol who knows 1:02 pm

Eermmmmm hi. how are you, dear notebook? how indeed? uh I'm okay. I just woke up. I'm slightly exhausted. I didn't even stay up late last night. Fell asleep at like 5 am or something. It had been just me and Lindsay for pretty much the whole call. Destiny was there for parts but mainly just me and her typing (I couldn't talk—family) and giggling and oh, my rowling email it was the best.

lol. Valerie's chickadee needs to be easy to duplicate so I can draw adorable adorableness TOO.

eats banana *feels awkward* *glances at banana*

throws away banana this actually always happens.

So I was thinking. when we're done sending this around once, we should send it (and maybe another one) along again so we can all see what everyone wrote. It could be an endless cycle, yeah?

idk it sounds good to me, what do you all think?

ps. I'm totally fine with you all violating my personal writing space by writing/drawing things in my . . . personal writing space : D

Ps.ps. I ship writing/drawing so hard

Saturday, October 3- 1:59pm

OK. before I start apologizing for not writing, let me tell you a few things. I have a cold, and last night was epic amazing awesome fantastic incredible sauce. Yeah, I went to a Draco and the Malfoys, Harry and the Potters, Whomping Willows and JFF & the Sugar Quills concert. It was just AH.

I don't go to Wizard rock shows OFTEN, but the ones I do go to always have the same people from MA chilling around and I'm finally getting to know some of them it's GREAT. :D

Yeah but anyway, I got a shirt and pins and a JFF bag and and and oman I love Wizard rock. ahhh.

Oh and MEREDITH, Paul DeGeorge's girlfriend, who is a merch girl is incredibly awesome and added me on Facebook! Stopping squeeing now. God, I'm friggin awesome.

Hmmmm okay before the show for oh oh I almost forgot but I swear I didn't. See, I was going to maybe kind of bring The Stalker Notebook with me to the show but I FORGOT so instead I got this thing for you all (that are into Wizard rock, anyway)

So guys. I'm going to send this really soon. I don't think I'll write anymore in it, but idk.

I love you all so much. My life is really stressful and before finding the vlogbrothers, nerdfighteria, you guys, I wasn't you know dead, but I really do feel like I have so much more in my life. Sure, it's still not complete, but even listening to you guys' static makes my life feel a little bit more bearable. You're all the best, all of you. And when I say you, it's not just a line. I REALLY DO pretty much kind of a little bit love you. A little. : D (sometimes emoticons on paper are a bit scary.) (btw I'm finally sending this on December 26, 2009. :))

OOKBAY <3333

(It's not too spectacular but it has HATP's signatures, and you can't see them until Leaky 11 because they're all MA-y? I love it, anyway >:))

Exact date unknown

Freaking questions ok:

Valerie's idea: You can answer this/these question/s if you'd like to, whoever you might be. And then ask things if you want. Just so yeah just so. Man dogs have good ideas if we just LISTEN!

1. Do you like mustard? Is there a reason for liking/ not liking it? What about ketchup? mayonnaise? Is there some other random, possibly disgusting thing you like/detest? Do share!!!!!!

2. DO YOU POP YOUR KNUCKLES/anything else (you know, like your neck : S) Freakin' weirdos . . .

3. If you were a giraffe, and you really wanted chocolate but were stuck in a cage/zoo/caged in area, how would you escape/break out/kill all the guards and what would be your weapon choice? You can only pick one, unfortunately. You are, after all, just a giraffe. Not that giraffes aren't special, but I mean there's only so much you can carry.

4. What is one thing (whether it's being on a cereal box, graduating from high school/college/

other lame place, alive or whatever) you want to accomplish in the next year or so?

5. What was life like before you were a nerdfighter? How did you *find* nerdfighters? Do you remember your first reaction lol

k, real bye now <3

    -Esther

(this is like Skype, where I freaking can't say bye.)

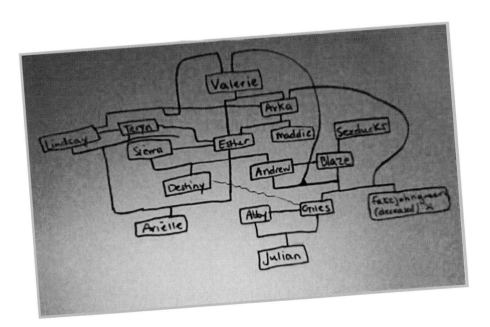

Catitude Chain of Command,
STALKER NOTEBOOK, **2009**

"THANKFUL" VIDEO
November 25th, 2009

I've tried blogging, I've tried making a video, um . . . I'm
not really prepared to make this, but I'm gonna make it
because I wanna have this made, like . . . uhh, I just, I have
a lot of things to say and I wanna be able to see that I
said them, later on. It's not like for you, whoever you are.
I mean you can watch it, that's cool. But, like this is . . . I
don't know. I don't know what I'm even saying.

But anyway . . . Thanksgiving is the time to be
thankful for what you have. And it's more about
dinner and what you're gonna eat for . . . uhsshh
turkey, nowadays, um, for most people. But, I actually
was thinking about it today and I realize that three
years ago, 2006, a few days before Thanksgiving I
was diagnosed with thyroid cancer. And, um, ah that
made me like just realize it, and . . . um . . . so that
Thanksgiving I spent my . . . I mean yeah, that year I
spent my Thanksgiving in the hospital. Um . . . and I had
like a tube in my side and we didn't really know what
was going to happen. Because, I had been sick and my
parents thought that the worst that was gonna happen
was that I was gonna have pneumonia. Ahh, then I, then
they're like, oh?

That wouldn't be so bad now.

But... the next Thanksgiving, but then all that stuff happened—it's a whole 'nother story. Next Thanksgiving I spent, I spent my Thanksgiving at home. We were living in France at the time for 2006 and 2007. (Uh, for a whole 'nother story!) And that Thanksgiving I spent my Thanksgiving at home. With this oxygen tube (points to cannula), except you know, a different one, just the whole thing all over the house, just connected to the machine that would make oxygen. And it was way downstairs and my bedroom was way upstairs so the tube would travel the whole ground and my parents would step on it. And it would be funny kind of, like just, you know ... whatever. But, then, the next Thanksgiving I spent ... we were in America. We came back to America so that I could go to a hospital that knew more about "cancer health" in children. Um, and then yeah, I spent that Thanksgiving at home in this person's house we were staying at. I think, I don't even know. Next Thanksgiving was this Thanksgiving, which is today, so Happy Thanksgiving!

But, yeah I wanted to say like ... being diagnosed with cancer, you know, I haven't really had ... well I've been pretty close to dying multiple times, err ... you know, pretty close to dying. Thought I was like literally ... last Christm ... last, um, last December, November.

Whoa Really? Last December, November. Oh, yeah, it
was like last winter. I was like literally pretty close to
dying. And, um . . . so that just makes me thankful for
being alive basically. Um . . . huh, you know if I had died
that wouldn't have been cool. Oh my voice is quivering.
Uhhh, yeah . . . I yeah . . . I'm just, I'm just glad that I'm
alive and thankful for the doctors and for medicine and
for, like, oxygen, and for like, you know . . . all that stuff
that keeps me from dying. The pills and stuff like that.

Umm, this Thanksgiving is good though, 'cause
I'm a little better even though I'm still kind of sick. I'll
still always be kind of sick, but you know, I'm glad that
I'm healthy, healthy . . . slightly healthy now. And I'm
at home and I have "aliveness" (uses air quotes), and
I have my family, and I have nerdfighters and . . . the
Internet and awesome friends that I've met through the
Internet. And I honestly don't know where I would be if
I hadn't um, had that horrible Thanksgiving where I was
diagnosed with thyroid cancer. I don't know if I would
even . . . you know, I don't know . . . I might have died a
different way! Heh, that's a really happy thought, ha, oh
my! . . . yeah, just, um . . .

So, I don't usually like . . . think, *think* about what
I'm thankful for . . . like, I just kind of sort of think
about it. But I really am thankful for . . . just being alive.
And I'm thankful for my family because my family is

awesome. And I'm really thankful for my friends because they're really cool even if they're . . . most of them are not physically present in this world. I mean in <u>my</u> world! In my world, in my town, most of them are in the computer. They're pre . . . um hmm, most of them are present in this world, I mean in, in, in the world. Oh yeah, this is what happens . . . when you . . . don't have a point to what you're saying except you kind of do, but you're trapped in your thoughts . . .

Alright. I hope you guys have a nice Thanksgiving because Thanksgiving is cool. Just, you know . . . remember that you're lucky even if you don't think you are. Because there's always something you can be thankful for. And, yeah, I know. Okay.

Friday, November 27, 2009 9:17 AM, EST

Happy Thanksgiving, everyone!

It was the best gift of all to celebrate the day all together, enjoying turkey, stuffing, smashed potatoes (we leave the skin on!), sweet potatoes, roasted veggies and the important condiments. We went around the table to say what each of us were thankful for—everything from family, to jobs, to food, to Wii were mentioned!

Esther continues to hold her own. We had a recent scare when the nurses heard skipping heart beats—as many as 5-9 in a minute. But after complete testing by the cardiology and EKG departments, we've been told not to worry. Her team of doctors at several hospitals is also meeting in the next 2 weeks to discuss her continued treatment. She's had more pain in her feet (a bit like having internal blisters), which is a side-effect of the experimental chemo she takes. She started an additional medication for the nerves which is supposed to help manage the discomfort.

Three years ago this weekend we found out Esther had cancer. The next year, Thanksgiving 2007, was when Children's Hospital finished their review of Esther's medical history, and stated that we were looking at maintaining, not curing her cancer. Then during Thanksgiving 2008, Esther had just come out of a month in ICU, where our family came at the doctors' request to say our goodbyes—just in case. For all seven of us to gather together at the table for Thanksgiving 2009 is a cherished celebration of life! So, if you haven't done it, thank God for your family and friends, and look someone in the eye today and tell them you love them.

From our home to yours.

Lori

Saturday, January 23, 2010 2:07 PM, EST

Esther has been doing well, attending high school about three days a week. She loves photography and French, and is doing well in her English class. She has a tutor for Algebra at home, and is doing her history course online. This past semester she was on the highest honor roll at school!

Healthwise she has been doing good, until this week's episode with her bi-pap machine. Her hair has grown back, so after Christmas she went back to school "au natural," without her wig. She has been having a lot of pain in her feet, so her medical team just decided to give her a "drug holiday" for 2-3 weeks to see if the nerve damage will diminish.

However, this week Esther had a tough week. She uses a bi-pap machine at night to give her breathing support, and the machine didn't work well Monday night. The therapist came out to fix it Tuesday, then 1/2 hour after Esther went to bed Tuesday night, the machine quit. I thought she'd be ok for one night (this has never happened since we started using the machine in November), so waited to call them back Wed morning. They finally came at 1 pm Wed. Esther couldn't sleep all night—she was upset, exhausted, emotional, and her lungs hurt. The company gave us a loaner machine, so Esther put it on for the rest of the day. Thursday we had clinic, and she was so tired she used a wheelchair—something she hasn't done for a couple of months. Then unbelievably, Friday morning about 6 am the loaner machine quit! Again, it took the company until 1 pm to bring us another machine.

The sober lesson from all of this for me has been to see how compromised her lungs really are. I knew using the bi-pap added to her comfort level; I didn't know NOT using it compromised her health to this degree. Now we realize that the huge gains Esther has made this year might simply be attributed to the support she's been getting for her lungs. Without that machine at night, I'm not sure the chemo or G-tube would have made any significant improvement in her health. Having that support has given her the energy to eat more, to gain weight, and to start school again. It's given her a feeling of improved health and wellbeing.

Anyway, a couple of long paragraphs. Our hope is that by Monday she'll have recovered her equalibrium and be back to feeling better. Just in time for her midterms next week! It's been a reminder to me to rejoice in each good day, and we hope you will take that to heart in your own lives as well . . .

Blessings,

Lori (for the Earl clan)

March 17, 2010

There was a quote on an episode of *Lost* one day, though I forgot what it was wait I typed it somewhere? Yeah: "you've just spent so much time running away to realize what you've been running toward."

Deep, right? ha. I like it. *Lost* has been my new love for a while. I love its biblical references and mythological feel. It's quite good. Sad it's almost over waaaa.

I'm in a lot of pain right now, lol. I mean not too bad, just regularly I don't really have . . . *any* pain. I did something screwy with my left leg (stretching I think?), and now it hurts when I move it at *all.* waaa yay. It's not too bad though because I haven't moved really at all the past week/ or so. Why? lol. Because I have a smidgen more of fluid in my lungs (like, literally a smidgen; they barely considered it more. but, because my lungs notice everything, I feel it. ugh) Anyway, it kind of feels like something is pressing on my lungs. Ugh. when I wake up it's the worst.

But I feel like a butt for complaining! Because there are kids who suffer so much more and yet do *good* for the world. :|

Ok. Gonna listen to music/doodle.

Bye.

have... *any* pain. I did something
screwy with my left leg (stretching I
think?), and now it hurts when I
move it at *all.* waaa yay. it's not
too bad though because I haven't moved
really at all the past week/or so.
why?. lol. because I have a smidgen
more of fluid in my lungs (they littera-
a smidgen; they barely considered it
more. but, because my lungs notice
everything, I feel it. ugh) anyway, it
kind of feels like something is pressing
on my lungs. ugh when I wake
up it's the worst.

but I feel like a ~~butt~~ for
complaining! because there are kids
who suffer so much more and yet
do *good* for the world :-)

OK.   gonna listen to music/doodle.
bye.

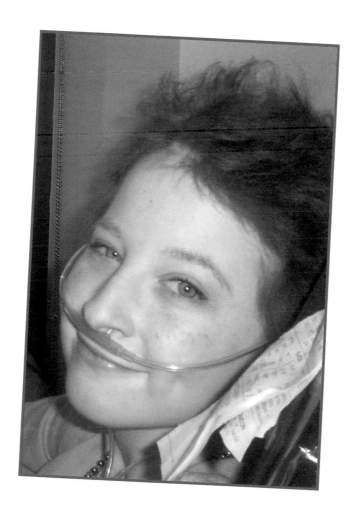

Star of nerdfighteria,
BOSTON, MASSACHUSETTS, 2010

Thursday, April 29, 2010 6:48 PM, EDT

Loved Ones,

Esther is not doing well. Next week they will be putting in one or more shunts (tubes for draining fluid) into her right side. All the fluid, and more, that they drained out a week ago is back again. This is very likely a sign of tumor growth. She's uncomfortable and tired a lot and has asked for a hospital bed so she can sleep for longer stretches. Our health care team is looking at yet another experimental chemo and maybe something more. We are willing and Esther is game to keep fighting, so we're not giving up hope!

Still, suffering seems a useless business. I see no value in my daughter's pain. I know the standard answers ("redemptive" "result of sin" "an evil attack" "bigger purpose"). But the only reality is mystery and that sucks. Our faith remains but is changed; we have "put away childish things." We talk about death and dying and living and loving and we wait, and try to dream a little together each day. Esther knows more about these things than any 15 year-old should. The grief for us is like a tightening of the chest, a closing in, a sadness and an anger and mostly, a helplessness. I can't do anything to make my little girl's pain go away! And she's so perfect, to me.

I wish I could tell you more but those treasures are ours for now. Thank you for waiting with us.

Wayne

May 2, 2010

I don't think we're going on the road trip (the one to visit the majority of my friends). Seeing as I've been sicker.

I want to invite friends out here.

Where? some hotel?

Who: Abby, Lindsay, Katie, Teryn, Maddie

Maybe also: Blaze, Arka, Destiny, Sara, Geri, Arielle

What we'd do: watch TV (The Office, DW, Community, w/e), baguette duel . . .

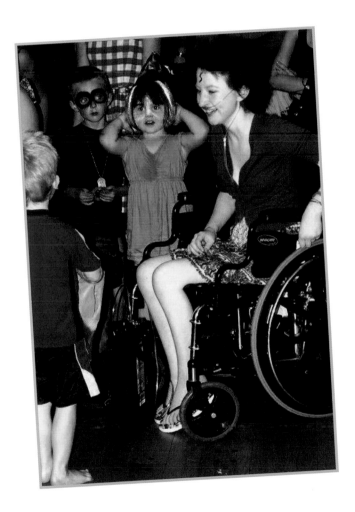

"Friends of Esther,"
SQUANTUM, MASSACHUSETTS, **2010**

Friday, May 7, 2010 12:48 PM, CDT

To our friends:

Esther just came successfully through a chest catheter procedure last night, and she is recovering in the Intensive Care Unit. The doctors removed another liter of fluid and put in a permanent tube during the hour procedure, and within a few hours she was able to go down from 5 liters of oxygen to 3 liters—so her lungs definitely have more room to work with the fluid gone.

The CT scan they did a few days ago showed something suspicious in the right shoulder—once she is a few days out in recovery they will do an MRI to see if the cancer has spread to her bone.

She is on frequent pain meds right now, but is stable and lucid and once she can go off the IV pain medication and they teach us how to use the fluid pump on the chest tube we should be able to go home in a few days. Right now they are draining off the fluids again, trying to get out some air trapped in the lung cavity.

Last night Esther said how thankful she is to have doctors who don't just do their job, but really care about her. Our team at Dana Farber's Jimmy Fund and Children's Hospital is the best of the best! We are grateful. Thanks for caring, and we'll keep you updated.

Lori

Sunday, May 9, 2010 11:52 AM, EDT

Esther is still in ICU, struggling with getting a handle on her pain and her breathing. Obviously taking out the fluid has improved her ability to use her lungs, since her settings went down to 3 liters of oxygen. Her right lung is not fully re-inflating, however, so we've gone up on her bi-pap settings, and she has been staying on her bi-pap rather than a nasal tube all but 2 hours or so a day.

She's been running a low-grade fever, so today they are going to start her on 48 hours of antibiotic while they wait for the cultures to indicate whether there is any infection. Switching her from morphine to another pain med over the last 24 hours brought on a migraine last night—so they're bringing in the pain team to help find the best medicines for her.

So . . . Things aren't dramatically worse, but they also aren't improving much. It's hard not to fear the future as I contemplate bed-ridden days of pain and increased interventions for my 15 year-old. Perhaps with new chemo we'll have months of better days . . . Not knowing is hard. Seeing Esther struggle with anxiety and pain is harder. We hope for reprieve, and pray for acceptance.

Isn't it sad that so often it takes facing death to appreciate life and each other fully? I hope you are making a difference for someone today . . .

Lori

Chillin' with Graham,
QUINCY, MASSACHUSETTS, **2010**

Saturday, May 15, 2010 11:52 AM, EDT

Wow! The power of the internet, twitter, and especially nerdfighters! Once John Green got the word out that Esther was sick and needed encouraging, the awesomeness coming her way has been an amazing thing to see. As her parents, we thank you for brightening her days with your messages.

On Wednesday Esther moved from ICU to the oncology floor, and into the most amazing room they have! It's like a hotel suite, with 2 tvs, a couch, a queen size hospital bed, and our own microwave and fridge. Even better, it looks like we're on track for her to come home by about Tuesday of this next week.

Her prognosis hasn't changed, and her cancer is pretty advanced. We have hope, though, that if this new experimental chemo she started kicks in, it could halt the cancer for a while and give us some time. She'll be coming home to an electric bed that moves up and down (Abe has already been experimenting on it!), and with all the pain meds, and breathing apparatus that she needs to be as comfortable as possible.

Thank you for all your notes. Esther has been reading everyone of them . . .

Lori

Esther and Pancake in her bedroom,
QUINCY, MASSACHUSETTS, 2010

Friday, May 21, 2010 8:26 PM, EDT

Esther came home from the hospital on Tuesday, and is settling into her newly designed downstairs room (the dining room converted to better things!). We have good care daily from the Brockton Visiting Nurses who come in for an hour or so to check on vitals, do labs, and drain her chest catheter. Some days are good, some just okay. This afternoon Esther sat for a while on our porch, and earlier she watched 2 episodes of Doctor Who with her brother Graham (Abe is too little for the doctor . . .).

She says thanks for all the great messages and internet love and hugs . . . They really make her happy.

Lori (mom)

Thursday, June 3, 2010 7:49 PM, EDT

Esther is doing okay. She has been more tired lately, and more nauseous—probably the new chemo she's been on. They are giving her a one-week break this week, so hopefully that will help. She is comfortably moved in to her downstairs bedroom, and it's wonderful since people can pop in and out, and her brothers can check on her. It's a close walk to play WII with them, or join us in the kitchen or the porch for a bit.

She is excitedly planning a Make-a-Wish "reverse" trip right now, where they are flying out several of her close friends to visit her at a hotel in Boston. That will be over the 4th of July weekend, and since we get to be there, we are excited about it too!

Esther had a wonderful time with Grandma and Grandpa this past week, visiting from South Dakota. We managed one special dinner out at a favorite restaurant—but mostly just hung out in her room.

Also, big sis Abby recently arrived home from Germany, which is a great encouragement to everyone!
We'll update again soon.

Lori

June 5, 2010

It's the Adivan. It's the bloody Adivan and I know it but I'm still feeling emotional and . . . well . . . shitty—Annette said when you take Adivan, you lose your inhibitions— the emotions you already have are just amplified.

So basically: I'm sad. I'm incredibly lonely. I've no one to talk to except Lindsay, who I feel doesn't deserve this Adivan-shitty-mess talk (plus she's busy right now) or like Mom/Dad. Kind of sad.

What do I say to Angie? She's over there. On the futon. I could ask her about her "bf" Bill. Or her friends. Or booze or weed. Or angst. There are things she'll talk about with me. I could ask what she thinks about. If she ever wonders when I'll die. Because, let's face it, we just picked out my spot in the cemetery. Very literally. Nice spot, nonetheless.

"I think that's why I go out all the time. Because I don't like to think."—Angie. Yeah, okay. Angie and I are two extremely different people—

Oh dear goodness I haven't hugged anyone for a hug in a long time. I feel sad. And a little angry. At what, I don't know. I miss Angie. I want people to ask if I'm ok; if I'm scared; if I'm unsure what the hell I'm feeling.

June 5, 2010

it's the adivan. it's the bloody
adivan and I know it but I'm still
feeling emotional and... well... shitty-
Anette said when you take adivan,
you lose your inhibitians — the emotions
you already have are just amplifted.

so basically: I'm sad. I'm ireeeedibly
lonely. I've no one to talk to except
Lindsay, who I feel doesn't deserve this
adivan-shitty-mess talk (plus she's busy
right now) or like. mom/dad. kind
of sad.

what do I say to angie? she's
over there. on the futon. I could ask
about her "bf" bill. or her friends.
or booze $ or weed. or angst. those
are things she'll talk about with me.
I could ask what she thinks about.
if she ever wonders when I'll die. because,
let's face it, we just picked out my spot

My cancer? suspected to be in my shoulder.

adivan
is quite a little
asshole.
excuse moi francais
although . . . .
it helps
me sleep
and it isn't
taken until
the nighttime.

Wednesday, June 9, 2010 1:28 PM, EDT

A quick note: we are soon off to the hospital as Esther continues to have ups and downs. Last night, Oma and Opa (Lori's folks), Abby, and mom and dad were together for big sister Angie's high school graduation (yeah Angie!). It was a gorgeous evening here in Quincy and Esther was simply "***radiant***" (as Charlotte said to Wilbur). Now, today, she's having trouble breathing so mom and daughter are leaving soon via ambulance. I'll meet them there.

Just last Friday evening Esther strolled (or rather was pushed by Angie in a wheelchair) around a local cemetery where she picked out her spot. Am I saying this? What parent helps their child choose a plot? This is not what we want. The joy and sadness of watching two sisters roll the grounds and simply be together was surreal. I cannot explain why hope sustains us even in the presence of innocence undone. Very few people in our culture talk about death and dying or if they do it's "embrace the light/suffering" or "fear not, heaven will reunite us with loved ones." I do not worry about death, at all, though I do not welcome Esther's dying. I do not care about joyous celebrations there, I want to give her away in marriage here!

Heaven is Esther doing cartwheels again, her cloud of fire-white, brittle hair shining, waving at waiting earth.

—Esther's dad

Thursday, June 10, 2010 10:57 AM, CDT

A BETTER DAY

I'm sitting beside Esther now. After a frightening yesterday, she's waking up, the fog of last night's morphine finally lifting. She finds it best to rest leaning back like a seasoned sun worshipper. No tan though, as her skin's a porcelain white. She's more than a beautiful young lady and a mature version of that wild hair, now chemo ravaged and of uncertain color, has returned.

Once she's able, our goal is to get her back home to her cats, around her family and visiting friends and in her own room. Besides, she's behind on three Doctor Who episodes and Graham simply won't watch one without her! Her Make-A-Wish is scheduled to come true in three short weeks and she is more than a little excited about that. Then follows her 16th never-been-kissed birthday party (and, no we are not looking to change that status). Esther has always been my muse and tolerates what I write here (from "oh, dad" to "that's good") but it's your guestbook entries that really touch her and give her hope. She sends her love.

—Esther's dad

Saturday, June 12, 2010 10:39 PM, CDT

Just a forewarning: my entries are much less poetic and reflective than my dad's. lol ;D

I woke up this morning around 8 am, having slept the night pretty soundly (I mean, hey, I was only woken up by my dad's snoring a few times). At some point- 9, was it?- I started getting a headache, so one of my favorite nurses gave me a massage and I fell back asleep. Nothing much there!

At noon, my two sisters and brother Graham were standing over me, shaking me slightly and (what sounded like) screaming at me to wake up. I was completely confused as to what was going on, but they handed over a large box with a pet logo on it and set it on my lap. By this point I was gaining consciousness enough to think they were giving me some sort of cat-shaped cake, but, no! Upon opening the box a BLACK CAT JUMPED OUT. Hello, Pancake!

Yep! Apparently, my fam and one of the really nice ladies that works here at Children's worked together to get my cat, Pancake, snuck into my hospital room! He's currently purring happily on my legs and it feels so nice to have my kitty with me, even be it in the hospital.

So, although I'm stuck in the hospital for now, I'm happy. I like the room I'm in (it's the same, huge one I was in last time. score~), I have my kitty, I'm feeling good, and I spent the entire day playing games with my sisters, Abby and Evangeline, and older-younger bro, Graham. My cat visiting being the biggest news as of late is quite a nice thing to say. Hope you're feeling well this nice evening, and remember to give your pet a hug.

Don't forget to be awesome -love, Esther

Pancake and Blueberry,
QUINCY, MASSACHUSETTS, **2009**

255

Saturday, June 19, 2010 11:28 AM, EDT

Seems like Grand Central Station around our house these days! Several friends have stopped by for visits, grandparents have come and gone, wonderful meals get delivered three days a week, the visiting nurse is in at least three times a week, and then there are sisters, brothers and their friends . . . ! Abraham came home with 3 friends from school on Thursday, and they entertained Esther with their 6-year-old rendition of "Shake your booty . . . " It was hilarious!

We do pace the days for Esther, as her breathing issues have continued. Oxygen is up to 7 liters, but the new PICC I.V. line allows continuous meds that help keep her comfortable.

Most of the excitement around our house is the upcoming Make-a-Wish event. Our family and 6 special friends of Esther's will be staying at a hotel in Boston from July 1-5. Activities include a harbor luncheon cruise, a celebrity visitor(!), a Harry Potter movie marathon, a concert, games, food, fireworks from 7 floors above the Charles River, and more! Esther is EXTREMELY excited . . . ! Watch for photos and info after the fact.

With several eloquent writers in the family, my role tends to be the pragmatic one . . . From our house to yours,

Lori

Boat Cruise!
BOSTON HARBOR, MASSACHUSETTS, **2010**

Monday, June 28, 2010 11:16 AM

Wooh Hooh! Make-a-Wish event is this weekend, and gets started early with the arrival of two of Esther's friends on Wednesday. Thursday we go to the hotel in Boston, and the other 4 friends arrive. It will be a busy, busy week for Esther, who is normally overstimulated by an hour or two with a visitor (like the recent visit with her cousins Victoria and Alex!), or the exciting weekly visit to the Jimmy Fund Clinic!!! And of course we have lots to do, what with getting a hospital bed and oxygen tanks delivered to the hotel, airport pickups, house cleaning, packing about 1000 things for Esther, and our own bags with swimming suits and party gear . . .

Pray and hope for health and strength and joy and awesome memory-making to last a lifetime . . .

Lori

MAKE-A-WISH WEEKEND
by Lori and Wayne Earl

A few days before the Wish weekend began, a bulky package arrived and everyone got their first view of the deep lime green bracelets which would become synonymous with hope and with Esther. (In fact, from that moment on, this color would be referred to by her friends and family as "Esther Green.") On the bracelets were etched five simple words: THIS STAR WON'T GO OUT. Included in the packet was a note:

> *Dear Esther and the Earl Family,*
> *The enclosed were created by the world design team of Alexa Lowey and Melissa Mandia. We hope you enjoy them. Approx 80 people are already wearing them and we will be ordering more shortly – the demand by those who know or who have met Esther has been huge. Remember "This Star Won't Go Out!"*

Alexa later explained that she and Melissa had been considering different phrases when this phrase suddenly "just came" to her.

Esther's Make-A-Wish event was actually two years in the making. She just couldn't decide what she

259

wanted or needed. The Make-A-Wish counselors plied her with suggestions: Disney World? "With an oxygen tank?!" A trip to meet a celebrity? She couldn't think of anyone else she wanted to see, or meet. She flirted with the idea of a shopping spree at Sephora, since she loved eye shadow, nail polish and makeup brushes . . . But once she came up with the idea of meeting her Internet friends from Catitude irl (in real life), she was 100% focused. Though it was an unusual request, the folks at Make-A-Wish, helped by local "Friends of Esther," did a great job at making her dreams come true.

from LINDSAY BALLANTYNE

I often asked Esther about her health, and seeing her regularly on video calls made me sure I knew what to expect. She warned me that she was in a wheelchair most always since she didn't have much breathing strength, but there was no way to grasp the full scope of her condition until I saw her in person. It was a wake-up call, but also a privilege to help care for her basic needs even for such a short time. I said good-bye to Esther during a marathon recovery sleep session, feeling that was the last time I would see her in person and doubtful she would even remember it.

from KATIE TWYMAN

The weeks leading up to Esther's Make-A-Wish trip were packed to the brim with planning. We were so excited to see each other, and we wanted to make sure we took advantage of every single second we had in each other's presence. Hours were spent coming up with the most ridiculous ways to pass time together. We put a lot of them in a list, which contained the following ideas, among many others:

- go to waffle house at 3 a.m. and eat cheesy hash browns and read books aloud
- Speak in British accents at least 40% of the time
- LARPING IN HOTEL 4EVA
- Hugging Abe (& others not as important)
- BAGUETTE DUEL
- generally making Arka uncomfortable

Obviously not all of our ideas made very much sense, and ultimately only a few of the things on the list ended up happening. Once we were finally all gathered in Boston, it didn't take long for us to realize that what we actually did was not nearly

> as important as the simple fact that we were
> doing it together. Hours were spent cuddling,
> gorging ourselves on candy, and laughing at
> nonsense. Mostly cuddling. And when I think
> about the trip, those are the memories that come
> to mind first. After all, that's what the trip was for:
> spending time with people you love and finding
> little ways to show that you loved them.

For several intensely exuberant, emotion-laden days and nights, seven of Esther's tight-knit Catitude friends, along with our whole family, stayed at a Marriott hotel on Boston's Tudor Wharf with views of the USS *Constitution* from the hotel patio. The first night at the hotel, the revelers enjoyed a catered dinner and general silliness with one another, a special visit from Esther's medical social worker, Jenn, and an energetic visit from Prof. Dumbledore himself! (Who brought along Andrew Slack, the co-founder of the Harry Potter Alliance.)

The highlight of the weekend for Esther was the planned visit the following day with her favorite YA author and friend, John Green. That morning, her dad met John Green in the lobby of the hotel to express his gratefulness that John would go to the personal expense of coming to Esther's weekend. Wayne asked him if he'd ever thought of himself as a kind of *Doctor Who*. When

John looked a bit puzzled, Wayne went on:

"Well, I've been watching *Doctor Who* episodes with Esther and it seems to be a story about an amazing, but lonely alien—with two hearts, by the way—who is full of love for humanity and who goes around the universe doing extraordinary things, one of which is to periodically drop out of the sky in order to choose a surprised and lucky passenger to accompany him on what he calls, his 'next adventure!' After promising to turn the would-be passenger's world upside down, he always gives them the chance to decline. Of course, they choose to join him and by their journey's end, they are changed and the Doctor is changed, too, always for the better."

Esther's father then looked John in they eye and said,

"I think you are the Doctor and Esther is your present passenger. I don't know why you chose her now, but thank you for inviting her along for the ride. Mostly, though, we know that you love her. That's the easy-to-understand part."

A few minutes later they went up to the hotel room where everyone had gathered, waiting for this

singular, thrilling moment when John Green himself
would enter their world. Just as the door opened—
like some old-time gunslinger—John pulled out his
video camera and began filming. They spent the entire
magical day with him, eating pizza together, playing
games and talking, and crying, too. The group played
the game Serious Ball, which involved tossing around a
foam volleyball covered with questions to which each
friend had contributed. When the ball was tossed, the
recipient would have to answer the specific question
underneath wherever his or her right thumb happened
to land. A few of the questions included, "Biggest fear
with the future?" "What's impacted you the most in past
five years?" "Your happiest moment and why?" "One
goal by end of year?" "What do you care about?" "What
would you say to J.K. Rowling if you had chance to meet
her?" and "What one thing would you change about
self and why?" Later that evening they drank espresso
with John in the nearby Italian North End, an event
Esther later described with one simple sentence: "We
walked into the North End, we got gelato and espresso,
and John was fun to just chill with." Outside the café,
John purchased two roses from a vendor, handing
one to Esther. The other he gave to fellow Cat, Arka,
saying, "Well, he's the only other guy and I don't want to
discriminate."

Before John left the hotel the following day, he wrote a note to Esther. Written on hotel stationery, he drew an arrow pointing to the printed words on the top of the page which said, "IDEAS WORTH SAVING" and added his own thought, scribbling, "I can't promise that, actually." He continued,

> Dear Esther:
> This was the stationery at the hotel where I spent one of the most important nights of my life. Thank you for the gift of that day, for your generosity, and for your pizza. I feel very lucky to know you—and as far as I have seen, to know you is literally to love you.
> What a star shines on our little planet. I pray for a miracle so that I will never have to miss you —but know this: So long as I remember anything, I will remember you and the unprecedented gifts you've shared with me.
> Love,
> John

Later that day, everyone (except Esther, who was feeling too exhausted to attend) was escorted via limousine to see the movie *Eclipse* at the IMAX. Then the group collected Esther for a lunch cruise around the Boston Harbor islands. She and her friends ended the day escorted by limousine to a Wizard Rock concert in Quincy, which was staged just for them. Featuring groups Draco and the Malfoys and Justin Finch-Fletchley, the partygoers were in heaven as the bands' loud voices and electric guitars wailed on with their Harry Potter-related lyrics. The final day was spent together lazily at the hotel. Esther was visited by her endocrinologist, Dr. Smith, who stopped by with her own family in order to celebrate her beautiful young patient. That evening, from the comfort of the sixth floor at Mass Eye and Ear Hospital overlooking the Charles River, everyone sat together at a private event—with more pizza!—and watched the Fourth of July fireworks light up the sky.

It was a time of bonding and healing for those who participated. Esther had an amazing few days and said her favorite part was definitely the people: her family, Catitude, and the daylong visit with John Green. Throughout the extended weekend, multiple laptops within reach, Esther and her friends were piled up on couches, hotel room floors, and scattered on the beds like so many popsicle sticks! As busy as those days were, there was still ample time to sit together and enjoy the quiet.

IDEAS WORTH SAVING.

I can't promise that,
actually.

Dear Esther:

This was the stationery
at the hotel where I spent
one of the most important nights
of my life. Thank you for the
gift of that day, for your
generosity, and for your pizza.
I feel very lucky to know you—

Residence
Inn®
Marriott.

For r
visit residencein

IDEAS WORTH SAVING.

and so far as I have seen,
to know you is literally to love
you.

What a star shines on our
little planet. I pray for a miracle
so that I will never have to
miss you — but know this: So long
as I remember anything, I will
remember you and the unprecedented
gifts you've shared with me.

Love, John

Residence
Inn®
Marriott.

For reservations or information
visit residenceinn.com or call 800.331.3131.

"Make-A-Wish,"
BOSTON, JULY 2010

Abby Drumm, Arka Pain, John Green,
Katie Twyman, Teryn Gray, Madeline
Riley, and Esther
OUT FOR ESPRESSO IN BOSTON'S NORTH END

with Evangeline

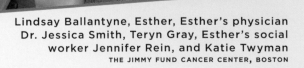

Lindsay Ballantyne, Esther, Esther's physician
Dr. Jessica Smith, Teryn Gray, Esther's social
worker Jennifer Rein, and Katie Twyman
THE JIMMY FUND CANCER CENTER, BOSTON

Katie Twyman, Arka Pain,
Teryn Gray, John Green,
Esther, Abraham Earl,
Lindsay Ballantyne, Abby
Drumm, Madeline Riley

"Puff fight,"
JOHN & ESTHER

July Fourth
"Roar" with Teryn

Abraham Earl

Lindsay and Esther

269

from TERYN GRAY

One of my most favorite memories of Esther is from July 4th, 2010, during the Make-A-Wish trip. We had just finished watching fireworks high above the Charles River and everyone else was riding back to the hotel in another van, but Esther and I had ended up in her family's car. It was a quiet ride back; the full day's events had exhausted Esther of the energy she had. After a few minutes of sitting next to each other in silence, Esther reached out, grabbed my hand with both of hers, and pulled it to her lap. She put her head on my shoulder and stroked my hand with her thumb for the entire car ride back. She whispered to me, "I love you. I love you a lot."

And that was really all I needed to hear for everything else to disappear. Esther made me feel like I was so important, and so loved. And I was so scared to lose her. But she kept on stroking my hand as we both cried quietly.

I'm not sure if it was entirely sadness that caused the tears, but there was so much love. And that's all that mattered. Despite the fear, despite the sadness, despite the pain, there was love. To me, that's how Esther was. She was all things human: imperfect, flawed, scared. But to me, what makes her so remarkable is that she was also so, so full of love and so willing and eager to share it.

Catitude continues to be imperfect, flawed, and scared, but we have a lot more love in our midst thanks to Esther. And we love her so much for that. I love her so much for that. I miss you, E.

There were others who didn't come to Boston but who also loved Esther and wanted to encourage her. Along with members of Catitude, several online celebrities responded with letters for a scrapbook that was created to cheer her up. Wheezy Waiter, Cute with Chris, Lauren Fairweather, Harry and the Potters, Julia Nunes, and others contributed pages, and Catitude's own Katie Twyman presented a large scrapbook to Esther when they met during the Make-A-Wish. Katie Twyman also wrote an introduction:

> Dearest, AWESOMEST Esther,
> This book is a reminder that there are so, so many people who truly and deeply love you from the bottom of their Made of Awesome hearts . . . you have given us SO much. You've given us laughter and smiles and inappropriate smirks. You've given

us pride and confidence and self-esteem. You've given us strength, encouragement, and bravery. But beyond anything, you have given us love.

Arka Pain, Lindsay Ballantyne, Esther, Teryn Gray,
BOSTON, MASSACHUSETTS, 2010

THE GIRL WHO IMAGINED BETTER:
Making a Difference "With Esther"

by Andrew Slack

co-founder of the Harry Potter Alliance

A group of kids I was working with in 2002 encouraged me to give Harry Potter a try. I'd been reluctant to read it—I thought it was just a fad—but as soon as I started the first chapter, I was hooked. I closed the book, turned to the person sitting next to me, and said, "This book just changed my life." Hogwarts opened up a world of freedom for me, a world of wonder.

Then I discovered the Harry Potter fandom and my mind was blown. The people who were growing up with Harry had created an entire online culture around him. Together they had created new Websites, podcasts, conferences, fan fiction, an entire sports league, musicals, and hundreds of Wizard rock bands.

And while I was thrilled to be surrounded by people online who didn't think I was crazy for being crazy about Harry, I was also frustrated. Harry Potter would do a lot more than simply celebrate being Harry Potter. He'd fight injustices in our world the way he fought injustices in his. After all, Harry literally starts a student activist group named after his mentor Dumbledore, called Dumbledore's Army.

I felt that if the entire online Harry Potter fan community could become a Dumbledore's Army for our world, we could revolutionize a culture of first-time citizen heroes engaged in their communities and around the world. We could prove that fantasy is not an escape from our world but an invitation to go deeper into it. Predictably, most people thought I was crazy.

Then I met a Wizard rock band called Harry and the Potters. Harry and the Potters are two brothers who look like Harry Potter, dress like Harry Potter, and sing indie rock songs from Harry's perspective. They are wildly popular and they loved my idea because it was crazy. With their help, and the help of my best friends, the Harry Potter Alliance (HPA) was born.

By the time I met Esther Earl in 2010, the HPA had tons of chapters, sent cargo planes loaded with supplies to Haiti, built libraries across the world, funded the protection of thousands of civilians in both Darfur and Burma, won J.K. Rowling's praise in *TIME* magazine, and made significant progress on issues around marriage equality. Hundreds of thousands of fans had joined our cause, feeling empowered to become heroes. It felt so gratifying to show the world that the power of our stories can change the story of our world.

And I knew we could do so much more, grow even bigger, but we needed funding and street cred. Not surprisingly, when your nonprofit is called the Harry Potter Alliance it's hard for many big donors to take you seriously. We just needed that first windfall with the hope that the rest would follow.

Having spent her childhood devouring Harry Potter with her sister Evangeline, Esther found solace in Harry's experiences. Similar to me and so many others, for Esther, Harry's triumphs were her triumphs. Harry's losses were her losses.

Esther was a Harry Potter Alliance member who yearned to make a difference in our world. Making a difference in our world is a wish that Esther and I shared. Esther had lamented to her parents that she might not live long enough to make a difference. As the cancer progressed, she grew more tired. She was often bound to her home or bed, feeling disempowered and frustrated. Esther also yearned to make friends and be part of a community. Her physical condition made this next to impossible. But then, there was the Internet.

Social media and the Internet have certainly earned a bad reputation for being a space that can be both dangerous and desensitizing to our human experience. But the story that is often not told is that of a teenager dying from cancer, and reaching out to others through Harry Potter fan sites, Facebook, YouTube, Twitter, and Skype. Esther did all of these things.

When the Make-A-Wish Foundation asked what Esther wanted, what she really wanted was to meet her best friends IRL (in real life). Though I only knew a little about Esther, she was a big fan of the HPA and I lived locally, so her mom, Lori, invited me to come for a weekend that would change my life.

As I entered the hotel, Dumbledore puppet in hand, I was taken aback by the unbelievably positive atmosphere in the room and how everyone was in such good spirits and full of so much laughter (with such irreverent jokes!). But I was mostly taken with Esther. Our friendship was instantaneous. Esther had a rare sweetness. She could look at you and see something in you; see you as you would like to see yourself. Through her kindness, warmth, and love for life she allowed others to be themselves.

None of us knew that Fourth of July weekend that something very special was about to happen. That we were one day away from the moment when the love Esther had for the world would become contagious. She was about to inspire a difference in the world.

Just days before the Make-A-Wish weekend began, the HPA entered the Chase Bank Community Giving

Challenge. Approximately 10,000 organizations were competing for votes on Facebook. The organization with the most votes would win $250,000. If we could somehow do this seemingly impossible task, it would be the game changer that we had been looking for.

Although we had scores of volunteers throughout the world working day and night for us, trying to get votes, though we had Harry Potter fan sites and Wizard rock bands pushing for us, in order to really come in first place, we would need something truly seismic to happen. During the Make-A-Wish weekend, Esther must have talked with John Green about the campaign, inspiring John to make the Vlogbrothers video, "With Esther."

> All night long I was thinking about how grateful
> I am to know Esther and trying to figure out a
> way to, like, give thanks for our weird Internet
> based cross-generational friendship. And then
> I remembered that the first amazing night of
> amazing I spent with Esther was at LeakyCon, a
> Harry Potter conference. And after all if it weren't
> for Harry Potter, I would have no Esther, and
> also there probably wouldn't be a nerdfighteria.
> Then I thought about the fact that Esther is a huge
> supporter of the Harry Potter Alliance, a charitable
> organization that nerdfighteria often partners

with. Like remember when nerdfighteria and the Harry Potter Alliance raised $123,000 to help Haiti heal and we had the SS *DFTBA* load up and go over to Haiti. Right, *that* Harry Potter Alliance.

The HPA is currently in this huge contest to potentially win $250,000 to dramatically improve the amount of worldsuck they can decrease. The HPA is currently in third place but what if we all go and we vote and we tell our friends to vote, and they win the $250,000 which allows them to continue their work, getting books to kids around the world from the Mississippi delta to Rwanda, and allows them to grow the work they do, advocating for human rights around the world. And also it is a small little way of saying to Esther, hi, thank you for being awesome. I'm not going to say that we should win this contest *for* Esther, because if I say that she will throw up in the back of her mouth and hate me. I think we should win this contest *with* Esther. So if you wanna give thanks for the existence of nerdfighteria and the existence of Esther and the existence of wonderful boy wizards, please go to the link and vote for the Harry Potter Alliance. So please go vote and thanks again to everyone in Boston. It was so fun to hang out with you guys.

It was now Monday July 5, 2010. I was scanning how many votes the HPA was receiving in the contest. We were doing well, averaging about one vote every couple of minutes. And then suddenly, when I hit refresh, we had fifty more votes. Then one hundred more votes. Soon five hundred. Soon over one thousand more votes.

The video changed everything. Thanks to that video, thanks to John, and thanks to Esther, we won first place in the Chase Bank Community Giving Challenge, nerdfighters all over the world celebrated, tweeting, "We won it WITH Esther."

As for Esther, she couldn't believe it. The "With Esther" video had made her something of a star on the Internet. She was getting tons of fan mail over Facebook and e-mail. People were telling her their problems and she was offering a helpful listening ear. Her wish to make a difference was coming true.

One week later there was a big Harry Potter conference in Orlando, Florida, where Chase Bank came to present us with a giant check at a press conference. At the last minute, the HPA tried to bring Esther and her parents to Florida for the event. Unfortunately no commercial airline had the capability of maintaining her oxygen machine at the last minute. So I scrambled to get a video

Skype call to take place during the press conference, so Esther could be there the entire time.

At the end of the press conference, we turned on the screen and I said, "We couldn't bring Esther to the conference so we're bringing the conference to Esther." Everyone saw Esther sitting at her home, smiling at them, and the entire room broke out in a standing ovation. Over a hundred people lined up at the computer to say hi to Esther, to thank her for being so awesome, to let her know what an inspiration she was to them.

At the end of our life, author Jack Kornfield says, the most important question is not how hard we worked or how much we accomplished. It's "Did I Love Well?" And Esther loved well. It's rare to see any human being love so well. And while Esther, and I, and so many of us yearn to make a difference—even to save the world— our world needs love more than it needs "saving." For all of the problems on this planet, we are not here to save the world. But we are to here to fall in love with it. And if that love can only spread as Esther's has. If we can do what she asked and find creative ways to express love and gratitude for the people we care about and the people we don't know, it can elevate the human condition and allow Esther Grace to multiply one wish that she already received: to have made a difference.

Andrew Slack announcing HPA's win of
$250,000 "with Esther,"
BOSTON & ORLANDO, 2010

Esther with Professor Dumbledore and his
handy assistant Andrew Slack,
BOSTON, MASSACHUSETTS, 2010

THEN (oh yes, I'm not done.) . . .

at (#1) 11:43 am July 13 2010 John Green texted me! "Hpa won. 250K." *

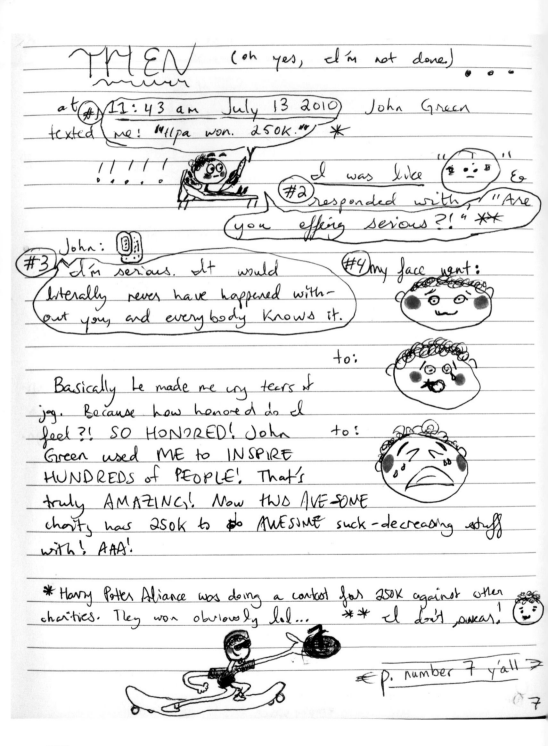

I was like "T_T" & (#2) responded with, "Are you effing serious?!" **

John:
(#3) I'm serious. It would literally never have happened without you and everybody knows it.

(#4) my face went:

to:

Basically he made me cry tears of joy. Because how honored do I feel?! SO HONORED! John Green used ME to INSPIRE HUNDREDS of PEOPLE! That's truly AMAZING! Now tHIS AWESOME charity has 250K to do AWESOME suck-decreasing stuff with! AAA!

to:

* Harry Potter Alliance was doing a contest for 250K against other charities. They won obviously lol... ** I don't swear!

p. number 7 y'all

7

282

THE WEAPON WE HAVE IS LOVE

by Paul DeGeorge, *Harry and the Potters*
and co-founder of the Harry Potter Alliance

My brother and I have written a lot of songs about the Harry Potter book series. Some of them are silly and weird and shaded with irony. Some are romantic, some are trivial, and a few are just wholly sincere. "The Weapon" falls into the latter category. At its surface, the song is a self-assuring statement of purpose lending Harry comfort and encouragement in the developing war with Voldemort. But the song also broaches several of the major themes of the book series: selflessness, overcoming death, and the power of love as an enduring and potent weapon in the fight against evil. These themes resonate strongly with Harry Potter readers and our song has, I've been told, played a role in deepening that connection for some fans. The refrain of the song, "the weapon we have is love," became the de facto motto for the real-world Dumbledore's Army, the Harry Potter Alliance, and it is with that backdrop that I performed the song during the HPA press conference following the victory in the Chase Community Giving competition. Esther was in attendance that day, her face projected comically large over the stage through a satellite feed. It wasn't the first or last time we would play the song for Esther, and I later learned that this was actually one of her favorite songs. It makes sense. Esther was always involved in a larger battle than her fight with cancer. She was playing her own part in shaping our world for the better. She wanted the power of love to be recognized and accounted for, and she worked selflessly to decrease worldsuck and to increase awesome.

I can see the success of her fight. It's manifested by her family, by her amazing friends in Catitude, by the Harry Potter Alliance, by TSWGO, by Esther Day and by the work of John Green and all nerdfighters who've been inspired by her existence. Everyone who has met Esther understands that in spite of life's difficulties, even in spite of death, ours is an incredible and beautiful world and we must take seriously our role in preserving and improving it. Those same ideas are at the heart of our song "The Weapon." The most difficult performance my brother, Joe, ever gave was playing this song at Esther's funeral.

THE WEAPON

written by Harry and the Potters (Paul and Joe DeGeorge)

We may have lost Sirius Black
But we're not turning back
We will fight till we have won
And Voldemort is gone

I'm gonna do whatever it takes
I don't care what that prophecy says
No I'm not afraid

Cause there's one thing that I've got
One thing that you've got inside you too
One thing that we've got
And the one thing we've got is enough to save us all

We taught ourselves to fight
And now we know that neither can live while the
*   other survives*
And I know that that means me
So I'm glad we've got our Army
We're gonna take down the Dark Lord's crew
The Death Eaters will all be running from me and you
And you and you and you and you and you and you

And there's one thing that I've got
One thing that you've got inside you too
One thing that we've got
And the one thing we've got is enough to save us all

The Weapon We Have Is Love

With Paul and Joe DeGeorge of Harry & the Potters,
SQUANTUM, MASSACHUSETTS, 2010

July, 2010

Happy Father's Day   by E. Earl

prelude: explanation

Ah, so we meet again, eh? Dad, I was going to do something really fancy—cut some shapes from construction paper, glue them all around . . . but yeah, all I got was some beautiful sticky fingers. Not the best present? So anyway, I decided to stick with #2 dad gift (#1 being, as we all know, a colorful tie): A letter. Hope you enjoy it, and I also hope it's legible. lol.

chapter one: getting off track

I've always remembered thinking throughout my life (all 15 years, my friend) that you look about 30-something, as well as Mom. But now, as life goes on and you age, you're starting to look in your forties. But aren't you, like, 50? lmao.[1] If you can call me Danei,[2] I can forget your age. Agreed?

[[1] *"lmao: laughing my a** off. I'd say lmbs, but it looks too much limbo"* [2] *". . . and Abby, and Graham, and Lori, and Abra . . . "*]

Anyway, the point of that paragraph was that you're quite young looking. However, I remember one time in the Aix hospital (I think it was before I was diagnosed); I was resting in bed, kinda grumpy, after having my catheter put in (btw, [3] I've decided I like my current cather mucho more than that one . . .), and I looked up at you. You were watching me sleep and I, being grumpy from meds, got annoyed and stuck Mickey over my head. Now of course when I think of that moment I feel really bad, and I also remember how tired your face looked, although you were slightly smiling. Seeing you tired and old-looking makes me feel horrible. And being the cause of that makes me feel . . . horrible. But I know you would never blame me for anything. [4]

Mom, let's say, has never looked a day over 23. Right, dad?

Chapter 3: home is where the fam is

In Williamstown, we had a hamster, yeah? Oh, William was his name? Who the heck knows.

But anyway, me and Evangeline used to take building

[*3btw: by the way. we're pretty smart, eh? 4unless, let's say, I broke a table playing games or something. *cough* . . . angie . . . *cough*] blocks and VCRs and blocky things, and we would build a maze-thing. Then, we would stick William in the maze and run around, playing "tag." Willy would always cheat[5] by sneaking through the cracks in the maze walls, and then he'd bump our feet. Then someone else would be it and . . . yes. Exciting. Why'd I tell you that? Oh I don't know but there you go. [6]

Story #2: Graham is watching a video right now of Doctor Who. It's an episode where the Doctor (David Tennant) and Rose travel to future London. They encounter nurses with the faces of cats who test medicines on humans (mean!). There is also (subplot, hello!) a woman who is currently "the last human on earth" because she's the last original human from earth . . . anyway, this woman (Cassandra) has a man/alien who for some reason is devoted to her. So later on, blah blah, the human test subjects are saved, Cassandra's conscience is inside of Rose, man/alien/Cassandra devotee is SUPPOSEDLY dead, and Graham says, "I hope that guy is still alive. He was very nice."

[[5] *that dirty, dirty cheater*

[6] *these are my emoticons, btw. emoticons are like smileys*]

I love his comments on things, seriously. So at the end,
Cassandra's conscience goes into man/alien (which of
COURSE Graham had figured out), Cassandra/man/
alien goes back in time to past-Cassandra, C/m/a says,
"You are so beautiful" then dies, and Graham naively
(but cutely) says, "Oh! Maybe Cassandra went into this
girl and the nice guy will live!" Graham is so great!

I lately have been just kind of sitting around with him
lately. Usually, he asks to watch <u>Doctor Who</u>, but w/e.*
I enjoy his company, and he really seems to not get
frustrated around me. Yeah, I believe he'll do
alright, honestly.

Abe time. He just went to the dollar store (oh trouble is
here) with Mom and came back with gifts pour moi—a
tattoo, a plastic, ducking chicken,** and got himself the
whole store.

Abraham is adorable. He just knows how to be cute.
He also knows how to be whiney . . . oh, that little butt.
But (lol), he's a great kid. He says some
profound stuff. That whole, "but who made
him? And who made him? And who made

[*w/e: whatever. oOoOo, challenging
**I really don't know . . .]

him?" thing makes my head all 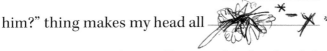 *

Some memories I have of him are his first birthday; it was in the Plymouth house, and we made him Mom's really good chocolate cake. We went out on the porch and Abe sat in his high chair while we occupied the glass table (that wasn't ours? or something . . .). Next, Abe used his hands and squashed the cake with his mouth. I think it was his first time eating cake, too. It was a cute experience. Oh, I don't think he liked the cake for very long. lol.

Another memory from not too long after that is when Abe smartly decided to lock himself in the bathroom. And then, the door smartly decided to not have an outdoor lock. And then you freaked out, lmao. Then Abe cried. Then I, not to sound cocky, saved the day with my big, tanned, glistening biceps by climbing through the window and KAPOW! unlocked the door.

[*"*blew my mind, basically*"*]

KAPOW!

Let's talk about Angie? She's a character, to be certain. Earliest memory of her is either the whole beetle dumping thing in Saudi or saving the kitty those jerks ~~(a jerk)~~ (in Saudi) were throwing around.

← me

We hid that cat in our closet for 3 days before you found it, you know. Oh yes, we're good.

Another memory? Going jogging at, like, 7 in the morning in Albertville. We were trying to "get fit" (12 year old me & 15 year old Ang, lol). So, I remember running almost all the way to the Briggs's (their house was far, OK?) and then suddenly, without warning, I had to poop. **Badly.** What was I to do?! We were so far from home! But we ran, fast — past some goats,* past some morning starers,** and I ran to the toilet and KAPOW! pooped. You know that feeling when, oh dear goodness you have to poop, and then you do? Yeah, it felt like that. It feels... like... AMAZING

#1 ← me

#2 (literally) me

*rem those

** wer weari short wife ers...

292

Let's talk about Angie? She's a character, to be certain. Earliest memory of her is either the whole beetle dumping thing in Saudi or saving the kitty those jerks (in Saudi) were throwing around.

We hid that cat in our closet for 3 days before you found it, you know. Oh yes, we're good.

Another memory? Going jogging at, like, 7 in the morning in Albertville. We were trying to "get fit" (12-year-old me and 15-year-old Ang, lol). So, I remember running almost all the way to the Briggs' (their house was far, OK?) and then suddenly, without warning, I had to poop. <u>Badly</u>. What was I to do?! We were so far from home! But we ran—fast—past some goats,* past some morning starers,** and I ran to the toilet and pooped. You know that feeling when, oh dear goodness you have to poop, and then you do? Yeah, it felt like that. It feels ... like ... *amazing*.

After I got sick I feel as though Angie and I faded a bit. We had not much in common, with her having a "teenage life," and me having a "lazy-butt invalid" one.

Actually, quite recently we talked about that ... it's hard,

[*remember those? **we were wearing shorts and wife-beaters]

to stay in touch and be friends when you've
become used to the routine you're in . . .
I love that girl, and she has a freaking
lot of potential, and she can be so
strong. She's a good sister to have. I
hope I can make more memories with
her very soon.

There's something else I'd like to say about Grahambo.
After his <u>Doctor Who</u> episode he asked, "Again, why
do you have cancer?" And I, never being prepared to
answer questions well, talked about cells (which he
knew of! "from TV") and how sometimes people are
born with cancer in their cells. I'd have said something
more philosophical, but . . . I . . . didn't? Eh. Anyway,
Graham stated, "If I could have two wishes, one would
be to have more time to hang out with Amber. And
the other would be that your cancer would go away,
forever."

Abby is one of those good first children, You know what
I mean? Maybe she had a rebellious stage . . . I clearly
remember being with Alexa and . . . dropping her off?
when suddenly we had to drive to Walmart so you and
Mom could get Abby and Keri from security. Guess they
were there for <u>stealing a necklace</u> lol. Abby tells me it
wasn't even a good one. *

I have good memories with Abbs . . . playing "shop" in Saudi; it's where we'd** set up shop w/*** our beanie babies and like . . . trade them . . . much funner**** when you're younger, lemme tell you. Recently I tried playing this w/ Graham and Abe, and dear me it was boring. Woow.

But so and, I'm using a new pen, just so you are nicely aware. Lol jk*****, I found my fav pen again!!!!!!!!!!

Abby has always been a good sister. When we lived in Albertville, mainly Angie and sort of I didn't like hanging with the big A. Why? Well because! When she was there it was because she was VISITING from HER friend-space. And she was inVADING OUR friend-space. You'd always make us bring her with our group which was just HORRIBLE because everyone thought she was hilarious/great/a new face INCLUDING, Evangeline and mine's LOVE INTERESTS. Namely, Ryan and Bruce. How in the world could you?!

But besides that, I've always felt totally comfortable

[*this is a guy laughing so hard that his eyes are crinkling, PAR LE WAY. **we being Abb, Ang and I ***w/ means WITH, btw. ****MUCH MORE FUN I MEAN *****Just kidding—clever, eh?]

with Abbs, I mean, people are <u>meant</u> to feel comfortable with family, but sometimes you have a good connection with people, and I'm like that with her; she's great. She's also HORRIBLE in that she feels no guilt in teasing me despite me being a SICK, PALE CHILD. It's <u>disgraceful</u> if you ask me. **

Abby now is great, and she is so good at taking care of me. She really is. And as I said earlier, she has no problem teasing me***, which shows she's comfortable with my millions of cords. – <u>GO ABBY!!!!!</u> –

After all my Abby-praising I'd like to point out that she's not the only sister I look up to. I mean, Abby <u>IS</u> someone I look up to, but Angie is too, in some ways.

Angie's good at writing and gosh am I jealous of that. She's also really just a person I like, so yeah.

Another person I look up to and feel the need to talk about is someone we all know and love . . . KERI LYNN HINKLEY.

[*"WHY WOULD YOU DO IT, FATHER. WHY"* ***Idk what's up w/ this face.* ****and you always say I'm never teased . . .*]

So one of the first memories of Keri Lynn "Earl Sister" Hinkley is: Graham and I were playing a video game* on the couch in the Medway farmhouse when Abb and Keri walked in. I was about 8 so they were . . . 13/14? Lmao. that's so young, essh. So, Keri walked in, said hello, and the first thing I wondered was if she was Indian. Of course, I didnt ask. Oh no, I'm too busy playing dumb games and being shy. But w/e, I found out eventually that she is not, in fact, Indian – SHE'S JUST SO TAN, Y'KNOW? Is she Caucasian or like Italian or w/e???

And but so, somehow this tan, sarcastic girl wriggled her way into our family and now I consider her a sister. It's cool. Because like, even if Abb and Keri weren't friends we'd still have Keri in our lives. And I'm cool wit' that.

Keri a few nights ago slept in my room (the dining room one!) and we talked for a little bit about everything and it was nice. Very nice. Love that girl, seriously do.

Mom is such a wonderful person, did you know that?

[*"p. sure that it was Luigi's Mansion great game . . ."
*"no, I don't know how the smileys I'm using work. But they do, OK?!"]

297

If you weren't around (which would be unbelievable sad ), I know Mom would be just as amazing at what she does, and you know it! She's a really lovely woman. If she were a friend's mom, I'd be like "OYR mom is supAH cool!!" but instead, I'm like, "ya Mom is cool GET ME SOME BLUEBERRIES PLZ!!!"

But let's be srs* for a min; I love talking to Mom. About serious things or not serious things. I love hugging her and I love when she reassures me that things are okay; even when . . . you guessed it . . . they aren't. Mommy is amazing and I love her.

Now you on the other hand . . . I cannot stand you!!! I'm only writing this ten page letter to show you how much I don't love you.

Oh man, I had you good. Yeah, I actually CARE ABOUT YOU, Wayne! lol your face . . . oh . . . but I'm not gonna talk about you NOW so owned.

FIN . . . of chapter 3

Chapter 4: Esther is bad (to the bone)

Can I tell you a secret DON'T GET MAD I just feel I should tell you? Although I've never been kissed, (boo) there was this one time when you and Mom went to a date and the boys were at youth group. So, Ang invited Kelsey over and I decided to actually LEAVE my room and go downstairs outside to help them start a mini campfire. This was a while ago . . . so we (well, Kelsey and Angie and I watched) made a fire succesfully and were psyched. They were drinking a bit of wine so I had some (now now don't flip out I'm just telling stories). Wasn't really good but I had 2 glasses. (I've had 2 glasses in a row before that, in France.) By then Ang had invited over Adam and some friends of hers. And then I laid on the trampoline and the sky spun and my breathing felt super good and Angie looked in my eyes and declared me drunk.

Anyway I'm debating whether or not to rip this page off, but I'd actually like to share the story of my first* time drunk with you.

So, Angie and her friends decided they were gonna go to Kelsey's to hang out (AFTER picking up the boys). So Angie helped me upstairs, me wobbling and giggling a lot. She carried my oxygen, although—I don't know if it's the alcohol or what—I didn't feel out of breath. Coolness. So I get upstairs and she tells me to sleep and call her if I need her. Which I did, when I got hiccups. Finally they went away, though, and I fell asleep. Woo, rebellion.

Literally the first regular-teenager-in-America thing I've done, Ai ai ai.

Oh, despite my "date" w/ Yasser when I was still 14. We went to some movie together and with a group that afterwards went to the 99 to eat. But the whole thing was awkward and he had to leave during dinner I DON'T KNOW it was awkward, Lmao.

So other than that, the most action and "alcohol" I get are sleeping with Mickey and drinking a sip of Mom's Smirnoff. I'm <u>WILD,</u> baby!

Another "bad" thing I've done is this:* me and Angie loved Barbies for a while, if you'll remember. We'd have a bunch of clothes that we'd dress our Barbies in, and we'd build houses and rooms for them, and then we'd not really play. The set up is the most fun.

And but so, we always wanted new clothes . . . we'd go to yard sales and buy their bags of old Barbie-clothes . . . but it still wasn't enough (because we were greedy children).

So one time when we were "forced" to visit a "friend's" house who had kids, and those kids had Barbies—so we played with them. And then, when we were alone in there, we grabbed this (I still remember) red, Barbie dress that we thought was beautiful and maybe some other stuff, and STOLE IT.

I felt so bad but Isabelle and Skipper and Barbie looked so good . . .

Yeah but ok, that's the end of that story. Pretty sure we sold all our Barbie clothes in a yard sale. lol.

What do you think of me now? I've told you all my dirty secrets. Should I be hung, like that bro on <u>Twilight Zone</u>? lol jk plz don't do that . . .

Oh, 'member when Graham fell off the bed in Saudi? Ugh, I felt so bad, Dad, 'cause me and Amanda were jumping off my bunk bed and then poor Grahamy slipped off and broke his arm. : (I kinda remember going to the hospital, but Idk. Too little to remember, I suppose?

Do I feel guilty for anything else? I'm trying to think . . . Oh, here's a "serious" one . . . For starters, I know that you would never, ever blame me for anything caused by

[*"*this story also includes Angie, shocked?"*]

my cancer. But there ARE times where I feel so guilty.
Lemme explain:

- my cancer brought us back to America. I know
you were running low on money, but I also know
that you <u>loved</u> France. Makes me . . . sad.

- my cancer KEPT us in America. I know that's not
what we planned but, idk, sometimes I feel guilty.
I know I shouldn't, but feelings are <u>feelings.</u>

- there was one time (and before you read the next
part remember I love you lol . . .) in the hospital
where you and Mom were arguing over spilled
coffee (HAHAHA I'm so funny) literally and like,
mighta been the morphine, but I cried a little
because <u>me</u> being in the hospital was the cause
of your stress.

Gosh, I prob shouldn't tell you this stuff for your
Father's Day gift, I just wanted to . . . tell you things I
haven't before. And those are not constant feelings, just
feelings I have felt at one point (s). Still love you.

<u>Chapter 5: Love, hate, feel.</u>

Dad you do realize I'm a human. Which is always good.
And therefore I have feelings and thoughts (believe me,
I have a <u>lot</u> of time to think . . . ha). Which you realize,

thankfully. I'm sure there are many parents who think differently, but you and Mom are a-class 'rents.

w/e I do not remember what I was going to say but: hey. It's July 3 (well, it just became July 3 . . . I think it's like, 12:30? or something?) And guess what? John Green just went to his room to sleep after a full day of . . . J Green. lol. He is the greatest guy and ok I am going to write some stuff that may or * not make sense?

Earlier today, John played "fun" ball with us. It was all on freaking hilariously dumb questions like "choco. flavored poop or poop flav. choc?" and "painties color?" But after that, we played "serious" ball and it got quite serious.** Whenever we got a good question, John would make us pass it around in circles and state our various answers. John and Abby—the—friend filmed the entire thing basically. (Although Lindsay later filled me in that John would film everyone's answer until they got to me. Then he'd stop ahhhhahah . . .)

Serious Ball turned into hugging—and saying how much love we have—time which was nice. And tear filled. Afterwards we went to nap.

[*"or may not . . . **hello blue: it's _now_ . . . July 10 so im _memory-relying_ right now . . . uh?"]

Then we walked into the North End, we got gelato and espresso and John* was fun to just chill with. My friends Katie and Teryn and I took a cab back but everyone else walked home w/ Mr. Wheelchair.

Once back at the hotel, you guys had the photo flippy thing set up. <u>Slideshow!</u> You guys had the slide show set up! So we all watched it was well done. A little long, but it had my songs and I am so freaking cute.

I'm really enjoying sharing stories but I'm gonna wrap it up 'cause most of this part is stuff you already know.

[*"*and my friends!*"]

Monday; July 19
9:41 pm

My g-tube is infected. My g-tube is infected and it huuurts. I'm p. sure it's my fault, too; I put the new Mickey in and—BAM—pain around it. G'job, Est.

I don't know what I've been doing . . . people online are still saying things like, "thank you, you're an inspiration" "yr amazing" "wow you're famous" "you're so beautiful inside and out" But WHAT DO I SAY TO THEM?

"Oh, jgreen mentioned me in a vid along w/ my friends and then he made another vid saying 'Vote for the HPA WITH ESTHER' and oh before all that he made hundreds of NFs sign my guestbook. But I'm still Estee & I've done nothing else????"

Ya w/e that's a silly rant but okay look I feel so lazy. I realize I'm sick however how do I connect I guess with Ang? I don't think I try, tbh,* at least not that hard. It's just that, dude, to get into Angie's brain and have a talk where we were both exposed would take a lot of effort. Then I feel lazy . . . BLEH DUMBEST PARAGRAPH~~~

Ok I can't write right now (write right AHAHA) because I'm tired and like feel really bad/hurting on my tummy. I hope the anti-B we got today helps. Weeee ok.

*tbh: to be honest J

305

Wednesday; July 14 / Early Morning lol . . .
5:30 pm

Abraham is finishing my drawing of a roller coaster
or sommat so we're sitting in my bed together. Ok
nevermind he has moved on to another drawing of a
guy skateboarding. I love his little skate ramps that he,
in his mind, has been on. J

Last night was my first "late" night in a whole . . .
I stayed up until 2:30 am video-chatting with what
was mainly Abby D and Arka but also Maddie and
Katie. Therefore, I awoke at 5pm today. Yay, messed up
schedule . . . <u>NOT</u>!*

Anyway, I've been trying to think of stories I would
like to be remembered (therefore stories I can tell), but
nothing's popped up in the ol' noggin. Poop. :O I just
personally kind of like holding a pen in my hand and
writing words with it? It's soothing. Also I'm bored.

*taking a tip from the <u>nineties</u> HAHAHAOME B-)

Monday; July 26, 2010

Explained to Graham today how everybody is born
with cancer cells, and sometimes, in people, like ME,
the cancer cell comes "alive." Y'know, he seemed p.
interested in it.* I explained it through pictures?
Like . . . okay here: (you're probs not interested in this,
Person, but <u>I do not care!!</u>)

"Everybody's born w/ cancer cells. That baby's me." ☺

"You're chubby." <u>Blue</u> is white blood cells, (I explain those) red is red blood cells, & these . . . green ones are cancer cells." "They're green?" "Not really." "Ok." "So I lived for a long time without <u>cancer</u>."

☺

"Until France." "Kinda, yeah. Then, sometimes the cancer cells are . . . bumped or something, or they grow more. That's when cancer starts." "Okay [something about farts]."

—Me and Graham

Wow that is so a bad explanation lol lol lol lol

*For the record, "p." or "v." or . . . w/e . . . those things mean "pretty" and "very" and . . . whatever lol.

July 2010

My birthday is what in 5 days? That's p cool that's p. cool. Lauren Fairweather de The Moaning Myrtles is gonna come out with her boyfriend NONEOTHERTHAN Matt Maggiacomo who is not really that fancy at all. I fooled ya. He's from The Whomping Willows. Also A Slack is joining us with NONEOTHERTHAN his girlfriend something something who I'm anxious to meEcEeEet.

I don't know what I want for my bday or what people are going to GIVE me? I literally have all I want and that sounds very "oh what a cute cancer kid I've got watery eyes" but really it's just "I already own things of interest."

Oh my how I want to write a story in here but I haven't the energy. There's a dumb one and a lesser dumb but much more difficult story cooking up in my head. They seem okay . . .

And now I'm off to prance into bed and create a hide-and-seek world on paper!!! ~~~

So. I've done nothing today oh I made these silly "characters" for a "paper hide & seek" I'm making. Idk what [am] I even doing ha.

I also spent about three hours (making the characters :3) What do I even do bye.

Thursday/July 29/s.o.b*: tired.
Mood: thoughtful?

As I wrote out "tired," I noticed Blueberry staring, wide-eyed I might add, at me. "Oh that cat," I thought to myself, "he sure is a curious fellow."

I proceeded to slowly write th- , then look back up at his round eyes. And oug- o dear me, he was watching the pen's movements . . . ! htf- don't autistic kids do something familiar? u- watch things move (such as a mouse cursor, which Blue himself has stared down)? –l Perhaps Blueberry has some of the same traits as some autistic people do some of their life. Is that a possible thing? Ok.

*s.o.b: state of being, obviously bro.

You've come to Esther's UEDA
Thank you for watching.

Video transcript, nothing more than feelings,
August 9, 2010

First scans tomorrow. I feel scared that they will show up and the cancer will either not have been reduced, or will—there will be more. I feel scared that it will have spread to my bones. I feel kind of lonely because lately I haven't kept in touch much with my friends. And it's just something that I feel a lot of the time, seeing as I mainly sit in bed, occasionally on my couch, and, um, spend most of the time with my family or my cats. I feel tired, I've always felt tired. I'm confused, very confused. Oh my goodness, confusion is very, very high on my list of feelings right now! I'm also proud of, of pushing myself lately, because, I mean you guys don't know any of this because it's just a day to day life thing, like I don't record it, but I've been pushing myself lately to wake up in the morning and to do things.

I feel bored. I feel so many more feelings but there're so many, that I just can't even find them. I feel slightly overwhelmed by that, that I can't even figure out what all my feelings are. And I feel sad about things that have happened in my life. And I feel happy that I'm still alive, but I feel kind of ashamed that I'm not doing that much with my life. I feel kind of like I'm fooling people, because you know, in my videos, and in what John Green and all those amazing people have said about me, like, they say these amazing things about me but I feel like I'm fooling you all, because I'm not always amazing, and I'm not always awesome, and I'm not always strong, and I'm not always brave, and you guys should know that, you know? I mean, I'm not always this perfect person. I get pissed, I get, I do stupid things. I . . . I get angsty. I cry. I hate my cancer. I judge people. I yell at my parents. I . . . sometimes wish I'd never gone through this, and then I realize that if that happened I wouldn't be who I am, and then I get all like "Oh, that's just confusing." But then sometimes I do wish it never happened, the cancer thing.

If you are, like, a person with feelings, I kind of urge you to like, write this, write in your diary or your blog post or a video or on a Post-it, like your feelings, because it feels good to just like, kind of see what they are, and even if you can't figure out all of them, because, holy crap the brain has a lot of feelings! And your heart, or whatever, is an anatomy, anata, anatomicalla-cally correct. I will see you guys tomorrow. Probably.

Thursday, August 12, 2010 9:45 PM, EDT

Esther is 16 . . . (I can't possibly be the mother of children aged 21, 19, 16, 14 and 6!) Esther's birthday was low key, with several friends over and lots of intellectual and fun conversation. Dessert was Esther's favorite cake: Black Tie Chocolate Mousse Cake from Olive Garden. Mmm! She opened some very creative gifts, plus she's received cards, emails, and a few packages from friends and family near and far. Thank you, everyone!

Monday we were back to the routine, with a long day at the hospital for PET and CT scans, and blood tests. After review, the doctors say that the "smart drug" chemo seems to be slowing down her cancer for now, which is a good thing. It's also giving her very high blood pressure, so tonight she started on a new medication for that. The best news is that the cancer continues to be contained in her lung area, with no spread to bones, which they were worried about.

Last night we had a game night and played Harry Potter Clue; Abby won! Tonight Graham, Abby and Esther are watching The Lord of the Rings—sounds very exciting in there! We are blessed . . .

Lori (for the Earl clan)

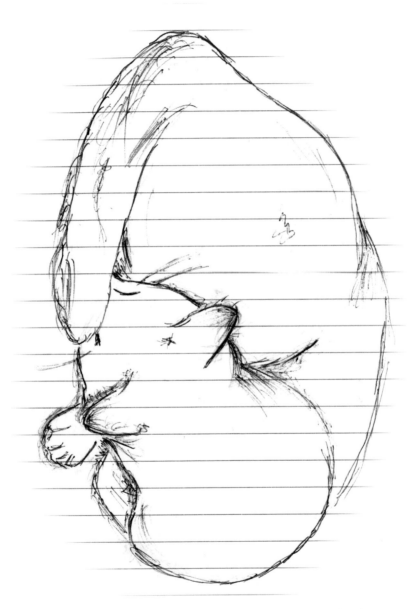

"An A+ drawing of Blueberry at his best,"
AUGUST **14, 2010**

August 14, 2010

- I just finished drawing it in pencil; hope going over it in pen (so it stays) doesn't ruin it too too much.

- Oh dang you, Current Dad! Neither you nor Mom are meant to see this journal until it is jam-packed full of entertaining anecdotes!!! and random drawings, mainly of cats. . . .

Oh this is August 13?—no, 14—and I drew this right now lol and it took about 45 min? Blue kept shifting positions HAH.

But yeah, I'ma go get make up'd and clothes and crap b/c*
Mom, Angie, Abby and I are going out to a movie called
<u>Eat Pray Love</u> that does NOT look like a chick flick at allll!
I've seen way too many of these in my lifetime . . .

1. happy guy/girl
2. sad guy/girl
3. crazy adventure
4. meet kooky lover
5. kiss
6. love

Okay there are a few different types of chick flicks, but that is one of them!!!

GOTTA GO OR THE EARL GIRLS'LL LEAVE W/O ME!

*b/c = because (I think I've told you that oh well it takes 3 times to remember, right?!)

Friday, August 20, 2010

I don't know what sparked Abe's current "need for Mom." For some reason I'm thinking it was after a longish stay in the hospital full of "is Mom going to be here tonight or Dad or what??" and it must have been/is hard on the guy.* It makes me sad to see him like: ☹

In other news I woke up this morning (7 pm) with a nose bleed. That's right; I woke up with blood all up in my Bi-PAP mask. It. Was. Fun—

Actually, so far, my day has only been like 4–5 hours long. I'm really going crazy with this "life" thing!!!!! I'm even lying here writing and my eyes'll close. Silly eyes, I thought you stood for: Escalating Your Eeeeemediate Stimulation ???

*I almost wrote " . . . it must have been . . . " EW I dislike when ppl do dat lol.

GOOD NIGHT.

Sunday, August 22, 2010 1:30 PM, EDT

Summer is zooming by . . . the Earls are getting ready for college, middle school, and first grade! And Esther has decided now that she is sixteen to officially withdraw from high school, and begin working on passing her GED. So we'll be ordering a few books and encouraging her to study. Plus, that will allow her to continue her sleep-all-day, stay up until midnight routine!

Medically, Esther's blood pressure continues pretty high, but is controlled. The newest complication is possible damage to her kidneys from the chemo. Which means daily blood tests until we see if her kidney will spontaneously recover. Wayne says cancer is like fighting a battle on one front, thinking you're winning, then finding out the enemy has snuck up from the side to engage you again. (well, he says it more eloquently!—that's my summary) All I know is that each day is new, uncharted territory.

We'll keep in touch . . .

Lori

"LOVE IS STRONGER THAN DEATH"
by Wayne Earl

"And those who are wise shall shine like the brightness
of the sky above; and those who turn many to
righteousness, like the stars forever and ever."
~*Daniel 12:3*

On August 17, 2010, Esther sat down to complete her 11th VEDA for the month. In what would be her final YouTube post, she showcases the downstairs of her home. Beginning with her trademark cheerfulness, she says playfully, "I know what we can do! Let's tour my house!" She then takes the viewer on a walk through her bedroom: " . . . now it's my bed, and now it's my lamp, and now it's my bookshelf, and now it's my Harry Potter shrine. Archie comics shrine! Oh and this is Denmark! You guys have never met Denmark. He's, um, my oxygen machine. I love him." She walks through the kitchen, entryway, living room and finally ends up in the bathroom where she concludes by saying, "Look at this! Lookin' at myself in the mirror! Lookin' at myself in the camera . . . in the mirror! Lookin' at myself—at you!" Finally, she pauses, smiles broadly and ends with a familiar good-bye: "Hey . . . *Love ya!*"

After that, her video shows a drawing of her cookie monster character at the bottom of the stairs and we hear her voice saying, "Lalalala, whoa! Stairs! Whoa! I do not pass. *You shall not pass!*" At the bottom of this drawing, Esther added the words: "And so he never passed the stairs again."

She recorded one more, brief video clip on Sunday, August 22nd as part of Catitude's group greeting for John Green's upcoming 33rd birthday. In it, she looks tired, and is obviously struggling to breathe, her face pale and puffy; but she is smiling. Uncharacteristically, her comments are brief as she offers a sincere, "happy birthday" and "I love you" along with a promise to contribute something more appropriate later when she's feeling better.

The following day, August 23rd, Esther was exhausted and spent most of her time in bed. That night, she sent what would be her final text message to a fellow Catitude member, containing two words: "love you." She also viewed various TED talks online and was struck by one discussion concerning developmental disorders in children and the relationship of such disorders to the brain. Thinking about its application to her brother Graham, she sent the link to us, writing,

"Idk it's interesting but probably irrelevant to Graham but y'know still interesting and it's only 10 minutes hey not too bad!!! °~°" She then commented on the same video via Twitter, saying: "I really like watching someone talk about something they are passionate about because as they talk they get all THIS IS A REVELATION, GUYS-y and to me that is entertaining/inspiring/hilarious . . . "

It was her last time on the computer.

Her attempt at sleep that night was impossible. She couldn't catch her breath. By early the next morning, it was clear that she needed more care than could be provided at home. We watched while the EMT's carried her out, carefully placing her into the ambulance. Lori got in beside her for the ride to Children's Hospital in Boston. Esther smiled bravely, though weakly through her oxygen mask, and then waved good-bye.

Before long, we arrived in the emergency room and gathered around our Star who was once again lying down on a familiar hospital bed. I went right to her side.

"Hi, Daddy, I'm glad you are here," she said groggily. "Where else would I want to be? This is the main event. After all, you're famous in this place!"

She smiled and took my hand, and held it tightly,

closely, like a child on her first day of school who knows she must soon part, and do so bravely, keeping the tears in check.

And then once again we were in a hospital elevator, going up and up. Although we would not have wanted to be anywhere else, at the time we thought of this ascension to the familiar eleventh floor of Children's Hospital as yet another necessary detour in Esther's ongoing treatment plan.

By the time she got settled in her room, her online friends had become aware that she was "back at the hospital." Soon, the comments, texts and questions on Facebook, Twitter and Esther's CaringBridge site mounted concerning her status. Blaze, from Catitude, tweeted, "I know most of you reading already know, but @crazycrayon is sick and she's all of my thoughts right now." From Florida, another online friend, *ericaeeks* wrote: "I <3 @crazycrayon, please keep her in your thoughts tonight . . . " and her friend, Andrew Slack wrote: "Plz send love, light, & breath to 1 of the brightest stars in the world w/a smile that lights up my heart: @crazycrayon."

Strangers too were feeling the anguish and sent note after note of encouragement. *Dripduke* texted: "I just had to leave class because I was about to start sobbing." Most of the messages were similar to the one by *hazmatbarbie* who declared, "Esther I love you!!! You can do this." *RebeccaActually* summed up the feeling of many when she said, "You've never met me, but I love you." *VerveRiot* confessed, "I normally don't pray. But tonight I might start to pray for Esther who is in hospital fighting to not die of cancer!" Throughout the day and into the evening, we took turns following this outpouring of affection, which brought much comfort to everyone, including Esther though she was in too much discomfort to respond.

It seemed to us that everyone online was talking about her! We shouldn't have been surprised. It was the natural response of Esther's online friends, collectively known as *nerdfighteria*. "A community," someone once said, that has "but one zip code." A "magical place where awesome is celebrated and where every member fights to end world suck." This was the family that Esther had come to know and love and now that one of their own was in trouble, they were standing with her. They could sense that their young Star was struggling, fading and they determined to keep praying, texting, tweeting, messaging, chatting and talking on the phone throughout that afternoon and well into the night. They were determined that Esther not go through this alone.

Esther continued experiencing much discomfort and was becoming increasingly unstable overall as

the fluid collected around her internal organs. At
one point, hospital staff decided to insert a urinary
catheter, a process she had endured more than once
and something she hated. One nurse explained that
it was necessary in case she needed to urinate, to
which Esther replied, "Yeah. Good. *But what happens
if I need to take a crap?*" Gratefully, by late afternoon,
the enormous amounts of pain medication she'd been
receiving began to calm her. She was less agitated,
and her breathing appeared less labored (with the
help of the ever present BiPAP machine). She was still
conscious but began keeping her eyes closed for longer
stretches, and spoke less and less.

The extreme seriousness of the situation didn't
really register for us until Esther's medical team arrived
and pulled Lori and me away, saying, "It does not look
good. She may very well go tonight . . . " After they left,
we returned to her side. Her eyes were closed and I
leaned down and whispered.

"Star . . . the Internet has been on fire all afternoon
with people talking about you! These people online
are amazing. Everyone is wishing you well."

She smiled. I had long thought of myself as Esther's
interpreter, or messenger, and had said on more than

one occasion that I would write her story should
this disease take her away. And I told her about the
conversation we'd just had with her doctors. I told her
that she might not make it through this time. I finished
our talk with a question.

> "Esther, do you want me to send a message and tell
> your friends how much you love them?"

I expected an immediate and affirmative nod, so
was stunned by her response:

> "No." she said, calmly, resolutely.

It was such an uncharacteristic answer but, as hard
as it was, I obeyed her order and in my next update
didn't mention that she was sending her love. (I am
sure her readers knew how she felt about them.) I made
the following entry on her CaringBridge site, mindful
that there would be a ripple effect and outpouring of
concern, grief and affection.

> After an agonizing night trying to catch her breath
> and get comfortable, we came into the hospital
> this morning and Esther is now in the ICU. She
> continues having a tough time breathing due to

what they call "fluid overload." This means that
her body, in part due to a compromised kidney,
is finding it increasingly difficult to expel fluid as
often as it accumulates. Her oxygen levels are also
dipping and she's flat out exhausted.

This visit is very serious. Our favorite doctor
said just now that she could go tonight. I told
Esther. She's still fighting and shows no signs
of wanting to give up! We are all here. Esther is
surrounded by her doting sisters and the staff here
who all know and care about her. We long for still
more days with our Esther Grace! I told Graham
earlier that she could die in the hospital but that
we'd rather bring her home and enjoy many more
star-lit evenings together. He agreed, saying that
sixteen was, "too young to die." Said Graham,
"seventeen is a better age to die. Or maybe twenty
because that is really old."

Later, I would understand that she had already entered
that forest, and had resolved not to look back. She had
courageously gone into that *valley of the shadow*, and,
like each of us, would have to face alone all that lay
ahead. Looking on helplessly, we took turns holding her
hands and stroking her amazing hair as she continued a
long walk into silence.

With the medication working its way through her tired body, Esther soon fell asleep and it became clear to us that the breathing machine and her powerful heart were the only things keeping her alive. Before slipping into unconsciousness, she had talked with each of us and responded gratefully to our tearful messages of affection, singing, hand massages, and face pats. She loved her family more than anything, and we were all there with her as she slipped away. She would have loved having her beloved cats nearby and they would miss her terribly. (From that day on they would relocate to younger brother Abraham's bed at night.) As Esther drifted in and out of consciousness, she suddenly blurted out the number "1842!" We were puzzled by this and went scurrying online to see if that date held any significance. I smiled thinking she might have just disclosed the answer to the secret of the universe!

Other than an occasional muffled mumbling, Esther continued sleeping. However, about an hour later, she suddenly opened her eyes, tried to sit up, and, looking directly at Evangeline (who was holding her right hand), said, *"I'm going, I'm going."* Asked by Evangeline where she was going, Esther responded, *"Oh, I'm just dreaming."* And then she closed her eyes and returned to sleep.

Those were her final words.

For the next three hours, the only sounds in the room were from the machine that kept her breathing, the words of comfort directed toward her and the falling tears of those who remained beside her.

Well into the early morning hours of August 25th, we made the impossible decision to turn the BiPAP machine off. With the loud whirring and wheezing ended, the quiet was immense. Within half an hour, Esther's unassisted breathing became increasingly strained as if to say, "I cannot go on much longer like this." Evangeline remained at her right side with Abby to the left. Lori stood next to Evangeline at Esther's side. Abby's dear friend, Keri, who loved Esther as a sister, remained next to Abby as we kept vigil. Our boys had long before fallen asleep nearby. I stood at the foot of the bed.

After several minutes of waiting, crying quietly and touching our beloved Star, she breathed out one final, unusually long breath, like she was giving it up, offering it, being pulled forward into a newer, richer life. Her dying appeared to us more like a birth than a death, a kind of willing submission, a sense that her struggle was complete and that it was okay to finish this final battle. Recognizing what was happening, I looked up toward the ceiling and, half crying, half laughing said to Esther, "It's okay, baby, It's okay. You can go! We love you!"

A few minutes later, the attending physician—who knew Esther—slowly took out her stethoscope, placed it on each, now silent lung and then on that beautiful heart. Looking at me from across the bed she softly shook her head from side to side. As we looked upon the stillness, we all marveled that we'd gotten to participate in so perfect and courageous and amazing a life. Evangeline smiled and said, "She looks peaceful." Lori commented that it was the first time Esther had "been without the use of her nasal cannula in a very, very long time . . . " and then her voice broke. Abby pulled up the hospital blanket just a little closer to cover Esther's shoulders and everyone laughed and wept thinking about that simple gesture, now unnecessary, the very first time any of us had been unable to bring comfort to our Star.

Slowly, carefully, we each offered a final good-bye.

****

Back at home, I sat down and wrote the following message on her CaringBridge site.

Aug 25, 2010 4:04am

Lovers of Esther,

Our beloved Esther Grace now belongs to the heavens. We were all together when she left us at 3am this morning. We are convinced she is more **truly** alive than ever but still our hearts are breaking . . .

-Esther's Family
DFTBA

Wednesday, August 25, 2010 1:01 PM, EDT

We awake to an empty bed . . . and empty hearts. There
is awfulness all around. We are sad. The weather is
sad. Esther's cats are sad. But Esther liked this kind of
day. She liked most everything. Esther liked. We would
stay doubled over but she would have us rise and
receive the grace that is a new day. And Esther loved
you all so much! She loved us, too. Esther loved. Thank
you to everyone near and far, known or unknown to
us. You helped to carry our light and life, gave her
hours of joy and purpose. She will miss you and we
will miss her banter with you. We're not so up for calls
and visits but appreciate your condolences, e-mails,
texts and tweets . . . nerdfighteria: you are awesome!
Remember: Awesomeness trumps awfulness every
time. Death is not the final word but the "next great
adventure" as Dumbledore said so well. Esther was
never an unhappy lady. She was always happily up for
adventure! In our hearts and exploring heaven; that's
where we'll find her now.

Our Star was a welcomer. Didn't matter who you
were or what badge you did or didn't wear, you were
welcome to sit and visit in person or by computer with
her. Esther welcomed. Whoever you are and wherever

you may be, we welcome you, too, to join us as we remember and celebrate her brief, but glorious life.

With Affection,

Esther's Family

"Carrying my heart."
QUINCY, MASSACHUSETTS, 2010

We feel for each other in the dark
We speak in code
and no one's sure how we made this work
but what do we do now?

We feel with each other through the dark Uncertain
of all things but the holes in our hearts and the hurt
and the loss and the disbelief and we know the same
things and we share such grief

I woke alone without the sun today
Found it strange that the day could change I woke
without the sun today

> —BLAZE MITTEFF of Catitude,
> who wrote these lyrics in the days
> immediately following Esther's passing

Three years and counting without Esther by my side, and yet she has possibly taught me more in these past years than she did during the eight years of our friendship. I could say that all of this surprises me—inspiring books as well as countless people and spreading so much love—but it truly does not. I cannot remember an instance that Esther showed negativity. She never sweated the little stuff, or expressed fear in an overdramatic way, and was always patient. I know she would not like to be called perfect, but if more people were like her, the world would be such a better place.

Not a day goes by that I don't think of Esther Grace. I think about all the fun times we could be having and all the laughs we could be sharing. It's frustrating that as time goes on more and more people won't know the presence she had when she was alive. However, it warms my heart to be able to spread the love that she is all about. Hearing people say "I love you" or seeing the TSWGO bracelets on my friends' and families' wrists brings hope and assurance that no amount of time will be able to dim her light because after all ... *this star won't go out.*
—ALEXA LOWEY

Friends and princesses forever, with Alexa Lowey,
MEDWAY, MASSACHUSETTS, 2003

On August 24, when we heard Esther was in the hospital again and this time the doctors were not hopeful, Catitude came together in a way I'd never seen. We flocked to Skype, starting a group call that lasted at least twenty-four hours. The day was spent anxiously awaiting any type of news. Most people tried to grab a few hours of sleep, but Teryn and I couldn't. I had signed up for text alerts on her CaringBridge journal, and when my phone went off at 2:00 a.m., I knew. Still, I went to the site and read the words I had been dreading all day.

I was frozen in place, my fingers hovering over the keyboard, shock and disbelief swirling around me. We still had the call open so I whispered Teryn's name. Andrew Slack had made us promise to notify him immediately if we learned anything new, so I gave Teryn his phone number, feeling unable to speak any words, but especially not these. When I heard her crying, trying to articulate this ostensibly impossible event, I completely lost it. Shaking and sobbing, we gradually called everyone back to Skype. For several hours not much was said, we just needed to gather together and hear the sounds of grief, the proof that we weren't in this alone.

"We all had that," Katy said. "We all did that together. We all suffered through the next few months, few years, waiting for our open wounds and our hearts to heal. And we had each other to piece together the confusing parts about love and loss and grief through the Internet. What do you do when the funeral is a $700 plane ride away? When John Green made a video about your friend, and people are grieving who didn't even know her? How do you grieve when no one in your family, none of your teachers, no one in your town knows about a girl in Boston who died of cancer?"

The pain was unbearable, and yet we got through it together, as much as you can "get through" such a loss. Everyone who had been at Make-A-Wish made it to the funeral, plus a few others. Wayne hugged me and told me he was sorry, that he wished we weren't meeting again in this way. The trip was simultaneously healing and scarring. It was something we needed to experience.

Katy continued, "A large chunk of Catitude came together for LeakyCon [in 2011], a Harry Potter convention. Esther was supposed to be there, but it was the first time so many of us were together in person after her passing. And we grieved like none other, but we also laughed like none other, and danced, and ate, and had panic attacks. It was amazing and beautiful and stressful— I'm not gonna tell you that trying to keep sixteen people together for a week in a different state wasn't stressful.

But being together made it worth it. We were still friends, without Esther, but she was still present. The mark she left on all of us wasn't going anywhere."

Years later our friendship remains strong. We're so lucky to have found one another, this support system of nerds with the same terrible sense of humor. People have said they feel Esther alive in us. I hope that's true. I know I always carry her with me, and to have a piece of her grace shine through me is a gift I will continually strive to earn.

—LINDSAY BALLANTYNE

One of the greatest gifts Esther gave me was something she never even knew she gave me. It goes back to a conversation we had early on in our friendship. We were talking about what we wanted to be when we grew up. At the time I was premed and told her I was planning on going to medical school to become a doctor. By this point in our friendship, I had known she was sick, and we had talked a bit about everything she had been through. I knew how much she loved her doctors and nurses for keeping her alive, and she thought it was so cool that I wanted to follow in a similar direction. I wish I knew her exact words from this conversation, but honestly, I don't think her words were as important as the effect they had on me. Her words touched my heart. She made me feel proud of my career aspirations. Just the thought of her thinking my becoming a doctor was the coolest thing has continued to inspire me time and time again and has helped me get through the grueling science-heavy course load of being premed. I ended up deciding not to go to medical school for various reasons, but chose to go to optometry school instead. Even so, I don't know if I would have continued on the path to become a doctor had it not been for Esther and her support. There have been many times over the past few years where I was ready to give up and follow a different path, but each time it was Esther's voice in my head that gave me the motivation to keep going and she still remains with me in everything I do."

—ARIELLE ROBERTS

Oh, Esther. I could never explain how much I miss you. But every ounce of grief and pain has been worth it a thousand times over. Thank you for introducing me to Catitude. Thank you for the nights spent laughing about butts and other silly things. Thank you for listening to me. Thank you for being beautiful, and for being honest. Thank you for the purest, most unconditional love I've ever seen. The burden of grief is heavy, but you gave me enough love and joy to get through anything.

Thank you for everything, E. I love you so, so much.

—KATIE TWYMAN

I don't notice you're gone, until I think about you. And then I realize that I'll never have a conversation with you again. I'll only hear the laughs preserved in your YouTube videos. And that's a pale imitation for the real thing.

When loved ones die, people always say, "Don't be sad. I'm sure they would have wanted you to be happy."

I'm sure that's true. But let's be realistic here, people also want to be missed. It is every person's nightmare to leave the world behind as if they had never been there at all.

But you don't need to worry about that Esther. You made a lasting impression on so many people, and we're not likely to stop missing you anytime soon.

You put up a really brave fight, Esther. You did so amazing. You lived so much life in so few years. You *changed* so many lives in so few years.

Esther Grace Earl, I will love you forever. I feel so proud and lucky to have actually been friends with you.

—MANAR HASEEB

Esther-
I give a lot of credit to a lot of different people for making the last four and a half years of my life as wonderful as they have been, but none of them deserve as much recognition as you. I'm not saying this because I think you are somehow better than everyone else in the world, although the argument could be made that you are, indeed, "better" than quite a large number of people. But I've heard people talk about you like that, as if you had reached some higher state of living before going away. And while I understand where they are coming from and where they see that, I'm not saying thank you simply because you were awesome or because you're some kind of otherworldly God-like being. We all know you are awesome, and I think you probably would have been upset about the latter. So, no. That's not it at all. But my life's never been very good . . . and you took all of that, everything terrible that had happened, and you listened to them and you genuinely cared and you didn't replace them but you brought a lot of incredible people that brought a lot of extraordinary experiences into my life. And suddenly, the bad things didn't matter as much anymore because I had too many good things to let the bad get me down for too long.

I had never experienced something like that. It was a brand-new thing to me, having a community of people who genuinely liked and cared for me that I knew would be there at any given moment. You were the leader that marched into my life with a ton of similarly spectacular people following behind; people who became my family and real source of support, and I could never show enough appreciation for that. You are my friend, Esther, and I can't tell you thank you because you're gone now, but I hope that you knew how much I love you and how absolutely miserable my life would have continued to be if we had never met. You opened up the door to a world where I was allowed to be myself and be loved for it. So I will keep on trying to make my life the best possible version of itself and spreading love in all ways that I can because that is the best way I know to honor you. And I'll keep the possibility of meeting you again in another stream of consciousness somewhere open.

I'm so glad to have met you. I am so glad to have had you around for any amount of time. And most of all, I am so beyond happy that I was lucky enough to have you call me a friend.

Love always,
DESTINY TARAPE

You were the first person from the Internet I ever met. I still can't believe it. I would never change that day as long as I live. I owe you so much. I remember I was way too scared to talk to Catitude at first. So I just talked to you. A lot. You told me about your medical conditions before you told the group. I felt like you really trusted me. That's when I knew I could trust you. I miss you a lot. But your memory lives on forever. It's amazing the impact you left on the world. While you were still here I never would have expected this. I feel like sometimes I take our friendship for granted, I feel guilty for doing that but I know you would love that. I miss you every day and I thank you for all you did for me before and even today.

—SIERRA SLAUGHTER

One of the worst things about losing someone young—and this goes doubly for losing a friend—is the sense that some kind of potential has gone unfulfilled. Esther doesn't/wouldn't have to worry about this: I am sure there are things she would like to have done on Earth instead of the between space where the beloved go (it's not for me to speculate on life after death although I believe pretty strongly there is one [haha, whoops, speculated]), but just by being herself and making good friends she's managed to impact a whole lot of lives in a profound way.

Looking back to when I first met Esther, I thought that she was very popular and outgoing and that she was much older and wiser than what you would think a young teenager should be. The more I grew to know her I became surprised how a mostly bedridden girl could be so warm and understanding to the sympathies of others. Esther was so wise that she seemed to only inhabit the body of a teenager as a temporary stage of a larger life span beyond the friend we knew. It seems almost ironic now that her story has reached so many and inspired people to hold on to her that she may not be forgotten. In this way its as if she gets to live out the rest of her life afterall, through us. —PAUL HUBER

Esther, I will never forget when I officially met you on Skype and Twitter during the 2009 Scripps National Spelling Bee. I have watched the bee every year since I've met you, not only because it is incredibly fun and it reminds me of the origins of Catitude, but also because it reminds me of you. You and the competitors shared a drive to constantly acquire new knowledge. Additionally, much like the spellers, you showed the courage to make mistakes and learn from them. But most of all, the fierce competition of the bee reminds me that you were a fighter until the end. To me, the bee will forever be a symbol of the spirit of Esther Earl. <3 —MORGAN JOHNSON

I guess, selfish as it is, I am still kind of reeling over my personal loss, and I'm worried about my friend not being imagined complexly enough—in my memory, by people who hear her story. And if that's the price to pay for getting people to consider everything from health care to mortality to interpersonal kindness, if we allow ourselves to take some direction from the person who I remember Esther to be: friendly, funny, sweet, above all a pal, well at least there's something there.

—ANDREW KORNFELD

"A Father and his Wizard,"
SQUANTUM, MASSACHUSETTS, **2010**

EULOGY,
Esther Earl's Funeral, August 29, 2010

by Wayne Earl

Thank you, Jim and Julie Salmon, and thank you Pastor Jim and Medway Village Church, for opening up your hearts to us; your home to us. Esther would have been so happy to see all these people, to know that she had so many friends that loved her. And she sang right from this stage, she was in the choir, and she enjoyed many good songs in this place.

And so, you may say, well, "Why are you up here making these comments, I mean *what do you know*?" Well, I got the front-row seat. And I got to see her close-up. It wasn't just box seats; I was in the dugout. I was right with her in her life. But more than that, I got to love her. And I got to be loved by her. And we got to love her. We got to be loved by her, touched by her brilliance.

And then, you know it's not coincidence that this was her name: Esther Grace. It's the only name we had for her. I mean if she had been a boy she might have been Herman Mudd or something, but she was a girl so her name is Star. I always called her *Star*. I always called her Estee. And Grace was just the reminder we didn't want to forget that it's all about grace. It's all about the fact that we don't deserve these good things, but they're ours anyway, to enjoy and to share and to delight in. She was a star! A star illumines, right? I mean when we see the light it's gone out. But it brightens something; in this case it shined its light—her light—of grace.

She helped us to see our flaws, but you weren't overwhelmed with that. She helped us see our potential, our life, what we could contribute . . . our awesomeness, right? Some relationships are bad for you, you want to get out of there as soon as you can, and others are good. You like them, you like them to stay that way. And others *change* us, and we're never the same. We walk away and we say, "Something happened to me, I am different . . . " The way I describe it is that I want to stand a bit taller, I want to serve a bit deeper, I want to love longer. I want grace to permeate my life. She did that. She lived. Esther lived! Sixteen years, but she lived well and she lived deeply and she was alive!

She loved to go fast, right? From the time she was small she was running and that hair was just flying everywhere. And it was just so bright and cheery and she loved things . . . I remember we were in Saudi Arabia; she was just four years old and she was on one of those motorcars with four wheels and she would take Evangeline ripping around the sand and up and down the streets—well sands—of Arabia.

She loved to create things. You've seen her artwork online; you've seen it up close. She was just in the middle of creating this wonderful game for Abraham and she didn't know where the game was going, but he thought she did. She loved her vlogs and all of those cards and texts, and monkey bars and playing in the snow and the beach; everything a kid loves to do.

She had a tremendous sense of humor. Were you touched by that? She was funny; she was funny and she was quirky and different and unique and alive. She liked chocolate milk, all kinds of food and culture, video games, colors and scents and people from different cultures. She liked . . . just the other day she was looking up . . . she said, "Dad, look at this, a website devoted to words in the English language that we no longer use." She described them for me. She said, "Maybe I can just string them together and make a paragraph or a sentence out of words we no longer use?" That's where her mind was.

On her Facebook she has a list of things she likes; you know, the 'Happy dance' by John Green, Skittles, and Wizard rock. You can see it—the list goes on and on. She liked *boys*. When she was sick and various friends would visit and crawl into bed with her sometimes—because she was, you know, she needed that connection. But one day I walked in and saw Arka next to her and there was a girlfriend on the other side and I said, "You know, if I ever caught a guy in bed with my daughter, that would be it, but I'll be graceful this one time."

She never kissed a boy (she said). But I was reading her journals this week, hmmm. And she, uh, where's Alexa? Okay, Alexa got her connected up with somebody named John and this John and Esther went off into the bushes at eleven years old, or whatever, and she said that was her first kiss. But then Alexa came back and disturbed them. That was a good thing.

We got to love her. We got to be loved by her. She also loved, loved so well. She loved so well and so deeply. She was passionate about all kinds of things, and passionate about, in Saudi Arabia, about stray cats. She and her sisters would bring in these abandoned cats that were just a mess of fleas and bugs and who knows what else! And, in fact they would say, "Dad, can we keep them, can we keep the cats?" "Yes, you can keep them *outside*, far away." She grabbed this big empty bottle of beetles and she filled it, she and her sisters filled it up with bugs and they came into the house and they said, "Mom and Dad watch" and they poured them on themselves and watched the beetles crawl all over them. "Isn't this cool how they crawl all over you?!" We were not humored.

She loved causes, she loved things that mattered. I didn't realize this, but she had on her wrist—I'd seen it before—but I didn't know she still had it on, but she passed away with a *"Save Darfur"* [wristband] that she had been wearing for a very long time. I don't know, maybe a year, and also the wristband that was made for her here. She loved her friends, she loved her friends, and she had so many for someone who was housebound and didn't get out.

She recently started this advice-opinion giving column. People would write her, they would say, "You know I'm struggling, my parents are really getting on my nerves, any advice for how to live with insufferable parents?" And she would write back, "Well I know what you mean, let's talk about it." And some of you have seen those entries; she did them personally for each person that would write in. It was becoming more and more common for her to get those kinds of questions.

She loved nerdfighteria and the last eighteen months that brought her alive. Are there any nerdfighters here today? Come on! There are those over here, okay, all right. If you loved Esther, then you are now an honorary nerdfighter, okay? She was a Welcomer. She believed there were no outsiders. She said everybody should be welcomed, and they were welcomed into her heart and into her room. I mean, she knew the difference between brokenness and people who were not real and all of that, but she just invited you in. I would just be amazed at how welcoming she was. It didn't matter if you were confused or depressed or perfect people who were confused about their sexual identity; whatever it was, she said *come on in*, I want to love you. I want to be your friend. I want to care for you. I want to understand. She didn't believe that there were insiders and outsiders.

And she also had this unique capacity for making you feel like you were the most important person in her life. You know, I could say I was the most important person in her life until somebody else walked into the room. And they just went out feeling great. And it wasn't that she agreed with you. I'd walk in and dump my stuff out and say, "Oh, this is driving me crazy . . ." And she would listen. I realize now that she never said she agreed with me. But she made me handle it. And that's what grace is: being there. She was there.

She loved her family. She loved Abe. You know, it was easy to do, because we announced his birth from this pulpit. Remember that? We were pretty old then (speaking for myself!). We announced that we were going to have another one, which was a surprise to everybody. You know miracles still occur! So what do you do with a fifth baby? Well, you give it to your *daughters*. We don't know what to do! We don't have the energy so Mom went to bed and I went to work and that was it. You raise this kid. So Evangeline had him for the first year and then Esther the second year when he was one to two. She took care of him, and she homeschooled, which meant, "Would you take care of the baby while I get back on my feet?" She loved Abe and you can see that. You can see that online. You can see that if you knew them together.

She loved her Abby. She thought you, Abby, she thought you were perfect, smart, and witty. And I think if there's someone she idealized most . . . you know, when she thought (I close my eyes and think, "man, who are those models out there, people I want to be like," I think of Esther)—she thought of Abby. She said, "Wow I want to aspire to where Abby is."

She loved Evangeline. Evangeline was there. Evangeline was there when she passed away. And her last conversations were with Angie. She thought Angie was the person that she most wanted to impress. Because Angie was so cool, Evangeline was so cool; she thought she was *perfectly* beautiful. She was absolutely right. She didn't like fake people; she didn't like doing mean things. But sometimes she did these *sneaky* things. This one time a few years ago when Evangeline, umm . . . when boys were still taboo, Esther created an online account for somebody named Chris and "Chris" began to e-mail Evangeline saying, "Hey I saw you at school and I think . . . "

How do I know about that? Yeah. Parents, they know all these things. There are no secrets and if there are secrets you only have to wait till weddings and funerals and they all spill out.

So yeah, "Chris" would write her and say, "Evangeline, I saw you at school; you're so cute, maybe you could leave a note for me?" Esther was just tricking her. Well, when Evangeline found out, of course she was livid and Esther wrote in her diary, she said, *"I cannot live with Evangeline mad at me."* And then they worked it out.

Then Graham of course, you know, he's wandered again. She loved Graham; she led him though the first five years of his life. Graham couldn't speak very well. Some of you remember that. Graham would come into the room and say, "Subalooga-de-ba-laba-be-abagaba" and we'd look at each other—my wife and I, and Abby and Evangeline—and say, I don't know. Then Esther would say, "Oh, he wants spaghetti with ice-cream and liver and onions on the side; a little bit of feta cheese in there and some sparkling cider to wash it down." She knew exactly what he needed, and what he wanted and she was *there* for him; a special relationship all the days of her life.

And then, for my wife, for Lori; nobody served her as well as you did and you were there night and day, usually not complaining. I helped out a little bit. But no one served her better. Somebody said to Lori recently that she did what none of us could do and Lori said, "No, no . . . " she did, *"what every one of us can do"* because we all have the spark of life, right? We are all alive; we all have something to give.

She not only lived well and loved well, but she died well, you know, which is no surprise. She knew when to go and it was way too soon. You know how people hang around sometime and you're like, "Weeellll, you know, I see that it's getting late now and I believe the last train . . ." and then others, you're like, "Yeah, well I guess it's about time to get going." And others you think, "Nooo! What are you talking about?! You can't go now." *We didn't want her to go now*. We had things to look forward to, so many things to look forward to, so many friendships that were blossoming, so much of an impact that we saw; that we could feel. Angie was with her and we didn't know it was the last moment; we didn't know it was the end. Her very last words, her very last words were, *"I'm going, I'm going."* And then she fell asleep and we were with her during those hours that she was sleeping.

I think about the things she's going to miss, and I can't, I can't get my head around it. The things, the anniversaries, the first things . . . the first time I'm alone. I don't know what that's going to be like. The first time when I see someone her age and I need grace and we need grace to bear up under it. And God promises that to us, to give us that kind of Grace.

Esther didn't have regrets; some of us live with lots

of regrets, you know. "Oh my goodness, I regret the shoes I wore today! I regret that I just yawned! Oh no! I regret that . . ." Esther was like, "Pfft, Dad, this is life, let it wash over you."

She died so well. I used to say to her—in the last year especially—I'd say, "Esther, when you . . ." (I believe, when we'd talk about heaven, I'd say I believe that life is *more* and she agreed and she said . . . she believed that . . .) I said, "When you die, would you just give me some kind of sign? Let's just work that out now so that I don't have to wonder if I got this wrong. Can you just tell me somehow, give me a sign?" And I had my last conversations with her, and I told her I loved her and I said this is very serious, but one of the last things I said to her was, "Esther, let me remind you, if you're going to go home tonight, would you just tell me?"—we had talked about this a lot—I said, "Maybe you could open your eyes and tell me that you see the angels and that you see heaven." This was a yearlong conversation; we never hid from death; we embraced life.

And she fell asleep. For all those hours we were by her side knowing that she wasn't going to come back. Then finally, right at the end, she opened her eyes, and she breathed out her last. And I just said, "Esther, you're going home! I am so happy for you!" And then she was gone . . .

But our relationship with Esther doesn't stop there. You think . . . the relationship goes on. It goes on! Esther's in your heart. Your relationship with her is unique. It goes on, it continues. If she isn't able to guide your life in terms of looking to her as an example of how we should live; if you don't have that hope in your heart that there's some other place, some other *meaning*. Believe me, Esther's life was almost entirely *this* world focused, as it should be. She believed that we are called to be here, to make a difference here, to be alive *here*, and to love here well and leave heaven with God. Let him take care of those details. She had her eye there too, she knew. But she believed in making a difference *now*. That's the only way, it seems to me, to live a meaningful life. She did justly, she loved mercy and she walked humbly with her God.

Dr. Seuss said . . . (I figure I need to quote an authority here), Dr. Seuss said, "Don't cry because it's over; smile because it happened." Right? I don't know about the first steps in a geography of loss, and I know that it's unmapped. I know that we all have to go by ourselves, but there's something bigger than us at work here. And Esther represents that and she's lighting the path and God is using her in amazing ways. *The Star lit up over our hearts and she poured out Grace.*

Now, is the story over? Come on as a congregation:

Is the story over? [Congregation responds, *"No!"*] Will this Star ever go out? [Congregation responds, *"No! No!"*] *Will this Star ever go out?* No? In memory of Esther, will you pledge to live a Life of Awesome? You're supposed to say *yes* right there. Is Esther alive now more than ever before? [Congregation responds: *"Yes!"*] Amen.

I got a front-row seat to her wonderful life. She's my Star. She's my muse. My kids know that. I've always been easy with Esther. She disarmed me. She brought out the best in me, she reminded me of the worst, because I could see it so clearly, but then she welcomed me into her heart. And so many times, like Monday, I said, "Esther, I don't know what I'm going to do without you when you go. I don't know how I can get along. What am I going to do?" And then I just expected her like always to say, "Well, Dad, let me tell you; here's what you do, A B C." But she said, "Come here." She just hugged me; held me close, didn't say anything, didn't say anything. And I realize now that that was . . . that's the best way to love someone. Hold them close, know that you're loved, *let it wash over you.*

We got to love her and she got to love us. Amen?

Monday, September 20, 2010 12:57 AM, EDT

> *"I will say you were young and straight and your*
>   *skin fair*
> *And you stood in the door and the sun was a shadow*
> *of leaves on your shoulders*
> *And a leaf on your hair"*
>
>   "Not Marble Nor the Gilded Monuments"
>   by Archibald MacLeish

Friends,

As you might imagine, we are missing our Star. In some ways, each day seems harder than the one before. There are so many sad moments: Abe asking who will finish the amazing game she was making for him; Graham wondering how he can possibly navigate the new season of Doctor Who without her; Abby and Angie missing late night talks and texts; Lori, and me, too, sobbing, railing against the unfairness of it all. The reality of her passing pushes hard against our need to keep her with us. A phone ringing, especially at night, can pierce the heart as she would sometimes call from her bed to come and adjust her oxygen, or remind us it was time for this or that med. We go to bed with difficulty and pray hard asking not to be awakened at 3 a.m. in a panic. But it was so easy to love her! And "love is stronger than death" as the Bible says which eases the pain a bit.

I loved to read poetry to her. She applauded my enthusiasm and made me feel pretty smart! I dedicate this poem to you, Esther Grace.

"I love the sea."
TOPSAIL ISLAND, NORTH CAROLINA, 2008

Saturday, September 25, 2010 1:49 PM, CDT

Friends,

Just got word about Esther's organ donations. How
amazing that two people can now—literally—see
again because each received one of Esther's corneas!
A man in Ohio and a woman in Maryland now see the
world through Esther's eyes. Imagine that! She
continues to give sight and light. When she learned
that none of her other organs would be used (because
of the cancer) she was saddened. However, she did give
permission for an extensive autopsy to be performed
(it was). This was a real gift to cancer research because
little is known about the spread of cancer in a girl who
goes through puberty while being treated (as she did).

She was an amazing, courageous, other person-
centered, young woman. If she, as a sixteen-year-old
teenager thought ahead and felt so strongly about this,
then so should we! I know a gentleman in Ohio and a
lady in Maryland that would agree.

Check out: http://organdonor.gov/

—Wayne

Saturday, December 4, 2010 2:50 PM, EST

Friends of Esther,

Thank you so much for continuing to honor Esther's
memory through your meaningful Guestbook entries
here. Sadly, this wonderful meeting place must now come
to a end. If you'd like to add another comment or two, you
have a few days left to do so as we will be closing this site
before Christmas. However, after that, there are several
ways that you can continue to keep up with all things
Esther. We've just begun a site dedicated to our new
foundation created in her memory. This organization
will provide resources to cancer patients and their
families as well as fund projects Esther would have loved.
Go to facebook and check out: This Star Won't Go Out.

Of course, Esther has YouTube and Facebook pages
which are still available to view and comment on (see
the links section on this site). We also have a YouTube
channel (go to YouTube and search: wayneandloriearl)
where we have been posting new videos of her. We have
hours of our beloved on tape and hope to edit and share
more of her creative spirit long into the future.

O friends, you cannot imagine how we miss our Star!

She is constantly in our thoughts and dreams. We wake each day and wonder how anyone could endure such insanity. Our kids are so young and their lives will be less breezy without her. Abraham will never really remember her. On Friday, we ordered the tombstone that she, herself, picked out. Yes, she'd be okay with what we said but what kid should ever choose such a memorial? We carry a perpetual sadness. Was it worth it? I can't believe you'd ask such a question! One minute with Esther was worth all that any pain can throw at us. Sixteen years beside such a soul was a privilege, the greatest of honors. Watching her unroll a daily patchwork of grace left us inspired and humbled and very, very proud. She was regal but also completely in the moment, "wickedly awesome." Estee walked on earth gently and deeply. She loved well and without exception. Her life is her true memorial, a living monument that will outlive us all.

With Deepest Appreciation for Your Support of our Esther Grace,

Wayne & Lori

Sunday, December 19, 2010 9:52 PM, CST

Such Grace!

This little book has now come to its natural end.
Esther really enjoyed your many kind expressions of
encouragement. Thank you for that. You helped to
make her struggle, and our part in that, bearable. We
are convinced that love never dies, that it transcends
anything that may come our way! We have memories of
an amazing human being and an abiding hope that this
is but a temporary separation. She loved her family and
friends with such grace. It was easy to love her, too. Life
was easier for everyone with her here.

Thank you for loving our Star!

Wayne and Lori

MAY 15, 2011
Wayne's blog

by Wayne Earl

"Love is Stronger than death."

—Song of Songs 8:6

Hope is the thing with feathers
That perches in the soul,
And sings the tune—without the words,
And never stops at all

—From "Hope" by Emily Dickinson

Dear My Star,

I finally went to the cemetery earlier today to see you.
In such places, I wonder, is anything more powerful
than death? Spring-time says yes, and just this week
thawed the ground enough to allow the installation
of your tombstone. And it is perfect. The Red India
granite stone is regal, yet welcoming, just like you. You
chose it well even if it is the second most expensive
stone on the market! I was surprised (and relieved?) to

see that you weren't there. This concerned me as I've been accustomed to meeting the dead in cemeteries.

But you were there. And yet, you weren't. If there is a there, there, then you are, there (whew!). Mystery. I took the first photos of the site for your friends and even recorded some of my thoughts a la Esther, on your Flip camera! My comments were totally unrehearsed except that I've been having similar conversations with you all along over these, long nine months. I know you thought I was your friend but I'm really just your dad and I've been worried that you might be lost somewhere, in trouble somehow. I have had nightmares but I cannot dream directly about you and you know what a dreamer I am. I want so much to see you! I can't go into a store without thinking, "This would be excellent for Star." You were so easy to buy for and so grateful for anything I brought home. "Oh, a tomato! How thoughtful, Dad. That's perfect." "Awesome! I have never heard of the 'Infinite and Dreary Chronicles of Drooling, Alien, Sumo-Wrestling Babies' but, hey, can't wait to start reading!" Many times I have wanted to tell you about my day or get your advice or watch the newest *Doctor Who* episode with you (you'd love them now!). No one around here likes espresso. Someone said you'd now be forever 16 but I don't think of you that way. To me, you are, at once a chipper five year old holding her new star pillow and an ancient bodhisattva-like wise young woman listening, blessing, ever ageless.

What does one do when a great party ends? Clean up? Relish. Remember. Is that enough? Esther! One young woman got a tattoo with a star and 'This Star Won't Go Out' printed right on her wrist! She put it there because that's where the cutting starts and, now, with such a reminder, literally right in front of her, hope has enlarged, self-harm is diminished. People are talking about you and are inspired to overcome all kinds of things in your memory. I understand that. You were a burden sharer and burden bearer. But we needed you here. I need you here, now. If I had a wish, it would be to see you, but, if I could draw you up from the underworld, you'd be horrified to think I'd used my wish on something so trivial! Still, I am angry that you are gone and I guess that means I am in denial. So be it. I am a denier, then. This is what I deny: death does not win (said with an undignified small d). Love is Stronger. Love and hope are conjoined, if you separate one, you kill the other. If hope survives then love endures. Where even a sliver of love exists, the thinnest of hopes has room to grow.

I left the cemetery and headed straight to the tattoo parlor. "Love is Stronger than death" has been etched on my heart for some time now so I've decided to make it official. That phrase, along with your name, "Esther Grace" and a shooting star, will soon appear on my body for all to see. Perched where I am, that's my understanding of your final, resting place. It ain't final.

Love,
Daddy

Little Sister,

A life is not meant to be half lived. It is meant to be fully, wholly embraced. If you want to make a change in the world you have to be strong. You have to take chances. You have to persevere. Sometimes you must blindly go in a direction that you may be unsure of, but one that you have faith will lead you to the right place.

This is what you have taught me, Esther.

I feel you around me at times, and it gives me strength that what I am doing is something you believe in. You said that you looked up to me, that you admired me and believed that I could do anything. But I always looked to you for courage. I needed you to tell me that who I want to be, and what I want to do, was the right path.

When you passed away, a part of me did too. My strength, my hope, vanished. How could I make a difference in the world when my best friend, my soul mate, my confidant, my support, a half of my heart, was gone? Everything went blank. A fog descended and I could not breathe. My body became heavy, my movements stunted, I could not find my way out.

And then I planted a flower.

This, I could do. This tiny seed I could bring life to. I fed it, I watered it, I watched it grow, and one day a sunflower bloomed forth. I realized that with life comes death, and with death, life. It is a cycle that we are a part of. I knew that you were there, showing me how beautiful things can be. A flower bloomed and the fog disappeared.

I knew that I could not improve the world by missing you, alone. So I breathed. I breathed through the clearing in the fog. I breathed away my anger that you were gone. I breathed away the heart-wrenching sorrow that I would never again speak with you, hear your voice, sit by you and look into your eyes. As I breathed out my pain I felt a peace settle into my lungs. The easing of the pain was making room.

I looked at the sunflower, and I felt you standing next to me, holding my hand. I blinked and you were gone, taking away my sadness and giving me hope. I can give life. I can bring color and beauty into this world.

I now carry you with me; you occupy the part of my heart that broke when you died. But dying is part of this cycle, this cycle of life, and while I am here on this Earth, in this temporary place, I want to do everything I can to encourage beauty and life.

This is what you have taught me, little sister.

—Evangeline

AUGUST 2013

Dearest Est,

I freaking miss you, dude. Things have been sort
of, foggy, since you left us here on Earth. It's lonely
sometimes without ya. I don't have you there to e-mail
or text at 2 a.m. The prompt, genuine reply I would
always get. So honest and real. It was easy to hear what
you had to say, and to understand what you meant
in the advice you gave. The way you would just look
at me and say "Abby . . . " and I would know what you
were thinking, and that you were right, obviously. I
miss just talking with you. Telling you what's going on,
rambling about our boy or family troubles. Telling each
other what was going on in our lives in whatever crazy
country we lived in at the time. We lived apart so much
of the time, but you were always there, always in my life,
and I was always in yours. I really miss those nights of
endless online games we'd play sitting across from each
other in the same room. The hours of listening to music
and playing Yahtzee until four in the morning. I miss
all the laughing, and all the love. Lying in bed with you
with the whirring of the oxygen tank close by, watching
whatever TV show we were into, probably *Gilmore Girls*.
And your kitties were always there; the connection
you had with them, and with all animals was inspiring.
Speaking of cats, did I tell you, I named my car

Blueberry, after the infamous marshmallow white cat of yours, of course? She makes me think of you.

I miss the way you love and appreciate all the small things, and all the big things, around you. How much you love your family. I don't love as easily and as big as you could. But I strive to be more like you in that way each day. You love with such ease. Such genuine kindness and acceptance. I see how simple it is. Maybe you were so real and honest because you knew you were leaving, it came naturally because of the cancer. Through re-reading all your e-mails and letters from before you were sick, I know that was just the way you were. You were a lover. A giver. I know it's easy to talk about someone who has died so positively, but honestly, I don't remember anything negative about you. *Ha.*

I wanted so much for you. I wanted the good things and crazy things and awesome things this world has to offer each of us. Your time here was cut too short. You would have been such a huge blessing here on earth. Done such awesomeness. You totally did, actually. And you continue to inspire hearts, which is truly special. For us especially; to see your whole life and story and love alive and growing through so many. It is natural and obvious that you are such an incredible influence. It shines through your life story. You're still living strong, my dear. It's too insane for my little human brain to grasp what a huge audience you've already captured. So incredibly cool. I wonder what you think of it all. Are you totally stoked by all of this madness? You must be so awed that you are actually an author now. You're a pretty big deal kiddo.

I am listening to hear where you are.

Word. I'm listening to your old playlist. I do feel you and hear you. I know you aren't gone. In the sunshine and the blue sky. In the wind at the beach. In the joy I find in the little things. The comfort of spending time with the people I care about. In dancing. I so wish we could dance together. I look forward to that. To dance, and sing loud, and jump around just me and you. Vang and I went and it was so much fun. I've been dancing lots, it feels so free and natural. I always feel you around me in the music. In the uncontained movements, in the smiles and talents of the musicians. In the freedom. I had so much fun in Oregon, and you were totally there. Enjoying each fiddle-filled note and each spin of the hula hoop. I miss hearing you jam on the piano; I'll have to start again.

Then there's the thought of us growing old as sisters. All having families and crazy insane lives. The thought of keeping it real as the Three Earl Girls. I'm sad we can't make any more memories like that. You and Inka are so special to me, though, and I do have some pretty awesome ones. You brought us together, you know. You allowed us to be more real with each other and I am grateful for that. You are holding the family together. Just like you always did being the middle kid. Thank you for loving us each so separately but so entirely.

Will you hold my hand when I go?

I totally did that night, love. I don't know if you remember very well, but we were all with you. Keri too (your other "sister"). Abe was asleep in the window seat. We painted your nails—really awesomely with stripes and dots. It was so late, and I was so tired, and I so didn't want it to be over, but at the same time, was so ready for it to be over; for you to be comfortable again. So ready to be done with the disease. You were peaceful. You were quiet.

Love is watching someone die.

I don't remember your last words, but I remember the feeling. The feeling of watching you sleeping, and that all I could do was sit there and hold your hand and think of how much I love you. And then the feeling of it not being you anymore on that hospital bed. You weren't waiting around, you were off on your next great adventure. We were all there in that room, but you were long gone. Your body didn't look like you anymore. Your soul, or spirit, or whatever we truly are was flying around or actually probably running around taking huge breaths, and laughing loud with joy. Off to bigger and better things. This is what you want for us too. You want us to get up and live, not stay lying on the bed holding your hand. It was raining hard on the way home and we listened to Dave Matthews. We're coming up on the three-year anniversary of that day, not one of my favorite memories, except for the fact that I know you were liberated from disease that night. That you got to start fresh.

I miss you, dude. Like so very much. With each little part of me. I've been avoiding your absence. Not thinking about it. Not remembering fully like everyone else, not talking about you so much. Just trying not to remember that you're over. But I've finally actually realized that you are so not over. You are so alive and present.

Just be happy, and if you can't be happy, do things that make you happy. Or do nothing with the people that make you happy.

You are so wise. We're all following you out one day, so my hope is that we can be more honest with one another. That we can love more simply and enjoy every little ordinary stupid hilarious thing more fully. That we find joy in silly online videos and nerdy songs and stupid jokes. I want us to take advantage of the awesome things that we have at our fingertips on this crazy beautiful planet. To send out more positive energy and to live in your example of love. That's what I want for me, and our wonderful family, and for everyone.

I guess I should go, this is getting pretty long and you probably have more important things to do, like upload videos for your Astral-Tube channel or some alien rock show to party at. I didn't tell you enough, thank you for being an awesome little sister for all those years, it was tons of fun. I'm so lucky to have had you around. Thank you for all that you've done for me, I happen to love you more than I can say. And like you said to me once, "Without you, oh geez, I would be in a family of psychos. Not that it's not anyway, baha!" Thanks for keeping us sane and being a spark of joy in our lives.

Love you always, little sis,

Abby

AUGUST, 2013

My Poem for Esther

1. Star, when I first saw you I knew you were the right sister for me.
2. Your heart reminds me of you because you are so sweet and thoughtful to me. You were always there for me when I needed you the most and you never gave up on me.
3. Dear, if you are dead or alive, I will still love you no matter what.

Graham Kenneth Earl

SEPTEMBER, 2013

Esther's Legacy

Her legacy is amazing, but her promise was even greater. Her heart was for love, and this world, and others. She would be answering an advice column, and creating life-changing blogs (alternately with super crazy, silly ones!), and volunteering with kids, and doing so much. Maybe putting on photography shows in a gallery, or writing children's stories, or interning with John Green. Instead, she is gone. And we are left aching for the empty spaces, and undrawn pictures, and the unloved stray kitties that will never know her quiet hand.

Still. We have so much—and especially so much more than so many with our loss. And that is a gift. She was a gift. Somehow that has to be enough. That, and loving others for her.

Lori Earl
JANUARY, 2013

In the spring of 2009, Esther mentioned that she had written a letter to her "future self." As she explained the concept, I listened, thinking nothing more than that it was a genius moneymaker idea for someone else. I think I responded with something like, "That's nice, dear," and then promptly forgot all about it. At the time, I simply had no idea how serious and mature my fourteen-year-old daughter's thoughts really were. Two and a half years later—on December 1, 2011—I opened a new e-mail and read these words, "this is a letter for the future Esther, that I will get when I'm . . . seventeen." She went on to explain that she'd sent it to our account "just in case" she wasn't around to receive it herself. At that moment, I remembered the brief conversation we had had. And then the sobbing began. Her every word was soaked with meaning, every phrase making it harder to catch my breath. I felt suffocated and ran outside to phone Lori, who was meeting with someone at a local café. I wanted to be sure she didn't open this final message from Esther in public.

—ESTHER'S DAD

futureme.org

this is a letter for the future esther, that I will get when I'm . . . 17. so you know that I'm really bad with words. I have emotions but I'm pretty bad at getting them out on paper. but this email is for you, and you'll understand most of what I'm saying (I hope).

yeah. I'm 14 now. I'll be 15 in 4 months. future me, I hope you're doing better than present me. I hope that if you still have your cancer, at least it will be gone enough for you to be off oxygen. and if it's not, just remember to use that Ocean Spray to keep your nostrils moist :] and I hope you've tried to talk to more people that also have cancer. in the world, there's not ONLY boring people with cancer. there are people that are awesome, but maybe you just haven't met them yet. you never will if you don't try. do you still even have cancer? do you still feel sick? are you back in school after missing so many years of it?

in the present, I'm a lazy person. I mean, with the health issues there's the fact that I can't do much, but come on man, I hope you've gotten off your butt! you've finally started doing physical therapy in the present, but you keep trying to get out of it. I hope in the future you are more strong willed and go through with things. remember how you always wanted to do something for the world? remember that? if you haven't done something amazing, don't forget to try. the worst that can happen is you fail, and then you can just try again until you succeed. those words don't work on me now, but just try to remember them.

graham is doing good, he's 13 in present, a teenager. and when you get this he'll be . . . 15. wow, that's older than I am at present. his speech problems have gotten better, and present me is a lot nicer to him now than past me. I'm glad of that. how is he in the future? is he doing good? give him a hug. play some games with him. he loves you and I hope you pay more attention to him. and abraham? he's what. 8 now? man, that's old. is he a sports maniac? does he play basketball, baseball, soccer, swimming—all the things he wants to do now? and is he a brainiac? he's so smart right now. he says the pledge of allegiance perfectly and can draw and say every letter of the alphabet. and he's learning to read.

oh, and evangeline/angie? are you friends with her again? when you were 12 and she was 15, you guys were best friends. we told each other everything. but ever since I got sick we haven't talked as much. I think maybe that might be because . . . I don't know . . . her problems seem unimportant compared to my health? maybe. I don't know. I wish that we could be best

friends again. it's kind of awkward to hang out with
her now, though. is that gone? please make an effort to
become, or stay, friends with her. you need each other.
is she 20 now? holy cow. seriously? that is soo old.

abby is 19 now, oh no, she turned 20 yesterday. wow.
twenty years old. I forgot to tell her happy birthday
yesterday . . . I never expected the day to come when
my sister has a two at the beginning of her age. it's
weird. future me has a sister named abby who is
22, eh? she's of legal drinking age now, haha. she's
at gordon now, and she wants to be a PA. she came
with me when I got my g-tube switched, and held
my hand as they freaking pulled the life out of me (I
could be exaggerating a little). she got kind of woozy
and fell off her chair, but I think that's because it was
me, someone she knows, in pain. I think she'll be an
amazing doctor if she goes through with it. cheer her
on, with whatever she's doing.

and then there's mom and dad. oh, mom, how is she?
is she teaching again? is she happy? she works so hard
now, everyday she's so exhausted. she does too much.
I love her, and remember to tell her that everyday. are
her and dad still bickering? all they talk about now is
money, since let's face it, we have literally none. the world
is in recession, and our family has ALWAYS been on the

poor end, but now we're living off of 300 dollars a month, really. dad just got a job as a mall security guard, it's only temporary, but he seems better now that he's not sitting at home job searching all day. I'm glad that he's doing something. does he still have problems with depression? don't get angry at him too much, he tries really hard and he loves you. if YOU had 5 kids and couldn't get a job, I'm sure you'd be a little depressed as well.

oh, are you still a nerdfighter? because right now that's a big part of your life. really pretty much all your life . . . I'm going to LeakyCon on May 21, to May 24, and I think abby or angie are going with me. if you have forgotten, it's a harry potter convention, and I'm going to get to see all the bands I love, and hopefully meet some cool people. the only problem is I feel really guilty for doing this, because it's so expensive. 250 dollars a person. but mom and dad know how much it means to me. it's just crazy how bad I feel for wanting to spend so much money. yikes.

still a fan of harry potter? the movies are over by now, aren't they? or is the last one coming out november 2011? I don't remember. but remember that harry potter is how you made friends with a lot of people, and don't shove him off once you don't need him anymore. and what about doctor who? I'm just getting into that now. I feel like it'll be a big part of my life, even though it's just a tv show.

how are your cats? pancake and blueberry? are they doing well? did you get anymore cats? or pets? blueberry and pancake are laying with me in bed now, and they're so warm. everytime one of them brushes against me, or lays next to me, they're warmth and contentment make me smile. if anything has happened to them, since I know blueberry's not the healthiest, don't worry about being sad, or crying. and remember all the awesome times you have with them. and how's Nibbs? do you still have him, or did you give him away? remember to show him some love, if you still have him. he's a puppy and he doesn't need the annoyance that's directed towards him. you know that. are you volunteering at animal shelters, if you can? if you're healthy enough, you should consider it.

what about, oh those silly things, boys? have you been kissed yet? amidst allllll the health problems and psychological problems, I still want to find a guy I like, who likes me back. I can't help it, it's just one of those stupid things I want. have you at least had a like who liked you back? geez . . .

are you still friends with alexa? and melissa? they're the

only people you're still in contact with that have known
you since you've been sick. they're good friends. and
even though you probably wouldn't still be "friends"
if you were healthy, they're awesome, and you need to
remember to talk to them more. if you haven't talked to
them in ages, why not do it now? and don't be afraid to
be yourself. you need friends, and there are other people
who need friends. the way to get friends is to reach out.

how is your mental state? are you still as confused as
ever? are you talking to god again? esther, god has been
with you through everything you've gone through, he
really loves you, and you need him. in the present you're
ignoring him, and I hate that. how do you think you
made it through that radiation, when everyone thought
you were going to die during the night? do you even
remember this stuff?

on thursday I'm going to get another CT scan, and PET
scan, and it will show how I'm reacting to the chemo. I
really hope that my lungs are improving . . . I'm nervous,
I've been feeling a little worse with my breathing
lately, and I just hope and pray that it'll be alright. hey,
remember to thank your doctors. dr. smith and annette,
they're fantastic people. and they're your doctors, don't
be afraid to tell them your worries.

to be honest, I'm not even sure if future me will even be alive. and for that reason I'm sending this email to mom and dad, since if I'm NOT alive, at least I know this email will be checked. man, what a way to end this letter . . . okay, future me, just try to be happy. try to do things. don't forget that many times you thought you'd never make it through the night. remember all the people that have helped you in the past. tell your family how much you love them. go to school—it may seem stupid, but doing homework and research can get your mind off the little, bothersome things. read. you're forgetting to read as much, and reading is a lovely thing. try to solve a rubiks cube again, you solved your first one yesterday :)

just . . . just be happy. and if you can't be happy, do things that make you happy. or do nothing with people that make you happy.

there was so much more I wanted to say, and maybe I'll send another one of these if anything happens. I love you, and I hope you turn out good.

ESTHER DAY
by John Green

When we realized how sick Esther was, Hank and I talked on the phone about setting up a perpetual holiday within nerdfighteria that would honor Esther in the way of her choosing, and that we would commit to celebrating as long as we made videos. I told Esther about it during her Make-A-Wish weekend: She could pick any cause or celebration, and then every year on her birthday, we would make a video about it. (I don't remember at the time whether we'd agreed to call the holiday Esther Day, but we had by the first Esther Day: August 3, 2010.)

Esther devoted a lot of time and thought to her choice, and in the end she decided she wanted Esther Day to be a celebration of love—not romantic love, which already has its fair share of holidays—but the kinds of love that are underappreciated in our culture: the love between friends and family and colleagues. While many romantic couples say "I love you" to each other many times a day, these other kinds of love, Esther felt, too often go unacknowledged. That's certainly the case with my brother and me: Before Esther Day, I don't think I'd said "I love you" to Hank since I was about twelve. But now, every August 3rd, I gather my courage and tell my friends and family I love them. Even my brother.

I love my family. *My family has supported me through my cancer and my crap and almost dying and everything and when I was, like, younger before I had cancer you know and I was all like little kid angsty, and I love them, and I love my sisters I love my brother I love my dad I love my mom I love my pets, they are included in the family category. I love my friends; my friends are amazing, the ones I've met online, the ones that I still have IRL, and this video makes me happy so I just re-watched it a lot and I just love, it's so lovely, and thank you for saying that you love Hank, I know you love Hank, you don't have to say you love Hank for me to know it, but I mean yeah, saying you love someone is a good thing, and I love you John.*

—Esther video, response to the first
Esther Day video, August 2, 2010

THIS STAR WON'T GO OUT FOUNDATION

by Lori Earl

The day after Esther's funeral, there was a knock on the front door of our home in Quincy. When I opened the door, standing there next to his bicycle was a young man, sweating profusely in the late summer's heat. He said he was from nearby Braintree and asked, "Is this the place where I can give a tribute to Esther Earl?" When I said yes, he handed me an envelope. He said he had written a note and had a small donation that he wanted to contribute to Friends of Esther. His name was Jarid, and it touched my heart so much because it's practical, local . . . I mean, on the Internet it's huge and it's across the world, but this was somebody from the next town over. I asked him, "Are you a *nerdfighter*?" And he said yeah and gave me the nerdfighter sign. And I just thought it was so amazing. I gave him a glass of water and a bracelet of Esther's—he said he was going to wear it until it broke . . . As he rode off, I opened the envelope to discover a five-dollar bill along with this typed note:

"In my experience, in times of need, every bit helps. Although I don't have much, I still would like to donate $5 to the Friends of Esther Fund. Esther was an inspiration to many. And no matter what adversity she was faced with, she always maintained a happy outlook on life. She never forgot to be awesome. She will be remembered forever."

This was the start of the foundation our family began in Esther's memory, named *This Star Won't Go Out*, after our own Star. TSWGO is committed to helping relieve

```
                          Untitled
In my experience, in times of need, every bit helps. Although I don't
have much, I still would like to donate $5 to the Friends of Esther
Fund. Esther was an inspiration to many. And no matter what adversity
she was faced with, she always maintained a happy outlook on life. She
never forgot to be awesome. She will be remembered forever.
-Nerdfighter Jarid from Braintree
```

the financial hardship associated with expenses related to caring for a child with cancer. It also has the mandate to give monies toward "other projects Esther would have approved of." A large portion of the donations have come through the purchase of the bracelets originally designed for Esther's Make-A-Wish event, and distributed by DFTBA Records. In addition, dozens of individuals and groups of young people have held amazingly creative fundraisers for TSWGO—shaving their heads, selling art projects, walking around walls and running races,

writing and performing songs sold online, rocking in
chairs all night long, and so many more! One twenty-
year-old in Germany even set up five thousand dominoes,
that, when released, illuminated a beautiful picture of
Esther. Two and a half years after it began, TSWGO had
given away over $130,000 to help more than sixty different
families, which, her friends and family agree, would have
made Esther very happy.

Lori Earl, TSWGO event,
NEW YORK, SEPTEMBER **2013**

Following is a sampling of ORIGINAL FICTION Esther wrote between 2007 and 2010. These pieces are all unfinished, the seeds of new ideas. They are rough—first drafts—and in them it is possible to see how Esther was exploring, experimenting, and starting to find her voice as a young writer. Edited for length and basic grammar, these are otherwise unchanged, as Esther left them—in progress.

Anderaddon [fantasy]

April 10th-May 1st, 2007

OVER IN THE FAR WEST of Ander Forest is a huge
rock shaped like a mountain. It is called Anderaddon,
a kingdom known for many, many miles for its great
strength, wisdom, kindness and mixed creatures.
Anderaddon is the only known ville to the country of
Topalville that has hedgehogs, porcupines, mice, the
spare (vegetarian) cats, and its original inhabitants,
ebitillies and ebitties. Ebitillies are young, fur covered
things: cousins of hedgehogs and porcupines, they're
said to be, since they resemble them much, though are
better mannered.

Ebitties are as well citizens of the same name
though are much more similar to beavers. They have
striped bodies, big teeth, a mighty, spotted tail, and are
the strongest creatures next to badgers. Ebitties have
ruled the kingdom of Anderaddon for more than 500
years.

Wiping dust off his glasses, Docknel the king slowly
raised himself from his chair, onto his two, frail old
legs. Two young ebitilly servants, Pobby and Fandiliny,
rushed to help him up, but the old ebitty pushed them
aside. The finishing of his scrolls was definitely making

him feel quite strong- as though he was young again. He smiled to himself, letting out an audible chuckle. Pobby heard it and wondered clearly what the old man was thinking about.

"Sire," asked he, hoping to sound more sure of himself than he was, "'tis only a truly drole thing that thee laughs at. Might'nt thee share what 'tis?"

"Why certainly, young fellow," said Docknel, inwardly smiling at the young one's nervousness. "I was thinking of the thought of being young again, trying to remember what I looked like, running around in the old days... Though all I saw was a young lad running around with spectacles and a wooden cane, scoffing people!"

Pobby chuckled appreciatively to this-but Fandiliny hadn't heard any which part. She was wondering with might what was written in the five scrolls Docknel held.

"King sire," Fandiliny said, with the not even the faintest sign of hesitation, "'tis impolite if one was t'be a'askin' thee what 'tis in thy scrolls?"

Pobby nudged her, nodding up and down. "Aye m'gel, 'tis the most impolite askin' one did ever hear! The king's business is his own!"

The three slowly descend the stairs, taking care not to go too fast for Docknel, for, if they did, Docknel was sure to get lost because of his bad eyes. The king didn't feel the need to tell them he knew the way around his

kingdom by his other senses as well as sight. He figured
it would be rude, and, if people knew this, not many of
the younger ones would go with him down the stairs,
and he liked the company of them. "But!" Fandiliny was
not going to give up that quickly! Besides, her curiosity
wouldn't let her. "S-sire, one loves the scrolls thou hast
written of stories thou hast learned over the seasons
and histories thou hast heard . . . Mightn't thy scrolls be
something similar to this?"

Hiding a smile, Docknel shook his head, sighing,
"Thou hast read all of them? Ma'am, you'll learn of my
scrolls maybe a little later. Right now we must talk of
something else. Are you two looking forward to the
festival this evening?"

Their eyes shone with happiness, both speaking
of what they loved that was happening in a few short
minutes.

"Oh, aye! 'tis what one hast always wanted!"

"Aye, one's mother explained we will be havin'
pudden . . ."

"And cinnamon cake . . ."

"And Honey Suckle cider- and- and sweets!"

"Flower-Jammed-Jammy-Jam!"

"Strawberry pie, garlic tea!!!"

"Brewed dandelion seeds . . . !"

"Wait," Docknel stopped on the top stair, looking

at Pobby with a puzzled expression. "Did you just say garlic tea?"

Pobby blushed, said a quiet "aye," and all three burst out laughing.

Choobly was trying to make an announcement, but only one listened. The party was over, the little ones in bed, the wine all gone, little food left (few people did <u>not</u> stuff their faces), and the ones still able-bodied were chattering away in talk. So the king decided to take matters into his own hands.

"HELLO!!!" he boomed.

All that could be seen from the font of the lawn where stood Docknel, were eyes, turned him in astonishment.

"Right, um, Choobly would like your attention, if you please . . ." The only ebitilly gave a smile and a wave of gratitude to Docknel, and announced in his fine, bubbly matter what he had to say.

"Well, now that one hast fin'ly gots thy attenchun, justa'wants toa'make cert'un thou art a'havin'a fun time?" A crowd of cheers were his answer, and a couple of hats and bonnets were seen in the air as well.

"'tis all thou wants to say?" one asked, after the cheering died down.

"Shut thy trap, young'un! Nay, 'tis not all one has need of a'sayin'! Just was a'wonderin' . . ." Choobly shook his head, and continued from where he had left off. "Ah, yes, right . . . one would like to a'have the plea'chur of a'sayin', that any of thee whoa'wishes to come up to a'perform cans't."

The early moon glowed off peoples smiles, and, after a bit of arguing about who would go, a young lad introduced himself as Macklen, and was up singing a favorite in his family.

Me, d'tis me, who can see
thy b'eetiful eyes.
Aye, 'tis thou, <u>only</u> thou,
who knows when one a'lies.
 'tis beautiful
Bugly ugly- 'tis B!
EEW- 'tis E!
Achh- 'tis A!
Ughhh- 'tis U!
Tachaww- 'tis T!
Icky!- 'tis I!
Fartsy- 'tis F!
U- though already know!!!
And Lowly yuck- 'tis L!!
'Tis how me spells,
thy b'eetiful feathurs!!!

The crowd cheered, and finally after singing to the request two more times, Macklen the young bowed, and sat. Another young one went up, but this time it was a young hedgehog. Her ears were not as pointy as others, though she was quite short and not as stout as others. She had golden brown skin, and sky blue eyes. She started, in a sweet but raspy voice.

"'Ello, people!" she smiled. "I oi is called Jennily, and I oi is the daughter of 'ee Carnilly, daughter of Jenniliny. I oi is to perfoi'm the poem oi found stuck 'twixt two rocks near the orchard gates, entitled . . . well, it's untitled, and oi also has reason to believe it's 'ee bit of a riddle . . ."

Cheering was once again enveloping the room, people laughing with joy at the thought of riddles. It was a favorite among Anderaddon. She nodded once there was silence and read from a piece of parchment she pulled out of her apron pocket.

"Oi am unknown to those
who are pure of heart.
But if ya found this,
here's something to start:
Me first has no shape,
nor 'tis living,
There's something to catch,

come, just dive in!
Without it we couldn't make pie,
and we would surely die.
Please look thoroughly-
No one good knows of this
as oi have toild,
Now this story,
'tis in your hands to save and unfoild."

There was silence for about two minutes as people
pondered, but people slowly began to clap. No one
could shake off the thought as the next though person
played a song: what did it mean?

Over to the Southwest of Anderaddon, on a small Island
called Killer's Isle, stood a castle. The creatures in this
castle were nasty sea-parrots, sea-rats, sea-weasels,
and sea-lizards ruled by their king, BladeSlip. BladeSlip
was an evil, gigantic parrot who was as slippery as an
eel when it came to trusting him. The last king, Jockle,
was a ruthless sea-rat, and his favorite out of the boat's
captain's was BladeSlip, at that time called BladeThrow.
When Jockle was sitting down at a festive dinner
celebrating the plunder his captains had brought
him that day, BladeThrow "happened" to let his blade
"slip" on the king's front paw. Jockle cursed him and

challenged him to a duel. BladeThrow, knowing the king was older than he and wounded, accepted gladly. Jockle was now just another carcass in the sea, come from Killer's Isle.

"'Hoi!"

"Ey, id'et, y'just soiled my new silk robe!"

"Oh sh'op, me a'int too sure Dog Killa ova there rip't me robe . . . He thinks it 'az ya!"

Mayhem was everywhere in the hall, people hitting each other, wine all over the place. The newly appointed king had given the captain's robes of velvet and silk, along with casks of wine to the crews. It was his way of "showing" them he was one to be trusted. And they all did.

BladeSlip stood up at the front of the two long, wide tables filled with food. He cleared his throat to get attention but they ignored him. He loudly asked for attention. No one seemed to notice.

THWACK!

A yelp of pain issued from a sea-lizard standing on the table. BladeSlip had thrown his dagger and it stood, sharp edge down, in the lizard's long tail. The whole hall stared at their king whilst the lizard nursed his wound. A weasel stood holding the blade of BladeSlip, staring in weasel disgust at the purple blood on the metal part.

"You! Weasel! Give me my blade!"

BladeSlip was enraged. He had asked them to look

and listen, but they had ignored him. He knew he had to do something to gain respect, and the only way to be respected, was to be feared.

The weasel scurried quickly to BladeSlip, too quickly, in fact. He tripped over an empty bottle of beer, and the ones around him laughed heartily. Though they quickly stopped to the icy glare of King BladeSlip, eyes twitching fiercely.

"You . . ." he started, spitting everywhere, "are . . . you are imbeciles! All of you! An' me? Well, oi am the only person with sense in this here <u>kingdom</u>! Might I remind you who the king is? ME! I AM THE KING! When oi say listen, I truly mean listen!"

Silence was the only sound for two minutes. BladeSlip knew by this time he had their full attention, and they obviously respected him more (the lizard's tale had completely fallen off). He didn't want them to hate him, though, so he began, in a different manner.

Clapping a nearby parrot on the back, he began, laughing:

"Aye, people sometimes have to blow their steam off, eh? How 'bout filling your goblet of wine?" The fellow people were startled by this sudden mood change, though they dared not question the mighty feared BladeSlip.

———

"Ah, my darling, have you come to join me?"

It was a glorious morning in Topal Land. The birds were singing, the sun was up, and Loolane was on a terrace, over-looking all of his ville. It was a routine of Docknel's wife, though rarely did he ever come to visit with her. He only came when they had to talk of important matters.

"Oh, Loolane . . ."

Loolane was worried at the stress in her husband's voice. Rarely did he see her, and she wondered aloud what it was this time.

"What should bring you to come up here this particularly wonderful morn? Surely nothing to ruin our good moods?"

"Nay, nothing like that . . . Just, well, I couldn't sleep last night, and when I finally did some young ebitillies came in and woke me. I . . ."

She waited a moment to see if her husband would pick up where he left off, though when he didn't she inquired, "Why shouldn't you sleep?"

"Oh . . ." Docknel hesitated. "Eh, I'm not really sure, actually. I had that poem the young hogmaid recited . . . though for what reason I can't say."

"Oh yes! Many people have talked of this poem,

though I was already inside, tucking young 'uns in bed when there was entertainment. Mayhaps you remember it? I have to say I love these poems young 'uns recite dearly!"

"Nay, marm, I don't remember, though if you don't mind I have to go speak to . . .What's her name? Jennily; yes, thanks!"

He gave her a kiss and rushed as fast as he could down the stairs. After five minutes he was in the great dining hall, asking if anyone knew where Jennily was. Many different replies were his answer from a group of porcupines.

"Aye, king sir, tha gel went thaddaway!"

"Nay, nay, Jennilimmigally nots—'er name was in that thur kitchen a 'snatchin' food."

"Hoi, thou art all wrong! Tha gel? She went ta tha archard, with tha other yun' 'ogmaids."

"Nay! Jennily is not there! She—"

A young churchmouse interrupted, giggling loudly. "Scuze me, but tha miz Jennily is in her bed, hiding from questions people have about the riddle! Heehee, youze is ah wrong! Heehee!"

A few of the porcupines tutted, horrified at the rudeness of the mouse.

"Thanks for all your help!" Docknel said to the group.

"But since she is her friend—"

"Ey! Best frenn'!"

Docknel sniffed. "Since she is Jennily's <u>best</u> friend—," the young mouse looked triumphant, "—I think shu'd know where she is more than you. But thanks!"

The porcupines nodded and walked away, scoffing him.

"Imagine! The nerve . . ."

Docknel was in the hallway in front of young Jennily's room. He knocked, though it seemed they were busy with something else.

"Sir, if'n you don't mind, I think I'll go in an' tell 'em someone's at the door, ok?"

"Aye, that works for me," he replied, smiling.

"He heard the hogmaid's mother, Carnilly, drop something she was holding, probably due to the fact that the king was in her doorway.

"Oh, 'ee deerie . . ." she mumbled, rushing around straightening things. "In 'ee door? Let the poor man in!"

The young mouse opened the door, rolling her eyes.

"Sire, come in, please," said she, adding under her breath, "though watch out for the Marm, she will mayhaps try cleaning you . . ."

He hid a smile, and walked in. Docknel moved a pile of books from a chair, and set a quite flustered Mrs. Carnilly onto the seat.

The old woman smiled, two dimples showing in her rosy, fat, pink cheeks. She straightened her apron and issued her daughter over, motioning for Docknel to sit in chair behind him.

"Soire, oi is quoite certain you is wantin' to see 'ee daughter about'ee riddle?"

He shuffled his large tail and smiled, embarrassed. "Aye, marm, but if she is not in a mood to talk about it, then please excuse me . . ."

"Nay, Soire," Jennily said, grinning. "Oi is quoite honored to be visited in 'ee gurtly b'izzy schedule . . . Mayhap 'ee wants to look at 'ee riddle?"

The king nodded, glad she wanted to visit now, for he had a strange energy that was sure to go away by the next day.

Jennily took out a large book of poems and opened it to the middle, where a piece of parchment lay. She handed it to Docknel and he read it, twice. They sat silent for a while.

"Soire?" asked Jennily, awkward at breaking the silence. "Does 'ee unnerstann it?"

He sighed. "Parts, ma'am, though I think we should consult with some others in the open air. I mean, if you and your mother approve . . ."

They both ayed, and so Docknel, Jennily and Rolly the church mouse were off to the orchard.

Esther Earl
Lime Notebook

Winter 2007

MY HEART WAS POUNDING. My head throbbing, and my side seemed to be hurting more than usual. I stared at the X-ray as my stomach butterflies flew around and my eyes welled with tears. I was nervous. Anxious. Scared.

"But what does this mean?" my mom asked the X-ray guy, her disbelief obvious by her raised eyebrow expression.

"It means there is liquid in her lungs, so her lungs are not properly expanding. We'll give a copy to you to take to your doctor, and he or she will tell you where to go from there."

Questions engulfed my thoughts, but I was too shocked and embarrassed to say anything. Is it a lot of fluid? Is it serious? Ever seen it before? Who knows? I sure didn't . . .

"Esther, he's asking you something." I snapped back to reality, focusing my available attention on the guy.

"Are you going to be able to walk to the doctor?"

I've lived with this stuff in my lungs for 3 months and he wants to know if I can walk a block away?

"Yeah, I think so," I answered, my voice a bit unstable.

"Good. The secretary will give you the copy of the X-ray, and then you go give it to your doctor. Ok? Please take a seat in the waiting room."

After pointing us where to go, we walked in and sat down. My mom thought her thoughts, and I thought mine.

Isn't it amazing how you can think a sore rib to be a pulled muscle, when it turns out it's actually liquid in the lungs? My parents thought that's all it was, a sore muscle. Well, it'll probably just be pneumonia or tuberculosis—hopefully not, though.

I could see my mom's eyes glaze over . . . she was thinking of something. Probably about living situations. At the moment we were living on a street near Cours Mirabeau.

[Note: The story now continues with the fictional "Carly" as protagonist. It is a continuation of the previous story and was written at the same time. These events as Esther wrote them are true—they really happened to her— including her quirky rendering of the French accent.]

Carly's parents walked back in the room; her dad's face was serious and her mom's face was blotchy, her eyes swollen. Just because she was crying doesn't mean it's bad news, she cried a lot, they might've been happy tears . . .

Doubts flew around, but somehow, sitting in her hospital bed with a tube coming out her side, she held onto a string of hope.

"Carly," a male doctor walked into the room, sullen faced, followed by Dr. Janie, and an unknown female doctor.

Dr. Janie put her hand on Carly's bed, a weak smile feebly on her face. By this, Carly could feel the tension in the room, hear the thick silence in the five, quiet seconds no one spoke.

"Carly." Dr. Janie said, her French accent playing along, "We 'ave to tell you some'sing important, some'sing 'ard to say. You 'ave 'ad trouble bree'sing for a while, and we learn 'sat is because you 'ad fluide in your lungs. Well, we 'sink it is because of pneumonia, but we learn it is because you 'ave tumor in your neck. And so on 'sursday we will send you to 'ospital in Aix en Provence because it is special in child cancer. We will talk to the doctors in Aix about your case, and 'sey are very nice, and 'sey will take good care of you. D'accord? On parles plus demain, mais je dois vais à un autre place. You are very special, Carly. Et on touts t'aime! Plus tarde!"

[Exact date unknown]

My dearest Sophie Amelia Bush,
How are you, precious? Does Suxburry find you
agreeable? I dearly wish I could visit you, but we are
just moved in to Delham cottage, and I cannot imagine
being settled for at least 3 weeks, and by that time you
shalt be gone. Love and kisses!

I am yours,
Esther G. Earl. etc. etc.

———

[Exact date unknown]

Dear Jane,
I sit here, at my desk, wishing dearly you were here, for
it is pointless and boring each day. I practice my French
each day, and Madame Dupont says if I continue at this
excelling rate, I shall be in France, with you soon! Oh! I
dearly wish to visit you soon! How is Patrique?— well, I
hope?
We all miss you, especially mama! Jane, she runs around
wishing you were here to 'see her get old'!

Ha, I laugh heartily when I think of that story you told about the mama getting old.

I have to help with supper. Des, bisous!

Love
Catherine Lilly Maffy
Your sister

———

[Exact date unknown]

Maria, Ma belle,

La France, c'est magnifique, je elit, c'est parfait.

Patrique continu à faire toret son traivaille, at je suis à la maison, sans rien a fay –Et ba! Catherine à m'euire hier, et ce dit que vous sont en ai ennui. Pluff! Moi, j'ai beaucoup d'ennir aussi.

Dit à mama que je t'aime, et je reviens depuis un moment!

Sincerement,
Jane Louise Maffy', la soeur

[Exact date unknown]

Dear Diary,   June 16, 1662

Today I sat thinking. What would I do if I lived in a later
time? Well, first of all there'd be machines that had their
own brains, and they'd do whatever I asked them to.
Second of all, I'd clear out the poor populations, and
people wouldn't die, unless they were wanting to. Then,
I don't know, for I am too tired to think.

Yours,
Marie Therise Muffiline

[Winter 2007 -Exact date unknown]

A RING FROM THE BELL on the desk made my heart jump, and I quickly ran to help the next person. My eyes focused on the girl at the counter, her eyebrows arched to the top of her forehead, an annoyed pout on her face. She looked me directly in the eyes, and exhaled impatiently.

"Aren't you going to ask how you can help me, or are you just going to stand there ogling me?"

I opened my mouth to ask "how to help" her, but all I managed to get out was a cleared throat. My mind was processing the fact that the prettiest girl seemed the most rude, which would result in me uncontrollably asking her why that was unless I kept my words inside my throat.

"Dude, what's wrong! Is there even service here?" the girl basically screamed, her hands, ironically, on her hips.

"Umm, why do the prettiest girls always seem to be the most . . ." I stopped myself, grabbed a piece of gum from my pocket and quickly stuffed it in my mouth. "Mmm, gum! Want a piece . . . ?"

Her eyebrows furrowed and she noticeably grimaced, "Can I see your manager?" she asked quickly.

"Oh . . . actually I'm—I'm the manager . . ."
I mumbled, trying to remove my eyes from her
twitching, hair nostrils protruding. I found myself
having the urge to reach into the work locker of Mandy
—my co-worker—and take her tweezers, then leap
across the counter and rip all the hairs out of the girl's
nose. Though I stopped myself, realizing that Mandy
had taken her locker keys home, and that might also
seem strange. My thoughts were kicked out my nose,
however, as I sneezed loudly, causing Brat to stop
midsentence.

"You," Brat started again, since it seemed she'd
been speaking earlier, "are the manager of Vidvine?"

Feeling hurt at her tone of impossibleness, I
nodded and began to ask, kindly, what she wanted. But,
hahaha, she interrupted me.

"You cannot be the manager. You are probably as
old as me—maybe younger. So, I need . . ."

"Umm," I said, dramatically placing my hands on
my hips, moving my head quickly.

"I'm seventeen, I'm graduated from high school,
and my dad owns this store—so I'm co-manager."

Brat raised her eyebrows, and rolled her eyes.
"Fine. What is the cost of this bag of chips, and do I
know you?"

I stared at her, my stomach lurching from

annoyance. "First of all, you were this pissed over a bag of CHIPS? Second, if I know you, it's from Drama class." In my head, I laughed at this joke, but I kept my annoyed face on for fun.

2009- Fiction about bullying
"Prologue"

WHO STARTED THE THING that says boys don't cry? My dad once noted that he had "never cried in my whole life." But, can I just ask, if a boy is absolutely devastated about something, is he just supposed to hang his head and sit quietly? What am I supposed to do—not cry? Well, I just have to say that if that's the case, its gonna be hard.

Me and Tom are great friends, you know, always have been. He may be only in 2nd grade, but he likes sports and some other stuff that I enjoy, so we get along good. Some people, like Rufus E. Copan, tease me for playing with a boy that's three grades below me. Rufus E. is a big football built boy who enjoys terrorizing little kids and kissing up to the teachers. Although his dad, Mr. Copan, owns a big law firm and their family donates a lot of money to the school so everyone—that's a teacher—loves Rufus E. I mean, I don't really care that he teases me, but it's annoying since it makes other kids do the same.

Take today, for instance: at recess, me and Tom went near to the pile of sand that's near the swings, the one we always go to. Anyway, we were minding our own business, building a sand town and smashing it with our giant feet, when Rufus E. and his "friends" came over.

At first, we tried to ignore them, but they're idiots who don't leave us be. They pushed all our tall buildings over and called us babies. I had a good comeback where I could say, "Yeah, I'm a baby because I find playing with younger kids fun, and you're not a baby because you pretend to be all tough and you tease people for more self confidence, right?" Rufus E. would then go, "Why you . . . !" but I'd punch him before he got to me. Instead of this brilliant plan, I stuttered while the bell rang and we, quickly, ran to our class lines, shouting goodbyes.

DOPP! The sound that could be heard was a soft thud, almost like a rotten apple, falling from a tree, in a dark, scary forest where no one could hear it's terrified . . .

"Rufus!"

Oh man! I was again awakened by the loud voice of my mom, calling from the bottom of the stairs. (Every time that dream comes, I'm interrupted, I couldn't help but noting.) I quickly jumped up from my cozy-yet-smelly dung bed, threw on my slippers, and ran down the stairs. The bright morning sun half blinded me.

"There you are, silly!" Mom said, giving me a peck on the cheek. "I was worried you would never wake up, the day's almost over!"

"Mom," I couldn't help debating, "you do realize it's only 1 hour past breakfast . . ." She looked down at me, her gaze not scorning, but curious.

"I know, honey, but if you sleep away the day, what will happen at night?"

Straining for a comeback, I plopped in my usual breakfast chair and half-heartedly gnawed away at my XXX, all the while thinking of why I slept so late. Sure, lots of people slept late, but I was normally up before even Mom, so why was today different?

Day after day, week after week, it was becoming a routine. For 2 straight months I had slept in every morning until 1 hour after breakfast, when Mom would call me and I'd, grudgingly scooch down the stairs. At neoschool I could barely pay attention, lunch was when I ate and doodled, hardly even thinking, at play-time I sat down, opened a book and pretended to read. When I got home, I'd take a bath, eat supper, then go to bed . . . Then all over again it'd start. Every now and again a jump in the pattern would reveal itself—a walk to Kiko Lake, a visit to the money tree—

but other than that, I was very, well, zombie-like. Mom was worried.

"Rufus," she'd constantly say, "are you eating your vegetables . . . ?"

Ce n'est pas Vrai Tu M'adores

[2010- Fiction, romantic]

AS I SAT THERE, watching her babble gleefully about the shoes she found, I couldn't help but wonder what her hair would feel like if I ran it through my fingers.

"So, would you?"

"Oh," I started, my brain trying to remember where I was. "Sorry? I was, um, thinking about . . . supper."

She looked at me, her eyebrows raised, then laughed, her smile wide. "Well, supper is quite important, right?" she asked, only continuing once I'd smiled. "Anyway, I was saying that on Friday I'm going to see a movie with Renée and Lily. I wanted to know if you want to come . . ."

"Like a double date?" I joked, winking hugely while secretly hoping she would say yes. Who cared if Lily and Renée were both straight?

Looking taken aback, she quickly stated, "No. No, no. Like a 'hang out.'"

I forced a smile, though it must have looked like I was in pain for she asked if I was all right.

"Yep, I'm good, thanks!" I said, smiling. "So, let's talk you. How've you been?"

"Haven't we been talking about me?" She gave a

grin, her pink lipsticked lips raising beautifully. "I guess you can't get enough of me, eh?"

As I was about to sarcastically respond, our food came. Usually when we go out, the waiter mixes up our order, giving me Kaitlyn's food, and Kaitlyn mine. This time was no different. "As I was saying," I continued, greedily grabbing à-la-fat-and-cholesterol Kaity had given me, pushing her salad away from her dramatic pursed lips (she often teased me as being a "meat-eater," disgusted by healthy foods), "How's work? I haven't seen much of you lately . . ."

Kaity looked at me with her bottom lip turned over, a smile playing in her eyes. She reached over and patted my non-hamburger filled hand, awwing, unaware of the tingling she left on me as she pulled away. "Poor baby, have we been missing Kaity-Waity?" she teased, giggling.

"Ha, ha," I responded, frowning. "You still haven't answered me . . ."

She stopped, taking on a mock serious expression and answering me—finally. "Well, to be honest to goodness, work sucks. I'd been trying to get that promotion, but it's already filled by some huge boobs, big butt, blonde psychochick."

Kaitlyn was an assistant's assistant (who knew?) at the "chicest"—I guess the other then chicest are wrong!—magazine in New York, <u>The Burglar's Purse</u>. Funny enough, it has nothing, nothing at all, to do with Burglar's but everything to do with purses and the like. It was about fashion, and her assistant had run off with the Editor's assistant. She was trying to get one of those jobs (the editor's assistant or her post-employer's), but, apparently, she wasn't qualified. I don't understand what qualifications you have to have to have to choose an aluminum foil pant suit for the number two "must have," like in issue 3, volume 7 of <u>The Burglar's Purse</u>, that Kaity forced me to read. It was torture, I remember.

"Your boss is a guy?" I asked, remembering none of this.

"I wish," she laughed, "but, nope. <u>She</u> is a lady, but I guess playboy bunnies are getting educations now-a-days."

"I'm sorry you didn't get the job," I said, meaning it, and also feeling awkward talking about boobiful girls with Kaity. "You deserve it—after all, they can get a job as a stripper slash bunny and you ca-"

Before I could finish Kaity leaned over and whacked me on the head, her eyebrows raised and her mouth half open, half smiling.

"For the record," she stated, "telling a girl she could be a playgirl or something like that isn't much of a compliment." I stared at her, wondering what she had just done. Okay, I thought slowly, she just hit me, right? And, and she . . .

"Um?" My thoughts were, as normal, interrupted by Kaity, her voice lost in hilarity and scorn for my comment, "Hey, Jude, you alright?"

If I had a penny for every time someone thought I was ill when I'd think things over, why, I'd be rich! A millionaire, even. Oh yeah . . . Kaity was asking me something.

"Hmm? Kaity, you, above anyone, should know I go off sometimes! And no," I cut her off, as she was saying something, "I'm not going to the doctor."

Silence. Chew, chew. Cleared throat.

This had happened when I'd told other people, but not Kaity. I've done this "and no, blahblah" before, but Kaity'd always laughed or something. Crap . . .

"Jude?"

I looked up from dipping my side french fries in ketchup.

"Yes, babe?"

"Jude, I'm . . . well, I'm," she stalled, as though her speech was temporarily disabled. "I- I'm . . . seeing someone."

"Um. Okay." That was hard to get out, huh?

"He's really great," she quickly said, doing her

nervous thing, "and nice. He's my boss's nephew's step brother's father's second wife's brother."

I gaped. "Wow."

"Yep, yep, yep. And my boss's niece came to one of our conferences, and she wants to be an auditor, I mean editor." Here she breathed and smiled at her own stupidity. "And she introduced me to a <u>picture</u> of this second wife's brother. Anyway, she came in again about a week later, and introduced me to the <u>body</u> of this dude, and turns out he works for <u>The Work of Art</u>!" she finished enthusiastically, waiting for my response.

I hid, as best as I could, my confusion, and instead stood up and ran over to hug her, forcing her up and shouting girlish like squeals. Wait, why was I excited?

"So he offered you a job!" I said, not wanting to hurt her feelings more as to find out if he did.

"What?" she stopped, and sat back down, her face confused. "Who? The picture boy?"

"Yeah—him! You went out with him and he offered you a job, right? That's why you're excited?" By this time I was, too, seated, and was embarrassed by the silence. "I mean, he's an Editor. That must mean something. . . ."

"Umm," she mumbled, coming out of her thoughts, "yeah, it does. Mean something, I mean. I mean," she seemed alert now, sipping her beer. "Editors have a say in who goes and who stays. But, Jude, that's not why I'm dating him."

I stared. I've only know Kaity to use men—not actually just date them. Hmm, maybe she's changed, after all. I looked at her for a second—her beautiful green eyes, her luscious red lips, sipping soda, her many freckles that she, unlike some girls, tried to get more of, her long brown hair, curly and tousled. She was more beautiful than the Mona Lisa, more wanted than the Eiffel Tower, more mesmerizing than Spain's spring ocean . . . the ideal perfection. And yet I was her friend; the one she shared secrets with, the one she joked with and the only one she'd let see her without makeup on.

After a pause she continued, "I'm dating him because, well, I really like him."

Did I mention I'm the one she talks to about her men? Yech. Joy, I know.

"He's—he's nice, and kind, sexy, funny, hott and, after that date . . ."

I must have mumbled something encouraging her to go on, after a long while of quiet. It was, "Mmph?" to be exact, when I was trying to say, "Are you sure he's not a <u>jerk</u> like your other shags? And what is the pause for?" because she continued.

"Oh Jude!" she sighed, as if she were on cloud nine, "he's great! On our first date we went to Le Diamonde—

you know, the French restaurant on second? Anyway, I got there after him, and he was up on the roof! Turns out he knows the owners, and they set up a special place for us up top. We laughed and chatted and really got to know each other. He's from Baltimore, and majored as a writer in college. Get this—he went to Harvard and Harvard Law!!"

I was emotionless. Outwardly, anyway. Inside I was fuming. This guy went to Harvard this and Harvard that while I barely graduated community this, and no that. This psycho majored as a writer, and was now editor of <u>The Work of Art</u>, while lil' ol' me majored as a lawyer and am now an owner of a not-known-stupid-icky-Italian restaurant, my salary being nothing (I well, am something, but nothing compared to Mr. Big Shots)! Mr. Stupid was dating Kaity. <u>My</u> Kaity! Well la-di-frickin'-da! I may have lost Kaity ten years ago, but that doesn't mean I can't win her back. Yeesh, I sound like a stupid sappy war novel.

"He wants to see me again," she finished, obviously unaware of how I felt. "Isn't that great?'

The last question was a bit rhetorical, but since I couldn't think of anything to say, I responded politely, by saying "Mmhmm, that's . . . great."

She smiled one of those huge, "I-just-won-the-lottery-which-was-one-million-dollars" smiles, her face glowing, her features more noticeable than before. Like, not kidding.

"We're going out Friday night," she said cautiously, for what reason I don't know.

There was a pause in which it hit me. Friday— that was when we, me and Kaity, were going bowling. We had been planning it for two weeks, since Kaity's schedule's so tight.

"Kait, that's when we were going to, um, go out, wasn't it?"

Her grin was fading along with her glow, and normally I would stop so she would get them back. But it was if I couldn't. I was hurt. I've liked her for so, so long, and every time I come a hundredth of a chance of telling her, she ditches me. Not purposely, but still. Ditching is ditching, right?

"Jude . . . we can reschedule . . ."

"Kaity, don't you ever want to spend time with me?" I tried to calm myself, but my voice was louder than normal. "Don't you <u>like</u> spending time with me? We've been planning this for so long! Geez, Kait. Maybe in between shagging any guy you can find you could find time for me."

I have a problem. Either I don't say enough or I say too much. And right now, when it's too late, I realized I said the wrong thing.

She looked almost angry, and sounded it, too.

"I don't—I don't—don't . . ." she stopped, and went from clenched jaw to a forced smile. "Well, Jude, I have to go. Thanks for lunch." She gathered her stuff and left, before I could realize what she just did.

I just realized I didn't find out picture boy's name. If I had, I might have been able to find him in Yellow Pages and beat him up.

I walked down the familiar street from my house to the subway, and all I could help but think was about, well, Kaity. And yesterday afternoon.

"Excuse me!"

I looked up from my thoughts just in time to see a man on a bicycle ride right where I would've been, had I not see him. But a girl with red hair did not seem to notice him, and the Bicycle Boy wasn't going to go out of his way to avoid a collision. "Watch out!" I screamed, ready to jump in and push her out of the way if she didn't hear me. Thankfully she looked up, saw me and then Bicycle Boy, and moved onto the street, where a passing mini-van came close to whacking her.

She walked right by me, her expression anything but stricken, and it seemed as though I was the only one in the world who had witnessed what Bicycle Boy had done. Rushing after her, I felt almost angry—<u>furious</u>

even. I just saved her a trip to the hospital, if not her life (that's a stretch, but hey)! I deserve a "thank you," thanks very much!

"Ahem," I coughed, not so conspicuously. She looked over at me, and I was startled to see bright green eyes looking straight into mine, with not even a hint of emotion.

She said, "Thanks for saving my life. It was, and will be, a great favor for my part." She had stopped by this point, and I found it weird that she wasn't more appreciative. "Thanks again," she finished, shaking my hand, and then continued walking.

I was stunned. Again, she barely acknowledged me, and as she walked on her pale blue high boots, I felt like a toy she had played with, but when she got a new one, and put me in a yard sale. Running after her again, I felt I was a pull-a-long toy, now.

"Excuse me, miss, but are you alright?" Smooth, I know.

She looked at me suspiciously, her feet still moving.

"I'm . . . fine, thank you." For the first time, she pulled a smile, and I was pleasantly surprised to see the way her red lips played with her pale skin. I looked down, again, at her boots, and this time noticed she was wearing red, tight pants. Whoa, they were really bright—no idea how I missed them before. Then I saw she had a tight, white tank-top on, (that looked very good on her, if you know what I mean . . .) with a black sweater, button-up type jacket, long, straight black hair falling on her shoulders.

    Wow.

"Friends of Esther,"
SQUANTUM, MASSACHUSETTS, 2010

ACKNOWLEDGMENTS

We would like to acknowledge that this is Esther's book. As her parents, we get to add our names to it—which we are happy to do! Our greatest wish is that you, the reader, will walk away with a deeper appreciation for the mystery of life, and the hope that comes with loving.

To Julie Strauss-Gabel, our editor, and to the entire team at Penguin Young Readers, especially Rosanne Lauer, Elyse Marshall, and Irene Vandervoort. Thank you for believing in us and for caring so much about Esther's story.

To our agent, Jodi Reamer, thank you for making all the magic happen. Can't wait to do it again!

To John Green, Esther's friend and favorite author. Her star shines more brightly because you chose to champion her. Your generosity and compassion have made everything a little easier for our family. We can never thank you enough. You are as kind and brilliant as people think you are!

To the medical teams at The Jimmy Fund and at Children's Hospital in Boston, thank you for the good work you did for us and continue to do for so many.

Thank you to nerdfighteria, and to Catitude, for being there for Esther, especially when things were really hard. You gave her a home online and you gave her hope irl. Without your love, there simply would be no constellation within which to set our Star!

To all the Shining Ones who helped with transcribing Esther's journals, writings, online media, and other stuff. You are a gift!

To Alexa Lowey, Esther's oldest friend, for all the memories and for creating the phrase we carry on our wrists and in our hearts, "This Star Won't Go Out."

Thank you to our extended Earl and Krake families, who supported Esther and us in every way, and who agreed from the beginning that our fuzzy haired, bundle of light was a gift to the world.

To our beautiful children, Abigail, Evangeline, Graham, and Abraham, who loved their sister perfectly and who miss her very much. Thank you for giving your mom and dad the space to grieve and to write. We know that your hearts are also breaking and even though we cannot protect you from pain, we will always love you, love you, love you, no matter what!

Finally, to *Esther Grace*. You were so easy to love! *Rest in Awesome*, Little One. We will *definitely* see you again.

You can read/watch more about Esther Earl, and Lori and Wayne Earl here:

Esther's YouTube: youtube.com/user/cookie4monster4

Caring Bridge: caringbridge.org/visit/estherearl

Wayne's blog: timeforhope.blogspot.com/

Esther Day:

John Green announces Esther Day: youtube.com/watch?v=ixr4YISTmck

Esther Day 2012: youtube.com/watch?v=VFX3uu6VyyU

TSWGO foundation:

Website: tswgo.org

Facebook: facebook.com/TSWGO

Tumblr: tswgo.tumblr.com

Thank you to everyone whose invaluable contributions made this book possible

LINDSAY BALLANTYNE is an inordinately tall female person from Colorado, where she works as a massage therapist. Her hobbies include yoga, concerts, boating with her family, and various projects for nerdfighteria, which is her second home. Twitter, tumblr, basically everywhere: itfeelslikegold.

SARA (CLEVERESTWITCH) BANFIELD is a culinary school graduate who met Esther for the first time in late 2009. She resides in Connecticut, where she spends her time playing video games, wasting hours on social media, being a nerd, and overanalyzing the world around her.

VALERIE BARR is an Ohio native currently studying English in Cleveland. She serves on the board of directors for the Foundation to Decrease Worldsuck and has plans to continue her education to attain a master's degree in library studies.

PAUL DeGEORGE and his younger brother, Joe, created the band Harry and the Potters in 2002. They are cited as the founders of Wizard rock (a genre of music based on Harry Potter) and have spent much of the past decade touring the US and beyond. Paul also co-founded the Harry Potter Alliance and serves on their board of directors and as their Director of Campaigns and Operations. He and his wife, Meredith Moore, own and operate Wonder Fair, an art gallery and design store in lovely Lawrence, KS, where they reside. Online: harryandthepotters.com. Twitter: @hatp.

JULIAN GOMEZ (@ittakesii) is a Film and Media Arts student at American University who is on the volunteer staff for the Harry Potter Alliance, which he was inspired to join in part by Esther's enthusiasm for and support of the organization. He is a member of Catitude, a nerdfighter since mid-2007, and just really misses Esther a lot. You can also find his videos at http://youtube.com/ittakesii.

TERYN GRAY comes from Ladera Ranch, California, and is now attending her first year at University of California, Davis, where she is participating in theater and competing on the women's rowing team. She has been a nerdfighter since 2008, a part of Catitude since its creation, and now spends her time performing, working with the Girl Scouts of America, vlogging, crying over fictional characters, and collecting cool socks. YouTube: holeysaintgeorge. Tumblr: holeysaintgeorge.

JOHN GREEN is an award-winning, #1 international bestselling author whose many accolades include the Printz Medal, a Printz Honor, and the Edgar Award. He has twice been a finalist for the *LA Times* Book Prize. With his brother, Hank, John is one half of the Vlogbrothers (youtube.com/vlogbrothers), one of the most popular online video projects in the world. You can join the millions who follow John on Twitter (@realjohngreen) and tumblr (fishingboatproceeds.tumblr.com) or visit him online at johngreenbooks.com. John lives with his family in Indianapolis, Indiana.

THE HARRY POTTER ALLIANCE is a 501(c)3 nonprofit that makes social change accessible to young people through the power of story. The HPA brings together fans, activists, and nerdfighters to form a real-world Dumbledore's Army that is actively working to decrease worldsuck. Since 2005, the HPA has engaged millions of young people to become the heroes they read about through their work for equality, human rights, and literacy. If you've ever wished for an eighth Harry Potter book, the Harry Potter Alliance is living it! Join today at thehpalliance.org. You can follow the HPA on Twitter (@ thehpaalliance) and tumblr (thehpalliance.tumblr.com).

MANAR HASEEB has a complicated, but fulfilling, relationship with her home state of Texas. One day she will launch a rap career, but until then she remains beholden to The Man and attends the University of Texas at Dallas.

PAUL HUBER is a college grad from St. Louis who has been involved in nerdfighteria since 2008. He is a Ravenclaw who loves books, heavy metal, and *Star Wars* among many other nerd obsessions.

MORGAN JOHNSON is a native Iowan currently in the College Student Personnel master's program at Bowling Green State University in Ohio. She has a penchant for cotton candy, nerdy graphic tees, the color yellow, and the Oxford comma.

ALYSIA "LYSH" KOZBIAL is an aspiring writer currently residing in Ohio. She's been involved in the Potter and nerdfighteria fandoms for a long time and enjoys long walks under the stars, knowing the brightest one is probably Esther.

ANDREW KORNFELD is a person who lives in the state of New York. He likes fun and good things, and maintains a measured and reasonable discomfort with bad things.

ALEXA LOWEY is from Medway, Massachusetts, where she was lucky enough to begin her friendship with Esther in first grade. In honor of Esther and along with their mutual friend Melissa Mandia, they created the green wristbands with the original phrase, "This Star Won't Go Out." Alexa said the idea for the name "just came" to her. She loves her family and friends more than anything in the world and is thankful to be able to have been part of this book.

BLAZE MITTEFF lives in Florida, where she attends community college. She was convinced by fellow Catitude member Lindsay to submit her writing for this book.

ARKA PAIN studies philosophy and literature at Boston University. He lives in Boston IRL and nerdfighteria online.

ARIELLE ROBERTS is a member of the board of directors of This Star Won't Go Out and has been a member of Catitude since its creation in 2009. She is an optometry student from Miami, FL, currently living in Boston, MA, who loves nothing more than curling up on the couch at the end of a long day with a good television show and a hot cup of tea.

Arielle created the font made from Esther's handwriting, used throughout the book, especially for this project.

ANDREW SLACK is co-founder and executive director of the Harry Potter Alliance (HPA) and on the board of directors for the This Star Won't Go Out Foundation. As a fellow at the Nathan Cummings Foundation, Andrew is working on the Imagine Better Network: an unprecedented movement that goes beyond Harry Potter to all fandoms.

A Phi Beta Kappa graduate from Brandeis University, Andrew has written for both the *LA Times* and CNN, and been featured on NPR, the *New York Times*, and the front cover of Forbes.com. A former full-time comedian, he is known for his inspiring yet funny talks, including at TEDx, Harvard, and as keynote speaker at the Nobel Peace Prize Forum.

SIERRA SLAUGHTER was born and raised in New York and is currently studying film at school in Michigan. The biggest sections of her heart belong to Jesus, Will Smith, One Direction, and claymation.

DR. JESSICA SMITH is Attending Physician, Endocrinology, at Boston Children's Hospital.

DESTINY TARAPE is a twenty-one year old nerdfighter who lives in the greater Seattle, Washington, area. Destiny has been a nerdfighter and part of Catitude for over five years and really misses being able to reach Esther at almost anytime of day—or night—online.

KATIE TWYMAN is yet another person from Catitude. She's from Minneapolis, and she has a special love for manatees and starting unrealistic projects. Twitter: @katiefab. YouTube: kaytaaay.